The point of Operation Black Rain was to put every outlaw in America out bad – to seize his cut, his motorcycle and his memorabilia, to rough him up, wreck his home, scare him and tell him "don't come around this club no more." It was, simultaneously emotionally, financially and legally devastating for the men involved. The point of the "enforcement effort" described in this book was never to punish "criminals." The point was to crush a set of seductive, romantic, dangerous, and maybe obsolete, ideas.

Cover photo of the author, center at the back of the pack, courtesy Suave, Mongols Motorcycle Club.

Out Bad:

A True Story About Motorcycle Outlaws

Donald Charles Davis

Contents

Hitman

In the lower left corner of a faltering nation, in a scintillation of street lights and swimming pools a dozen miles northeast of the Hollywood sign, two motorcycle outlaws leaned into a long curve where one El Lay freeway hammerheads into another. Motorists saw them heading south. Witnesses in cars looked, checked their door locks and got out of their way. Everybody looks. Americans must look though they rarely consider why.

The long curve is just inside the Glendale city limits, a klick south of Foothill Boulevard – which is the antique, raveled ribbon John Steinbeck called "the mother road, the road of flight." This greatest American escape route wends its final 25 miles from Glendale to the end of a pier. The pier juts 100 yards into the Santa Monica surf. And there the dead end of the American dream is marked not with a tombstone, not with a bronze plaque, not with a statue of weeping mourners but with a flashing, Technicolor Ferris wheel.

It was the last hot after the first frost. In the old cities in the East and Midwest, in places with winter, they call it Indian Summer but this frost was where it has been for the last 10,000 years – in the high sage desert north and east of Vegas. The cold, heavy, air there obeyed the laws of meteorology and physics. It tumbled south and down until eventually the cold wind rubbed like two sticks against the faults and passes that flow into Los Angeles. The stand-up comics and the Hustler Honeys who "bring" Angelinos their weather call it "frictional and compressional warming."

The priests and the Chumash knew better than that. They knew black magic, not happy-happy science chat, filled the basin with hot air. Los Angeles' Indian Summer is the season that sets Satan loose. The winds that fall out of the desert are the *Santana*s. When they weren't preoccupied with genocides or molestations the priests insisted the winds be called *Santa Anas*. The *Santanas* are the hot winds that whisper to serial killers, that pant hundred foot flames and turn the sky the colors of Halloween. The priests decreed they must forever be named in honor of Jesus Christ's grandmother. Raymond Chandler called them the "Red Wind" when, "every booze party ends in a fight. Meek little wives feel the edge of the carving knife and study their husbands' necks. Anything can happen. You can even get a full glass of beer at a cocktail lounge."

It was one of those nights and the two outlaws were coming from the kind of cocktail lounge Raymond Chandler must have had in mind. They were heading to Venice, a mile from the Santa Monica Pier. It was October 8th, 2008. The Ferris wheel was dark for the night. It was almost two o'clock in the morning. There was a quarter moon. It was 70 degrees. And, the two motorcycle outlaws were going 80.

Eighty is the *defacto* mandatory speed on all Los Angeles freeways in the middle of the night and motorcycle outlaws are always going 80, anyway. Or a buck. Or a buck twenty. These two guys rode with the Mongols and even if you know nothing about motorcycle outlaws, especially if you know nothing about outlaws, you know how dangerous tribes like the Mongols must be. These were wild, free, natural men. You couldn't scare these men. These men were the last of our pioneers, our mountain men, our last revolutionaries, the last gunfighters and the last cattle rustlers. They were as anachronistic as wild Apaches. Which is exactly why everybody must look?

Hitman and Porno Ron – their names were Hitman and Porno Ron – leaned back in their saddles with their legs stretched out and their hard hands hooked over ape hangar handle bars. They rode 19th Century gasoline engines bolted into webs of steel pipe balanced on bicycle wheels. Their motorcycles boomed the stuttering, hundred decibel roar that evolved politicians, corner office tough guys and concerned citizens all complain rattles windows, triggers car alarms, startles dogs, terrifies the elderly, elevates blood pressure, raises serum cholesterol and makes poor, little, sleeping babies cry. As if being two of the most dangerous men in America was not bad enough.

They were doing just what they would have been doing if they knew they had only seconds to live. Not every man knows how he wants to die but these men knew. Most bikers dream the same death – they want to die in the saddle with their boots on. And, as they entered that curve, if they were going exactly 80, one of them had 45 seconds until God pointed his swift finger and glanced his terrible glance.

The guy who died was named Manuel Vincent "Hitman" Martin. He was 30-years-old, tough and fearless. He looked dangerous. He had hard, sleepy eyes, a round face, a slightly asymmetrical goatee and a thin mustache. He also had a wife and two small kids. He did not drink, smoke or do drugs. The other guy, Porno Ron, was merely the victim of another, commonplace, Los Angeles murder attempt.

Neither of them expected trouble. If they had expected trouble they would have been riding in a pack and the pack would have been followed by a chase truck and the murderers would not have escaped. Everybody in that pack would have been tough, fearless and armed.

Hitman had a loaded Glock concealed in the small of his back and he had already passed that boundary between fools who like to pose with guns and men with the *huevos* to actually light you up. "Hitman would throw down," Peter "Bouncer" Soto, the man who brought Hitman into the Mongols said. "He wouldn't even think if he felt trouble. He would just do it and ask questions later."

Hitman and Porno Ron had been at a lounge called The Mix at 2612 Honolulu Avenue in Montrose – a badminton serve from Glendale. The Mix was accused by police of being haunted by several "street gangs" and that night was the beginning of its end. The night club had its power shut off the next month but managed to survive until March 15, 2010. It's final event, three weeks after it lost its liquor license, was a party for the 311 Bikerz Motorcycle Club which The Mix advertised by claiming a "fully stocked bar."

The 311, allied with the Mongols, and Hitman and Porno Ron and many other Mongols were at The Mix the night Hitman died to attend a going away party for another Mongol named William "Target" Owens. Owens was a tattoo artist who, in a certain light, before he got his Mongols chin tattoo, resembled Doc Holliday. He was also a recovering methamphetamine addict. He had been convicted of that crime which meant he had forfeited most of his Constitutional rights. So he had to prove his good citizenship by enduring warrantless searches day and night. And, one unannounced parole search of his residence discovered that he owned a functioning slot machine. So then he had to pay his debt to society for that. Hitman showed his love and respect for Target by staying until almost two. Then he headed home with Porno Ron. Ron was not yet fully a Mongol. He was a "hang around," which

4

is to say that he hoped that someday he might be invited to join.

They warmed up their bikes then three minutes after they left the parking lot Hitman and Porno Ron leaned into that curve. As they approached the Glendale Freeway a "dark colored car" in the next lane pulled up just behind them and opened fire. Only a very skilled or a very lucky assassin can hit a moving motorcycle from a moving car. The gunman shot at Porno Ron first. Hitman glanced back, with his sleepy eyes wide and his chin up, and when he did a look of recognition flashed across his often impassive face. The shooting lasted, probably, three seconds and a total of 11 shots were fired. Porno Ron's motorcycle was shot four times and the next day he found a bullet in his boot heel. Martin's motorcycle was shot five times before he managed to pull the bike to a slow and controlled stop on the narrow shoulder of the transition road. Martin, true to character, was remarkably graceful and composed for a man who had just been shot at. Then after he stopped, after he put his feet down but before he could climb off his bike, Manuel Vincent Hitman Martin fell over dead. He had been shot once in the chest. Which means that when he looked back, when that recognition flashed across his face, he was probably recognizing the man who killed him.

Porno Ron frantically called the Mongols who were still at the bar and they got to the crime scene before the police or the paramedics. One of them set the bike on its kick stand and pushed on the emergency flashers. A Mongol named Shawn "Monster" Buss started Cardio Pulmonary Resuscitation. Bouncer Soto grabbed Martin's gun and checked the magazine and the chamber. The gun was fully loaded and had not been fired. Bouncer hid the weapon.

Porno Ron fell apart. While Monster dipped his hands in Hitman's blood and refused to give up Porno

Ron danced Sufi circles in the fast lane of the freeway, "screaming at the top of his lungs," hoping to flag down a doctor or a wizard or a miracle. The doctors and wizards checked their door locks, refused to look and speeded up. One of the Mongols dragged Ron out of the traffic and threw him to the ground. Then while Porno Ron settled into the numb stoicism of grief the other Mongols checked their guns and waited for Martin's shooter to return. The California Highway Patrol, a freelance news cameraman, the Glendale police and paramedics came instead.

The paramedics took over from Monster. He walked over to Bouncer Soto and told him his "son" in the club was "done." That is what the Mongols think of each other. That is who they are. They call each other brother, father and son. Soto walked to the body, looked down for a few seconds then bent to pull off Martin's Mongols cut – the black leather vest with a cartoonish, Mongol warrior wearing shades and smoking a joint on the back.

The paramedic said, "You can't touch him."

Soto, who resembles Shrek and whose conversational voice is a growl replied, "Fuck you dude! That patch doesn't belong on the ground with him. And, that fireman just backed off. He didn't say shit. I took the patch off him."

The next morning, the snarky television take on Martin's murder was that it had screwed up way too many people's morning commute. Cheerful, bubble headed hosts speculated on when, if ever, the transition between the Glendale and Foothill freeways might reopen. As is their custom, the police worked very deliberately, closing down a half mile of freeway while they sipped their coffees thoughtfully, crossed their arms pensively, strode about importantly and told each other dirty jokes.

Only a few eccentrics here and there were more interested in the biker angle than the traffic angle. "It was all we talked about in the writer's room that morning," a Hollywood show runner named Kurt Sutter said. Sutter writes and produces a television series about bikers for the *FX Network* called *Sons of Anarchy*. In that show the Mongols are called the "Mayans." They are not the heroes. The heroes, for whom the show is named, are meant to represent the world's most famous motorcycle club, the Hells Angels.

But despite their relative lack of fame, in Southern California the Mongols are the show. The bad ass biker pecking order in Los Angeles has Mongols first, Vagos second and then the Angels. The Vagos and the Angels sometimes, but not always, get along. The Mongols and the Angels get along rarely.

The feud between the Mongols and the Angels is the second longest in American History – second only to the feud between the Hells Angels and the American Outlaws Association – and it is as violent as a Norse saga. The Hatfields and the McCoys only went at each other for 26 years. The Mongols and the Angels have been beating, stabbing, shooting and blowing each other up since 1977. It is personal. It is not about business. If it was about some drug business or whore business or gun business it would have stopped thirty years ago but it has become a tradition. It is self-perpetuating. Motorcycle clubs are not about crime or business. Motorcycle clubs are about brotherhood, honor and self-esteem. And the feud is centered in the Hells Angels' core belief that they are number one.

The feud is part of the baggage you agree to carry when you join either club. It is how young Angels and young Mongols prove themselves. Usually members of the clubs try to avoid each other. The violence is mostly hidden. As a matter of honor, nobody talks to the police. And, when the police learn something they almost never share it with the public. Sometimes the violence spills out into the open where all the citizens can see. And, when the feud appears on television all the non-combatants get their chance to stare at the men they imagine they could be.

The feud was boiling that Fall. Nine weeks before Hitman and Porno Ron took their last ride together a nasty brawl between Angels and members of a Motorcycle Ministry affiliated with the Mongols – the Set Free Soldiers – was sensational news in Los Angeles for a couple of minutes. Much of the appeal of this news was the shocking assertion that in the outlaw world there are "motorcycle ministries." Bemused news anchors, people who routinely employ agents and publicists, reported that the previously invisible and unknown Set Free Soldiers were merely a gang that called itself a ministry as a public relations pose. Sophisticated atheists and agnostics everywhere snickered.

The brawl began after Pastor Phillip Aguilar, the founder of the ministry who frames his left eye with a tattoo, and three of his Assistant Pastors met with four Hells Angels at a bar called Blackie's by the Sea in Newport Beach. When the conversation deteriorated, as conversations between Hells Angels and other outlaws often do, ten more Set Free Assistant Pastors entered Blackie's and surrounded the Angels. A fight ensued that lasted less than one minute. These things rarely last more than a minute. Two Hells Angels were stabbed. One of them had his throat cut. And, one Set Free Soldier was punched in the face with a pool ball. The fight wasn't actually televised but the subsequent Swat raids were.

The Angels-Mongols feud was in the news again around Labor Day. On September 2, a Mongol named Christopher Bryan "Stoney" Ablett shot and killed an Angel in a street fight near the corner of 24th Street and

Treat Avenue in San Francisco. San Francisco police, federal prosecutors and, in particular, agents of the Bureau of Alcohol, Tobacco, Firearms and Explosives – the ATF is the motorcycle club police – have deliberately obscured the details of the fight for years to preserve the secrecy of an "ongoing investigation." An ATF "confidential informant" or "source of information" may have witnessed the fight.

The dead Angel was Mark Papa Guardado. He was the bear-like, often tender and beloved President of the Frisco Charter and the Angels made the earth tremble and the air roar when they carried him home. Civilians lined the funeral route for miles to watch the long pack of bikes fly past. About the same time, three pipe bombs exploded outside the home of a Mongol in San Jose. No one was hurt and little damage was done. An anonymous ATF source told gullible reporters that the lack of damage only showed the Angels must be slipping. That detail, that blunt taunt, made most news stories, too. The anonymous source was probably an ATF Agent named John Ciccone. Ciccone is good at what he does and part of what he does is ensuring that the Angels and Mongols continue to hate each other.

On October 7, hours before Hitman and Porno Ron leaned into that curve, Stoney Ablett walked into a police station in Bartlesville, Oklahoma. Ablett, a handsome man with long, blonde hair and a large Mongols tattoo under his right ear, told the desk sergeant "I am not armed, but I am a fugitive, and I'd like to turn myself in." The sergeant did not believe him. Criminals do not behave like this. Only righteous outlaws do. When the cop could not find Ablett's name in the National Crime Information Center database Ablett helped him find the entry.

That same summer Hitman Martin had also been an active participant in the great and never ending feud. One smoggy day Hitman rode his motorcycle up behind a Hells Angel near the interchange of the 405 and the 118 Freeways in the western end of the San Fernando Valley and stabbed the Angel in the back. The stabbing never made the news. It was never reported to police but the ATF knew about it. "Brand new fucking knife and I left it in there," Hitman excitedly announced as he rushed into a Mongols party. "Now I have to get another knife."

When the sun rose on the morning Hitman died most of the news media in Los Angeles assumed that Martin had been murdered by Hells Angels in retaliation for the killing of Papa Guardado. It was the most simple minded angle. It demonstrated extreme naïveté about what actually happens in this subculture and no official ever contradicted the assumption.

All police routinely lie as an "investigative tool." It is a felony, punishable by forfeiture of your constitutional rights, for you to lie to any federal, state or local policeman but it is just good police work when the cop lies to you. It is routine for police to lie to the press and safe to do so on the subject of outlaw bikers because most reporters are terrified of outlaws. The police are completely blameless when a reporter repeats lies he has been told by his own imagination.

Sergeant Tom Lorenz of the Glendale Police Department identified Martin as a male motorcyclist in his thirties. Police refused to mention the Mongols because to tell something close to the truth would "violate department policy against publicizing violent street gangs" but everybody in Los Angeles County already knew Martin rode with the Mongols anyway. Television reports showed a 400 pound man who resembled Shrek and who wore a Mongols full patch tattoo on his back towering over three Highway Patrol officers at the crime scene and provided the context that "the Mongols are in a furious, bloody feud with the Hells Angels." All of the televised and published accounts also mentioned that Ablett had just surrendered in Oklahoma the day before.

A man named Tim McKinley provided the impeccable quote the *Los Angeles Times* needed to prove true the story the news media had invented out of old toe nail clippings and spider webs. McKinley, a retired FBI Agent who is an "expert" on "biker gangs," told reporters it had to have been the Hells Angels. "It is just game-on between the two groups and it has been for quite a while now," McKinley explained. "They're in a gang war." Of course, McKinley had no idea what he was talking about. But he did get his name in the paper and the *Times* had a reason to say what it wanted to say in the first place.

Meanwhile, the police who actually did have a clue were trying to lead the press on a different wild goose chase. A cover story was invented on the fly. The Glendale Police spokesman slyly stated, "We don't know if he was specifically targeted, it's a random situation or if this was some sort of road rage incident." An "associate" of the dead man was mentioned but not named. The press release issued that afternoon added the interesting detail that "thirteen shots" had been fired at Martin. Not eleven shots, one of which was carried away in that associate's boot, but thirteen. It was the kind of calculated detail that often appears in official police statements. It was a way for police to test whether reporters were actually listening. It was also a little on the clever side for the Glendale cops. It was more the sort of disinformation regularly provided by the ATF.

In detective fiction, in the sort of story Raymond Chandler did well, the detail about the thirteen shots exemplifies an *idee fixe*. The thirteenth letter of the alphabet is M, or as it is pronounced in Spanish, *Eme*.

The intriguing claim that there had been thirteen shots might have also been a good-hearted attempt to give journalists a lead to pursue but no journalist did because they didn't need to. The Hells Angels angle was too adequate not to play in a story that would quickly go away. The really important stories, as soon as the traffic began to clear that day, were the Dodgers and the Phillies; Britney Spears' refusal to cop a plea for drunk driving; an outbreak of *tourista* at USC; and Sarah Palin/Tina Fey/Sarah Palin/Tina Fey. The first, terrible, neighborhood-devouring Santa Ana fire of the season started the next day – the day Martin was autopsied.

After the autopsy the Glendale Police released more "details" about the murder: "Coroners were unable to determine if Martin died from the gunshot wound to his chest or injuries sustained in the subsequent motorcycle crash...." Although, there had been no crash. There was, news footage of Martin's bike sitting upright and undamaged with its yellow turn signals flashing, flashing, flashing but the press was too preoccupied with getting somebody to tell them their story to notice that. So, it was "reported" that maybe Hitman died of the injuries he sustained in his motorcycle crash. Or maybe he ate some bad shrimp.

The acknowledgement that "There was one individual with a Mongol tattoo," was a belated admission that Bouncer Soto was just too big to miss. "The Police Department has not ruled out any outlaw biker activity that may have caused this event.... This obviously started somewhere else and it culminated on the freeway while they were riding.... Detectives are trying to determine where the two bikers were before getting on the freeway...." This was 36 hours after a photographer shot a photo of three uniformed Glendale police officers standing outside The Mix which had been cordoned off with what appeared to be about a mile of yellow tape. It was also a day and a half after all

12

the Mongols at the scene told cops where they had been "before getting on the freeway."

It is easy to dismiss all this prevarication as a case of smart, hard cops having fun with soft, dimwitted reporters but the truth is worse than that. Most of this was reported either on television or in the financially distressed *Times*. Almost everyone from Sarah Palin to Tina Fey is cynical about television "news." But no matter how cynical you are about American journalism now, you may be disillusioned by the truth.

Even jaded news consumers wish and hope that print reporters are somehow more trustworthy than television reporters; that print reporters are investigators rather than merely the trusted cronies of sources or the rewriters of press releases. Actually, most journalists, including reporters for the *Associated Press* and the so-called "newspapers of record" are as overwhelmingly dependent on official sources to provide them "content" as their style obsessed television counterparts are. Most of the news copy read by television anchors and printed in newspapers is actually written by official sources. This blatant propagandizing is especially true when journalists attempt to report on American crime and punishment. The *New York Times*, *Washington Post* and *Boston Globe* may do a fine job with political gossip but they seem blind to the existence of the police-prison industrial complex. From time to time the American press notices when the police are corrupted by money. No one notices that police in America have been widely corrupted by power.

The press has always been bullied by corrupt police. Stephen Crane, while working as a journalist, had to leave New York after offending the cops. "Theoretically the first result of government is to put control into the hands of honest men and nullify as far as may be the ambitions of criminals," Crane wrote. "When government places power in the hands of a criminal (by which Crane meant a corrupt cop) it of course violates this principle and becomes absurd."

What is new within the last few years is the set of skills police departments in general, and particularly federal police departments, have developed for mass media propaganda. For example, police are regularly trained at taxpayer expense in ways to better to lie to the press.

"Media Relations has become one of the single greatest challenges facing Law Enforcement in America," the brochure for "Russell Ruffin's Police Media Relations Training" explains. "With every major news event from the September 11 Terrorist Attacks to the DC Sniper Case, Law Enforcement Officers are faced with the difficult and added burden of disseminating timely and critical information to the public. Whether you are facing the television news cameras daily or dealing with printed press releases, the public is turning to you now, more than ever."

"This exclusive training course, taught by working news reporters, will help you not only develop and refine your communications skills, but also leave you with a better understanding of the needs of the media. If your responsibilities include the management and distribution of information to the public, this course will help you recognize your weak points and build on your strong points. From body language to choice of words and phrases, you may be sending the wrong message to the media and the public. During the program we will turn the news cameras on you and ask tough questions to see how well you are prepared. The videotapes of your performance will then be critiqued."

The course, taught by "Emmy Award winning working news reporters," promises to teach cops, "how to overcome Ambush Journalists, deal with Tabloid News and to safely disarm 'Investigative' Reporters. You will discover how to become an effective resource

14

or 'expert' for the media, elevating you to a prestigious position that will empower you to not only pitch your own stories but routinely present yourself in a more credible position."

Another course taught by Angeline Hartmann, "a national correspondent for the *Fox* television show – *America's Most Wanted*" promises to teach cops "How to get the Media to Work for You."

This media manipulation might be tolerable if it was intended simply to make cops look like "heroes." There is much of that. One cannot live a day in America without constantly being nagged that the police are our most scared cows.

What many Americans of good will, conservative and liberal, faithful and faithless, black, brown, yellow and white, rich and poor might agree is intolerable is that all this propagandizing is mostly used as both an investigative and prosecutorial technique; to prevent justice from being done, to punish dissent, to pressure defendants and particularly to prejudice jury pools, judges and defense attorneys. Hitman Martin, whose name you have just now heard for the first time, was murdered in the context of

an implicit conspiracy to intentionally lie about life, death and civil liberties in America. Co-conspirators included the Department of Justice, the ATF, most of Rupert Murdoch's News Corporation, *The Associated Press*, Discovery Networks International and such venerable American publishers as Random House, Crown and HarperCollins.

The "thirteen shots," the lead that the stupid and lazy Los Angeles press was invited to pursue, was a "clue" that Hitman Martin had been murdered not by the Hells Angels but by another dangerous enemy of the Mongols. The night Martin died the Mongols, at least half of whom are *Xicano*, had only recently ended a five-years-long feud with the Mexican Mafia; which is both a prison gang and a confederation of Mexican street cliques that is important enough to have several names including the *Eme*, the South Siders and the *Surenos*. *La Eme* dominates California prisons and by, at the least, shear force of numbers they are very dangerous enemies.

According to a secret ATF Report of Investigation – an ROI – the Mongols had been "green lighted" by the Mexican Mafia about the same time Ablett shot Guardado. The ATF report stated: "…National President of the Mongols…talked about a Code 55 (telling Mongols not to display their colors) being issued because of the Mexican Mafia issuing a 'green light' against the Mongols and the shooting death of the Hells Angels San Francisco President. The President of the Mongols Boyle Heights Chapter said 'Fuck them! If they come after us, we'll come after them.'"

The report, however, was probably another police lie. The lies the ATF tells are like the iceberg that sank the Titanic. Ninety percent of their mass is hidden so any eventual, secret investigation is likely to find anything – which can then be readily contradicted by more anything. It is a bureaucratic strategy intended to subvert the useful concept of "reality." It is a system Jorge Luis Borges would have been proud to imagine. Regrettably for the Republic, it is no joke.

Although the ROI described an event at the beginning of September it was probably not written until after Martin died. By October, a truce had been declared between the *Eme* and the Mongols. The official report of the green lighting also contradicted another, super secret, contemporaneous report that stated that Mongols club officers had "met with Mexican Mafia representatives in order to resolve conflicts between the Mexican Mafia and the Mongols."

The Mongol who chose to go to war with the *Eme* was a man named Ruben "Doc" Cavazos. Doc Cavazos was the most powerful of the Mongols until he was voted "out bad" a month before Hitman took his final ride.

"Out bad" is what outlaws call a member who has been banished. The principal infractions that lead to banishment are drug addiction, abandonment, betrayal, cowardice, adultery, lying and theft. In a club like the Mongols the process of going out bad is always harsh. In most cases, besides losing all his friends, the banished member must pay a fine or forfeit his motorcycle or both. He must also forfeit all his club memorabilia and he must black out or remove all his club tattoos. In the most extreme cases, out bad is what happens just before your former club brothers show up with a belt sander to take your tattoos.

Doc was expelled from the Mongols on August 30, 2008 for stealing at least $190,000 from the club and for not stopping the feud between the Mongols and the Mexican Mafia. Typically, at the time Doc was negotiating to appear in a documentary about the Mongols with a producer who claimed to be affiliated with *HBO Films*.

That summer Doc's judgment was probably impaired by an apparent, escalating addiction to cocaine. Doc had begun rolling his shoulders and sniffing again and again like an old boxer on the brink of dementia.

At the same time Doc was becoming ever closer to three relatively new Mongols. Numerous sources believe they were the source of Doc's cocaine. Those three were named Gregory "Russo" Giaoni, Paul "Painter" D'Angelo and Darrin "Dirty Dan" Kozlowski. All three men became members of the Mongols Cypress Park chapter and they had an influence on the club far greater than would seem likely for new guys. The three were very ambitious for the

Mongols. The Mongols quickly became their full time job. And, they hoped to turn the motorcycle club into a blatantly criminal enterprise.

In another fullsome "coincidence," those three men rode to the party at The Mix with Hitman Martin the night he died. All three rode to the party wearing their Mongols colors as if they had nothing to fear from either the Angels or the *Eme*. But Russo, Painter and Dirty Dan left the party, wearing their colors, even earlier than Martin did, which was unusual. The three always stayed to the very end of every party but that night they abandoned Hitman to ride back to his home in Venice at the beach accompanied only by the hang around Porno Ron.

The three new patch holders all shared a house less than a mile from The Mix and that house was loaded with drugs. (A prospective member of an outlaw club is fully accepted when he becomes a "patch holder" entitled to proclaim his club identity on his back.) A glass table at the house "was always covered" with crank that other Mongols were encouraged to abuse. (In the sixties and seventies outlaws smuggled the methamphetamine they sold to truckers in their crank cases – so now a metonym for the drug is crank.) Russo who had a goofy smile and Painter who smiled sourly both appeared to have serious drug problems. They constantly bought drugs and gave them away. They gave some of the drugs to Doc. Both men carried nasal spray bottles filled with crank and sniffed from them frequently. One night that summer when Russo was tweaking he took his motorcycle apart and couldn't put it back together. All three had limitless access to money but nobody in the club was sure where the money came from. At one point the three even introduced Doc's son "Lil Rubes" Cavazos to one of his girlfriends. They were everywhere always. They were at the party in the

Valley when Hitman charged in and announced he was going to have to get another new knife.

Numerous Mongols noticed the three new members and either disapproved of them or resented them. Friction quickly developed between Target Owens and Dirty Dan because Target thought Dirty Dan looked like a cop.

Each time a new member joins the Mongols his photo is sent to all the club's chapter Presidents. When Target Owens, President of the Ventura chapter, saw Dirty Dan Kozlowski's photo he thought the new Mongol was a dead ringer for an undercover ATF Agent named Darrin Kozlowski who was pictured in a bestselling book about the Mongols. That book, by an ATF Agent named William Queen, was titled *Under and Alone: The True Story of the Undercover Agent Who Infiltrated America's Most Violent Outlaw Motorcycle Gang.*

When Target looked into this Random House literary product he saw what seemed to be Dirty Dan's picture in the photo leaves following page 118. Lil Rubes Cavazos did not have to look in some book to know that his new friend Dirty Dan was an asset for everybody. He told Target that Dirty Dan had already "done more for the Mongols" than Target had and to "shut up." So Target dropped it. But Dirty Dan never forgot or forgave the accusation Target had made.

Bouncer Soto became suspicious of Painter D'Angelo and Russo Giaoni after the two stubbornly refused to ride into Mexico with other members of the club. Bouncer suspected they were cops and he started calling them the TJs: For Tijuana where they had refused to go, and because they were never apart, and because they were both thin men of average height who both shaved their heads and wore goatees. "I couldn't tell them apart," Soto said. But Bouncer was a loyal soldier and when Doc assured him they were not cops he did not push the issue. "They were so far up Doc's ass all the time, you know…. I figured even if they were cops what difference did it make by then. Shit. What did they have?" Besides, motorcycle outlaws see cops everywhere and before the three were allowed to join the club they were all administered lie detector tests. One of the questions was "Are you a cop?" And, all three passed the tests which satisfied Doc.

When Painter, Russo and Dirty Dan got to The Mix the night Hitman died they immediately went looking for fights. "They were trying to say we were there to fight some Russian dudes, which was totally not the truth," a Mongol who was there said. "They tried starting shit with the bouncers there, and a few other people until Hitman chilled them out."

Among the few other people the three rogue Mongols "tried starting shit with" was a member of the Mexican Mafia associated Toonerville Rifa 13 clique. The clique is named for the old Toonerville neighborhood in Los Angeles, which in turn is named for an even older newspaper comic strip. Mongols remember the Toonerville gangster as "Lips" for a tattoo he wore.

Target and Bouncer were both right. Giaoni, D'Angelo and Kozlowski were undercover ATF Agents. They never left parties early because they stayed to gather "evidence." And, whenever they stayed out late a chase car stayed out late with them. The house they occupied was an ATF safe house filled with hidden microphones and video cameras. Their safe house was less than three miles from the Los Angeles headquarters of ATF in Glendale. And, the three were part of a three-year-long, multistate investigation of the Mongols that was eventually given the public relations handle "Operation Black Rain." As part of that investigation it was Kozlowski who wrote the ROI that claimed the Mongols were not wearing their colors because they had been green lighted by the *Eme*.

Contemporaneous with Black Rain was a federal investigation complete with wire taps of Toonerville Rifa 13. The wire taps were being monitored in a place called the "War Room." The War Room is a feature of the "Los Angeles High Intensity Drug Trafficking Area Intelligence Architecture Plan." The War Room was invented after 9/11 to coordinate the efforts of undercover agents and domestic spies from different police forces. The concept was realized about the time the war on drugs was being redefined as a national security issue and the original mission of the war room was to prevent undercover cops from shooting each other, which in Intelligence Architecture speak, is called "deconfliction."

"The War Room," according to police documents, "provides real time operational and tactical intelligence support by tracking, around-the-clock, all Federal, State and local law enforcement 'high risk' operations within the four county region." So that night the Drug Enforcement Administration, ATF, FBI, Los Angeles Sheriff's Department, the Glendale PD and the Los Angeles Police Department were all monitoring the party at The Mix.

None of the Mongols knew about either the Toonerville investigation, the Mongols investigation or the secretly reported green light but the three ATF undercovers all knew everything. The Field Agent in charge of the investigation and the man who actually typed up most of the ROIs, John Ciccone, knew. And, the Assistant United States Attorney who was officially conducting the investigation of the Mongols on behalf of a grand jury, a man named Christopher Brunwin, knew.

The night he died Hitman Martin knew something, too. For whatever reason, the night he died Hitman Martin experienced a sudden realization about Painter, Russo and Dirty Dan.

21

"Hitman came to me and Monster Shawn and said he had to see us the next day because we 'had to talk about the new dude that was hanging with the Cypress Park (ATF) brothers.' Mind you, in this entire investigation those Cypress Park guys never left a party early once. They rode in with Hitman. Yet, that night they left an hour or an hour and a half before everyone else. Why would they leave early? Right after Hitman came to me and another brother? Why did they leave then?"

One consequence of their early exit was that the chase car, presumably, got to go home early, too. So there were no ATF witnesses to the murder. So afterward the ATF Agents could plausibly deny knowing anything. But the next day, October 8, the three undercover ATF Agents all did their best to incite a war. In virtually the same hour that the Los Angeles press corps was being invited to connect the dots between thirteen shots and the thirteenth letter of the alphabet, Special Agent Darrin Kozlowski was telling every Mongol he could find that Hitman had been murdered by Toonerville Rifa 13 and that retribution should be exacted.

"Dirty Dan tried as hard as he could to get me to cosign on the Toonerville dude as being the shooter," a Mongol who had been at The Mix said. The Mongol refused because he had been standing outside the cocktail lounge when Porno Ron telephoned for help. And, as he stood there he saw "Lips" just getting into his car. "When that didn't happen he went to the National Sergeant at Arms and said that we were at the bar to start shit and he kept up his Toonerville hype. He even tried to get me and another Bro that was there that night in trouble over the shooting and thrown out bad."

Giaoni and D'Angelo, federal agents and officers of the federal court, were telling other Mongols

22

how eager they were to participate in the underworld war Kozlowski wanted to start. "Hey dude what's going on. Do you know who did it? Do you think you know who did it? Well you know, if you want us to go with you, if you guys are going to go take care of business. We're down."

The real Mongols mostly felt sorrow. Years later one of them said, "Nothing will bring back Hitman, that I know." After a long pause he slowly said, "He was a good brother. He left behind a wife and daughters in all of this. I miss him quite a bit." Not even a majority of Mongols think Hitman Martin was murdered by Special Agents Giaoni, D'Angelo and Kozlowski. But some of them do and it is difficult to separate the circumstantial evidence that those agents either killed Martin or provoked Toonerville Rifa 13 into doing it for them from the cold clarity of hindsight. Looking back, the three agents certainly had the motive and the opportunity to commit the murder. Most ATF undercover investigations are at their best unethical and at their worst seasoned with felonies so it seems unlikely that any of the three agents would find murder morally objectionable.

It is a fact that the US Attorney responsible for the case, Christopher Brunwin, knew about both the Mongols and the Toonerville investigations. Enough evidence exists to convict Brunwin of being a sophistical, amoral and self-serving bureaucrat; so that is his airtight alibi. Brunwin, a graduate of Boalt Hall School of Law at Berkeley, would never allow himself to get entangled in a murder cover-up. Allegedly John Ciccone, has called Brunwin a "pussy." When asked directly what he thought of Brunwin, Ciccone replied with a broad and smirking "no comment."

It is also a fact that after spending tens of millions of dollars to infiltrate the Mongols the government case had reached no logical conclusion.

Most of the crimes uncovered by the investigation either had nothing to do with the Mongols, were petty, were committed by a handful of members or were actually committed by ATF employees. So it is hard to imagine that Brunwin was anything but alarmed when he heard whatever he heard about Hitman Martin's murder. And, it is equally clear that he was not concerned at all about the undercover agent's safety. He already did not give a damn about the safety of any of the Mongols. And it is also a fact, like gravity, that on October 9, the day a coroner couldn't decide if Martin had died as a result of a bullet wound to the heart or a completely imaginary motorcycle crash, Brunwin tried to make the investigation stop. He convinced a federal grand jury to return a racketeering indictment against Doc Cavazos and 78 members and associates of the Mongols Motorcycle Club. That indictment, as far as Brunwin and the rest of the US Attorney's Office was concerned, was the official end of Operation Black Rain. Nobody in the US Attorney's Office in Los Angeles will confirm rumors of the big, happy, hand washing party held later that day.

It is another fact that the three undercover agents in Los Angeles and a fourth undercover agent in Las Vegas continued their undercover duties for another week as if they did not know their case was finished. Then it took another few days to orchestrate the big, mass media minstrel show.

The Bust

The raids and the spin began in the darkest hour of October 21, 2008. When the police come for you, they always come in the night. "For safety reasons," Ciccone's 96 page affidavit explained, "the best time to execute the warrants is before most of the occupants of the subject premises, and the population in general, have began their activities for the day. Moreover, in order to maximize the chances of recovering evidence located at the subject premises, the warrants should be executed as close to simultaneously as possible."

"Safety." They serve and protect you in the middle of the night for "safety."

The warrant services were enforced by at least 1,600 militarized police in five states. More and more in America, police like to dress up like the science fiction Marines in the second installment of the *Aliens* franchise. They encourage one another, "Let's rock n' roll!"

Since Waco, these recurring, ATF led, mass raids are directed almost entirely against members of motorcycle clubs and they serve two functions. First and most obviously they should be understood as dramas that advertise and glorify police power. Cops put on the skins of Tom Hanks and Matt Damon in *Saving*

Private Ryan but in these dramas only "bad guys" die. Second, and much less obviously, service of a search warrant by a special weapons team is a brutal form of extra-judicial punishment. These deployments are organized to shock and awe their victims. Police commandos break into homes in the night. They routinely kill pets, sometimes execute suspects, terrorize children, humiliate and brutalize women, literally wreck homes, and confiscate everything they can find. And, then they go "Ooh Rah!" Just like real science fiction Marines.

The warrants themselves come close to what the founding fathers tried to forbid. The "items to be seized" on October 21st included any amount of "United States currency in excess of $500;" "firearms, and ammunition;" "personal telephone and address books;" "telephone bills and utility bills;" "mail;" "all Mongols vests, colors, patches, T-Shirts, pins, stickers, and other memorabilia evidencing an association with the Mongols;" "all notes or minutes of meetings conducted by the Mongols;" "all editions of the Mongols' Constitution and records reflecting amendments to the Mongols' Constitution;" "photographs or videotapes;" "all knives capable of being used as a weapon;" "boots;" "memorabilia associated with rival gangs;" "computer equipment used to facilitate the transmission, creation, display, encoding or storage of data, including word processing equipment, modems, docking stations, monitors, printers, plotters, encryption devices, and optical scanners;" "any magnetic, electronic or optical storage device capable of storing data, such as floppy disks, hard disks, tapes, CD-ROMs, CD-R, CD-RWs, DVDs, optical disks, printer or memory buffers, smart cards, PC cards, memory calculators, electronic dialers, electronic notebooks, cellular telephones, and personal digital assistants." And, in case some of the police did not know how to turn on a computer, "any documentation, operating logs and reference manuals regarding the operation of the computer equipment, storage devices or software;" "any applications, utility programs, compilers, interpreters, and other software used to facilitate direct or indirect communication with the computer hardware, storage devices or data to be searched;" and finally, motorcycles. Motorcycles found at the "subject premises," including motorcycles that just happened to be parked there, were seized because, "members of the gang used their motorcycles and firearms to make their drug business work. This included use of the motorcycles to transport drugs, attend meetings and other gatherings where the gang's drug business was plotted and carried out, and to provide security and other support for the conspiracy."

All of this was seized on the basis of allegations made by the ATF Agents who rode to The Mix with Hitman the night he died and additional allegations manufactured by the undercover agent in Las Vegas, a man named John "Hollywood" Carr.

Further, another federal prosecutor named Frank Kortum, on behalf of the United States Attorney in Los Angeles, on Ciccone's recommendation, sought to seize every item in the United States that could be found that might be construed as indicative of support for the Mongols because, "there is overwhelming evidence that the defendants use and display the (mark) to promote their criminal enterprise and activity." The federal legal team asked Federal District Judge Florence Marie Cooper to order "all defendants in this criminal action, and any of their agents, servants, employees, family members and those persons in active concert or participation with them," be enjoined and restrained with the full force of United States law from "wearing, using or displaying" any Mongols insignia including the common English word Mongols "however used, spelled or displayed, whether capitalized, abbreviated, singular or plural, printed, stylized or incorporated in a symbol or article of clothing, whether used alone or in combination with any wording or symbol, and whether displayed personally or for the purpose of advertising or publicizing the activities of the Mongol Nation, the Mongols or any members thereof."

The naked idea of that was to convey the message that after they locked you up they could lock up your wife if she wore a tee-shirt that proclaimed "Free The Mongols!" They could lock up your kid if he wore a tee shirt that said "Free the M****ls!"

All of this evidence gathering and summary punishment was very expensive even by government standards. The police deployments alone that day, depending on what the police had for lunch, cost at least a million dollars. Late in 2011 all of Operation Black Rain and all that followed from it has cost at least $150 million. The number is the product of an informed but unverified calculation. Nobody knows for sure how much it has all cost because nobody wants to know. When asked, federal officials behave as if they have been asked something ridiculous, unknowable and unimportant. When asked whether it should cost $12,658 to arrest a man for what turns out to be suspicion of possession of a quarter ounce of marijuana federal officials respond as if the question is rude.

And, certainly nobody in the Los Angeles press corps wants to risk being rude to the police. No "reporter" dared be so rude as to connect the murder of Hitman Martin in any way to the police. The press did what it always does when covering grand police spectacles. The press transcribed the handouts. If they were rude, the next time the cops might not let them have a handout. They might get fired because the cops would not talk to them and their more reasonable replacement would get the handout.

The official story of Black Rain, of depraved motorcycle outlaw villains defeated by idealistic, selfless, courageous police champions, was told without a hitch. The Department of Justice Press Release, written by a pleasant fellow named Thom Mrozek, became the rough draft for all subsequent press coverage of the Mongols case. Mrozek wrote:

"Sixty-one members of the violent Mongols outlaw motorcycle gang were arrested today after being named in an 86-count federal racketeering indictment that alleges the criminal enterprise was involved in a wide range of criminal activity, including murder, hate crimes against African-Americans, assaults, firearms violations and narcotics trafficking.

"The racketeering indictment seeks the forfeiture of the trademarked 'Mongols' name, which is part of the 'patch' members wear on their motorcycle jackets.

"'In addition to pursuing the criminal charges set forth in the indictment, for the first time ever, we are seeking to forfeit the intellectual property of a gang,' said United States Attorney Thomas P. O'Brien. 'The name "Mongols," which is part of the gang's "patch" that members wear on their motorcycle jackets, was trademarked by the gang. The indictment alleges that this trademark is subject to forfeiture. We have filed papers seeking a court order that will prevent gang members from using or displaying the name "Mongols." If the court grants our request for this order, then if any law enforcement officer sees a Mongol wearing his patch, he will be authorized to stop that gang member and literally take the jacket right off his back.'

"Those arrested today include the former Mongols National President Ruben 'Doc' Cavazos, several chapter presidents, and various officials of local chapters. In addition to the arrests today, authorities seized dozens of motorcycles which allegedly are part of the gang's criminal enterprise.

"During the investigation into the Mongols, the ATF, joined by investigators from the Los Angeles County Sheriff's Department, the Montebello Police Department and the Las Vegas Metropolitan Police Department, seized 71 firearms, an explosive device and narcotics, including more than six pounds of methamphetamine.

"A total of 162 search warrants were executed today in California, Nevada, Colorado, Oregon, Washington, Florida and Ohio. In addition to the motorcycles seized today, authorities recovered numerous firearms.

"The Mongols are an outlaw motorcycle gang that was formed in Montebello, California in the 1970s. There are as many as 600 members nationwide, with approximately 400 based in Southern California. Many of the Mongols were recruited from some of the most violent Los Angeles-area street gangs, including the 'Avenues' and '18th Street.'

"The Mongols have been in an escalating battle with the Hells Angels motorcycle gang since 2002 when the two groups engaged in a massive riot at a casino in Laughlin, Nevada. The Mongols have also been involved in an ongoing and violent feud with the Mexican Mafia over Mongols drug trafficking activities in areas controlled by the Mexican Mafia.

"According to the indictment, members of the Mongols typically engage in crimes that include acts of violence – ranging from battery to murder – drug trafficking, money laundering, weapons trafficking, extortion, and, very frequently, violent attacks on African-Americans. Members also frequently conduct robberies, steal motorcycles, and engage in the theft of credit card account information to obtain funds for themselves and the organization. Members often commit their crimes and acts of violence with perceived impunity because they believe victims and witnesses are afraid to testify against them or to cooperate with law enforcement for fear of retaliation by the larger Mongols organization.

"During the investigation, four male ATF agents worked undercover and successfully infiltrated the Mongols to become 'full-patch' members. Four female ATF agents also went undercover to pose as their girlfriends. The undercover agents had to undergo rigorous scrutiny by the Mongols, including polygraph examinations, to be accepted as members of the Mongols. They also had to develop and maintain 'biker personas' to prolong their undercover investigation.

"ATF Special Agent in Charge John Torres said: 'Today, the leadership of the Mongols, one of the most violent outlaw motorcycle gangs, was taken down. For three years, four brave and dedicated ATF undercover agents put their lives on the line to infiltrate the Mongols. They made great personal sacrifices to protect our community and we are all extremely grateful.'"

Mrozek's release was full of loose ends. One obvious string to pull is that there were not four undercover ATF Agents in the Mongols when the indictment was returned. There were actually seven and three of them, on the East Coast, remained undercover for at least another 19 months. But not a single reporter was skeptical of any statement in the release.

Another talking point that might have been questioned but was not was the statement about ripping a symbol "right off" somebody's back. Actually the Mongols patch was not a "trademark" like "MacDonald's" which is registered as a legal notice to potential competitors that the name "MacDonald's" is already taken. The Mongols insignia and name were what federal law calls "collective membership marks."

And, as a matter of fact, in the United States of America no police department has the right to rip a Christian cross or a Republican elephant or a Masonic square and compasses or a boy scout fleur-de-lis or a Nazi swastika or even a Mongols patch or a tee-shirt with the opinion "Free the M****ls" off anybody's back because they are all constitutionally protected forms of expression. Newspapers and other mass media like to brag that they are in the free expression, rather than the police propaganda, business but nobody asked about that. The *Los Angeles Times* quickly rewrote the release. The *AP* picked up the *Times* story and the next day some version of Mrozek's essay ran as "news" in London, Hong Kong and Sydney.

The actual indictment, the list of crimes of which the Mongols were accused, which no reporter seems to have read, was full of "crimes" like:

"On November 17, 2005, defendant William 'Moreno' Ramirez is alleged to have possessed a .22 caliber rifle, a 12-gauge shotgun, an M-1 carbine .30 caliber rifle, a .45 caliber handgun, a .38 caliber revolver, ammunition, and numerous articles of clothing that identified his membership in the Mongols gang, at a residence in Montebello, California."

Or:

"On December 10, 2006, defendants Shawn Buss, Robert Vincent Rios, Abram Wedig and Joseph Braden attacked and beat an African-American patron at the Tokio Lounge in Hollywood, California, while shouting racist slurs at the victim." What that charge neglected to mention was that the African-American, in an apparent fit of madness, had just shouldered aside a Mongol to grab his sister's ass. And, the three Mongols who shouted the racist slurs were not named in the indictment. Their names in the club were Painter, Russo and Dirty Dan.

Or the mind-bogglingly contrived charge:

"On September 18, 2007, in San Bernardino, California, defendants Rafael Lozano, Harold Reynolds and Ismael Padilla and an unindicted co-conspirator armed themselves with firearms and arranged to purchase 33 kilograms of cocaine with an undercover law enforcement officer and a confidential government informant."

In the first place, the incident happened in Vegas not San Bernardino. Secondly, the allegation is a lie. What did happen was a chilling. It could have just as well happened to your grandfather. The video surveillance footage of this event, which is still top secret, looks like a student film homage to Woody Allen at his driest. But the allegation did allow the Department of Justice and the ATF to portray the Mongols Motorcycle Club as a major drug cartel.

Another interesting passage in the indictment read:

"On March 11, 2008, by telephone, defendant Cavazos discussed preparing a story on the Mongols with a news reporter, and Cavazos told the reporter that he could provide specific details about a Mongols murder committed at a tattoo shop and involving the Mexican Mafia, including information about the planning and preparation for the murder."

No journalist in Los Angeles ever wondered aloud if there should be a clear line between press investigations and police investigations. Instead the press kneeled and deep throated the official account.

Morning news anchor Frank Buckley of television station *KTLA* (owned, effectively, by the *Chicago Tribune* and the *Los Angeles Times*) tossed his viewers attention to a reporter in the field who had "live coverage of the arrests." Virtually every television news story in Los Angeles is introduced as "breaking news" or "live coverage."

The "latest on our top stories at 8:33," Buckley told viewers, was "breaking news out of Montebello. Police are rounding up suspects as part of a three year undercover investigation known as Operation Black Rain. *KTLA*'s Chip Yost is live in Montebello to explain. Chip?"

"Yeah. Good morning Frank. We're learning a lot more about this," Yost said. "Remember those Swat guys we've been showing you throughout the morning?" Nothing says journalism like a screen full of Swat. "They're up here on the roof over here. If you take a look at those guys, we could move the camera if we could, you see there where that guy's at in that area over there they have a holding area where they've been bringing a lot of these suspects, these Mongols, in there. We can show you some video we shot earlier of some of them coming in."

Actually, *KTLA* did not shoot any of the footage. In the television news business the footage is called "B-roll." The ATF shot all the B-roll and for the next three minutes while Yost "reported," sleepy and often defiant Mongols were instantly punished with public shaming.

After they were led past the assembled television journalists they were greeted inside by John Ciccone exultantly snarling, "You want to talk to me? You want to talk to me?" Monster Buss, who tried vainly to save Hitman's life was arrested that day. Porno Ron was not indicted. Trouble Turner was located in a hotel room with a woman. The police had already wrecked his mother's house looking for him. They threatened the mother with arrest if she did not help them find him. She called her son on his cell phone. He told the police where he was. When the cops arrived they beat him. Trouble fought back so they beat him some more. Of all the indicted Mongols, only Bouncer Soto escaped and remained at large. That morning none of the defiant Mongols wanted to talk to Ciccone.

"While we're doing that (watching the Mongols do the perp walk) we're going to talk to Tom Mangan of the ATF," Yost explained to his viewers. Then Yost threw a small bag of marshmallows, one by one, right at Mangan's talking head. "This was a really complex investigation. You had some of your own guys deep undercover with these guys." That is how Yost asked, "What is going on?"

"Yeah. Good morning," Mangan said. "It was a massive operation. Three years. Deep undercover. By four extremely experienced, ATF deep cover operatives. Uh, they seen the worst of the worst. We're very proud of today's operations. It was a massive operation, uh, reaching far beyond just California. Five states in total."

"And, these guys your agents, four of them in total..." Yost asked television style – which is a style of interrogation that resembles Rogerian psycho-therapy more than H. L. Mencken, "...actually I understand became members of the Mongols.

"That's right. Uh, they were so experienced and that became the purpose of it and they became full patch members of the Mongols which is an outlaw motorcycle gang. They were living and breathing day to day with those guys."

"Did it ever get hairy? I mean did they ever have a day where they thought their cover was going to be blown?" Like the time during the 33 Kilo cocaine deal in Las Vegas when a Mongol named Harry "Face" Reynolds, alarmed and dismayed to suddenly find himself in a room with all that cash and concerned for everybody's safety, leaned on a door that had a crouching, Vegas Metro Swat Team on the other side?

"There wasn't a day when they woke up that they didn't have to be in role and aware of the situation and the surroundings living those dual lives. Uh...they immersed themselves in it and quite frankly was very successful with today's, uh, look at the fruits of today's labors. It's a massive arrest operation, devastating to this gang, uh, and taking out the whole leadership of the Mongols organization."

"And, we're talkin' more than a hundred arrest warrants for everything from murder to what?"

"Just a hundred and twenty arrest warrants just in the Los Angeles area alone. Murder, attempted murder, firearms, narcotics violations, RICO, conspiracy, the gambit. And this is the gambit and the type of violence that's associated with this gang."

"Is there a reason why this was done today" Yost asked. It was the one interesting question he asked. He did not have Hitman Martin's murder in mind but his reportorial instincts were good. He was competent enough to wonder, "Was there something that caused this all to take place today?"

Mangan flirted with the truth. "Uh, you know again, if you look just with the last several months. Look at the violence associated with the Mongols. You had one of their own that was shot off a bike on the expressway. Uh, over a month and a half ago, a rival gang, the Hells Angels, one of their sworn enemies, the President of that gang was killed by a Mongol. Again, the violence runs with these colors and runs with these individuals."

"And, we always hear, you know I've done stories on some of these biker gangs before and they say we're clubs. We're not a gang. What do you say to that?"

"That's a joke. The Mongols are a gang. They recruit from the most vicious street gangs here in Los Angeles. They're nothing but a criminal syndicate on wheels. Uh, they're a motorcycle clu...gang and that's what they are. They're criminals."

Thom Mrozek later denied responsibility for the phrase "criminal syndicate on wheels."

"What do you expect this to be, the outcome of all this action to be," the television reporter asked. "Is this the end of the Mongols for now or will they come back in some form?"

"You know, like you cut the head off any snake sometimes," Mangan, a poet among ATF Agents explained, "you know, another one may pop up but we're very happy with today's operations. So far everything is being conducted safely, successfully and we have a lot of bodies in custody and we expect more."

And, then Chip Yost said, "Well thanks for joining us." The camera cut away before Yost offered Mangan his lovely parting gift.

Back in the studio Frank said, "Lot of information in that interview, Chip." Frank said that with a straight face.

The coverage on National Public Radio, the heavyweight champion of liberal social orthodoxy, was more creative. "Award winning journalist" Mandalit del Barco sweetened her "report" with motorcycle sound effects. "The Mongols Motorcycle Club has been around for 30 years, born in Montebello, an East L.A. community," del Barco told listeners. "Legend has it that they formed after the Hell's Angels wouldn't have them because they were Latino."

Yes, "legend." NPR actually "reported" a "legend." NPR also interviewed ATF author William Queen. "In the state of California, the Mongols run the outlaw motorcycle gang world," was how Queen introduced himself. "They pride themselves with being the most violent around – everything from just street beat downs to murder."

Del Barco explained to her radio listeners who was talking. "Former ATF agent Billy Queen went undercover with the Mongols for two years, resulting in many arrests. He went on to write a best-selling memoir about his experience. Queen says he wore a long goatee, drove a Harley-Davidson they stole for him, and had to earn his Mongol patch by proving himself."

"Whatever they wanted me to do," Queen said. "If it was stand by and assist in stealing motorcycles or hauling the drugs for them, whatever it was that came up, I did. I had my own little line in the sand, and that was rape and murder. I certainly wouldn't - gonna assault people to the point where they would be hurt really bad." By that Queen meant, by his own admission, that he nearly killed a man in a knife-fight but the loser did live so he could not have been hurt that bad. Queen did not actually cut off his victim's sexual organ or anything. "You know, they drank and they partied," Queen explained. "And if you got in their way, they'd just beat you down. They want to be king of the mountain, baddest dudes out there rolling."

"So as a former Mongol," del Barco continued, "Queen says he can appreciate and admire the three-year undercover operation the ATF's agents played in this recent sweep dubbed Operation Black Rain."

"These guys and girls worked behind enemy lines for three years with people that would murder them if they found out who they were," Queen claimed, arguing the motive Kozlowski, Giaoni and D'Angelo might have had for murdering Hitman Martin first.

A week after Martin's funeral, two days after the roundup and the press event, the four Agents who "investigated" the Mongols in Los Angeles and Las Vegas – Giaoni, D'Angelo, Kozlowski and Carr – dressed in biker costume, rode motorcycles, put on masks for their "security" and appeared on the Fox television show *America's Most Wanted* where they were hailed as anonymous heroes. The host of the show rode a motorcycle too.

"The mystique and the glamour of the Hells Angels and the Mongols and some of these outlaw biker gangs is just fiction," John Walsh, the creator of

38

America's Most Wanted explained. "A lot of them deal in drugs, teenage prostitution, they sell guns, they commit murders. And I've ridden motorcycles my whole life and raced motorcycles. And, I think it's gangs like the Mongols and some other outlaw biker gangs…give motorcyclist a bad name because they're…they take the low end of the spectrum.

"I got to meet these ATF guys who risked their lives to go under cover with the Mongols. I mean you can lose your life. If they know if you've come into the gang…it's like being an undercover narcotics police officer." Walsh maintained his journalistic objectivity to the extent that he did not volunteer to build the gallows or buy the rope. It might also be worth mentioning that three years after the conclusion of Black Rain John Walsh is the only journalist to meet the undercovers. In November 2011, Giaoni's, D'Angelo's, Kozlowski's and Carr's names have never been released or published.

"The ATF did something that's never been done in the history of outlaw biker gangs," Walsh explained. "Some biker gangs like the Hells Angels market their tee-shirts and their colors and stuff and if people really knew how you get your colors by doing some of these terrible things they probably wouldn't buy these products but the ATF is this close," Walsh held his fingers about an eighth of an inch apart, "to owning the Mongols logo and that if you wear a Mongols hat or a cut jacket or if you wear their tee-shirt it will be against the law. I think it's a really good way to hit them right in the financial belt."

Walsh, who is probably a well-intentioned man, did not elaborate on the implications of his theory that the Hells Angels and the Mongols are criminal syndicates funded by the lucrative and illicit tee-shirt racket. Instead he bragged that *America's Most Wanted* had been granted "special access" by the ATF. A journalist might have asked whether it is proper for a federal police department to grant or deny access to reporters depending on how much they are likely to flatter the cops. Walsh did not ask that.

Walsh, the victim of a terrible crime long ago who channeled his grief and rage into vigilantism is generally considered by Congressmen, Presidents and the public to be a credible victims' advocate. People who have been victimized by Walsh's broad brush find him less credible. "John Walsh should get hit by a car," Trouble Turner said.

At the opening of another segment, Walsh leaned on the handlebars of a "seized" bike in a "secret location," which was a police garage in Long Beach. Draped over the handlebars of the bike was a Mongols vest, patch-side out, displayed as a war trophy. It was great, gritty, television "realism." As with all of this new, stupid journalism, the image was intended to portray that Walsh and the ATF were "partners" in the story. The point of the coverage was not journalism but "realism." No one "reported" the Mongols case. The Mongols case is an example of what happens when reporting is replaced by something better – as the Paris in France has been replaced by the better one in Las Vegas.

But it is possible, despite government objections, to report a story about what led to and followed the murder of Manuel Vincent Hitman Martin. It is both an old and new story. You know it by heart and you have never heard it before. The story of Operation Black Rain is really the story of what John Walsh called the "mystique and the glamour" of motorcycle outlaws. And that story did not begin in October 2008. The beginning of this story was very long before that.

The Final Frontier

Motorcycle outlaws are ghosts from the American frontier which, during our nation's long rise to greatness was our national treasure and our refuge from repressive laws. In retrospect, the frontier became the basis for most American mythology and, until Vietnam, most of our national ideals. As recently as 1960, John F. Kennedy was calling for "a new frontier."

Six score years after its evaporation nobody ever asks the obvious question of how much longer America can go on without a frontier. Without a doubt, the disappearance of the frontier exacerbated the Great Depression. Americans escaped previous capitalist meltdowns by running west. The dispossessed fled the panic of 1873 by overrunning the Sioux lands and the gold they pulled out of the Black Hills helped end that depression and pay off the Civil War. People were still trying to run west in the 1930s. *The Grapes of Wrath* is about the bleak end of that. The absence of a frontier complicates the depression that began in 2007, which on television is usually called "the economic recovery."

Current scholars tend to describe the frontier as an "ideology" and argue that we are better off without it – without all the genocides, lynchings, gun fights, range wars, cattle rustling, drunkenness, drug addiction, racism, sexism, vigilantism, general lawlessness and environmental exploitation. Political correctness forbids the possibility that those sins might be the dark heart of freedom.

But the scholars are still at least half right. The idea that the frontier itself may be distilled into an idea explains the spread of outlaw motorcycle clubs around the world. It lends context to Vladimir Putin's remarks to the Night Wolves in Sevastopol in July 2010. "Bike is the most democratic transport vehicle," Putin told the Russian outlaws. "Bike is the most daring, challenging, as it gives its owner the tempting feeling of freedom. That is why one can say without exaggeration, bike is a symbol of freedom. You came here, because you are a free people and you can go wherever you want."

American outlaw bikers are also now a symptom of the escalating and infuriating unfairness of modern America. Outlaw clubs are kin to populist movements like the Tea Party on the right and Occupy Wall Street on the left. Bikers are predominantly libertarian. And, their members are the metaphorical and in many cases the literal descendants of men who needed elbow room from society and so they ran off to Kentucky, to Texas, to California, to Alaska and after that last gold rush, just before the Russo-Japanese War, even to Manchuria.

Admittedly, at first glance, it is a daffy notion to see motorcycle outlaws as lost time travelers or poltergeists but at least it is less daffy than insisting that these same men are gangsters or that clubs like the Mongols are hierarchical, profit centered mafias – like the banks or the oil companies – which happens to be the official view of the ATF, the Department of Justice and of quasi-official "biker authorities" like Julian Sher, Yves Lavigne and Kerrie Droban. Virtually nothing you have seen or read about motorcycle outlaws is true except as Stalin defined truth.

The truth about outlaw bikers is buried under a well polished narrative you already know. So, before you can begin to understand what the government of the United States did to a few hundred men who call themselves Mongols, because they defiantly called themselves Mongols, you should at least take another look at most of what you now assume to be true.

The story the cops and prosecutors tell always begins with an image of a drunk named Eddie Davenport who rode with a motorcycle club called the Tulare Riders. When he started drinking one Thursday afternoon Eddie had a lot of company. When the party broke up Saturday night Eddie was too drunk to leave. By the time the reporter arrived he was alone. Then Eddie agreed to help out a photographer who wanted to put his picture in the newspaper.

The photo was taken late on Saturday July 5, 1947 or the wee hours of July 6. The photographer was Barney Peterson. He worked for the San Francisco *Chronicle*. For hours the police scanner in the *Chronicle's* city room squawked about an out-of-control party in a sleepy, little, farm town south of the city. Eventually a night editor sent Peterson and a general assignment reporter named C. I. Dourghty Jr. out to find a story. The town is still there and comparatively unchanged. It is called Hollister.

Hollister sponsored a "gypsy tour" over the three-day weekend. "Gypsy tour" is a phrase from the 1920s that describes a gathering of motorcyclists from far and wide. Now these events are always called either "runs" or "rallies." The name has changed but the intent of these gatherings has not. The point of the continuing rallies in Sturgis, Laughlin, Laconia, Reno and a dozen other places is to invite a horde of motorcyclists to town and then sell them beer, food, souvenir tee shirts and accommodations at five times the regular price. The Hollister tour attracted a thousand riders. Ninety percent of them were young men and most of them belonged to motorcycle clubs.

Before the Greatest War, the Greatest Depression bloomed with clubs: Stamp clubs, sewing clubs, chess clubs, bridge clubs, the Masons, the Elks, the Knights of Columbus and motorcycle clubs. All these clubs gave ordinary people something to do and somewhere to go one night a week. They were a cheap source of joy and companionship. They were social networks. The Outlaws Motorcycle Club, now widely described as an "organized criminal syndicate," began as a way for downtrodden yeoman to share their misery and their enthusiasm for motorcycles in McCook, Illinois in 1935.

The War changed the tone of motorcycle clubs. Hollister, and Eddie Davenport, changed the sparks in people's brains when they heard the words motorcycle club.

After the Second World War rugged, simple, Army surplus Harley-Davidsons with flat heads and 45 cubic inches of cylinders were so cheap anyone could afford one. Jobs were so easy to get they were disposable. And some small percentage of veterans, like Larry Darrell in W. Somerset Maugham's *The Razor's Edge*, took some time to "loaf."

The young veterans did not quite fit into the old motorcycle clubs anymore. So, they organized a new generation of motorcycle clubs. And that is where the Hells Angels, the Pissed Off Bastards of Bloomington, the Boozefighters and the Galloping Goose came from. Hollister, out of innocence or greed, thought it might be good business to invite a thousand of these guys to town for July Fourth.

It now hardly matters what actually happened. But, what actually happened was dozens of drunken bikers raced up and down California Route 25 which Hollister still calls San Benito Street. Three of them were seriously injured in crashes. One of them almost lost his foot. Another helmetless rider fractured his skull. Thursday night the biker horde slept in haystacks outside town and in little Hollister's six public parks. At least one of the bikers urinated in public and was arrested for indecent exposure. The revelers littered and they defied traffic regulations. In short, a bunch of strangers rolled into somebody else's town and acted like they owned the place as college students would do 15 years later in places like Fort Lauderdale and Palm Springs, and as college students still do in places like Cancun. About 3:30 Friday afternoon, the local, seven man police force sent out a call for help. The next day the *Chronicle* sent in Peterson and Dourghty.

Dourghty called the tour an "outburst of terrorism" and reported "wrecking of bars, bottle barrages into the streets from upper story windows and roofs and high speed racing of motorcycles though the streets." He also said peace was restored only after 40 California Highway Patrolmen, armed with the threat, but not the actual deployment, of teargas, "herded the cyclists into a block on San Benito street, between Fifth and Sixth streets, parked a dance band on a truck and ordered the musicians to play."

"You just can't run everybody out of town," Dourghty quoted Highway Patrol Captain L.T. Torres.

Dourghty's report falls in the penumbra between plausible and fanciful. He probably never saw any of the mayhem he described. So, neither did Barney Peterson. And, so Eddie Davenport became the poster boy for American moral decline.

Dourghty phoned his story in to a rewrite man but, still, his quotes do gleam like a dead fish in the moonlight. Dourghty's wonderful detail that "bartenders halted the sale of beer, believing the group could not afford whiskey" should be true. The quote from a local city councilman that "there appears to be

45

no serious damage. These trick riders did more harm to themselves than the town," probably was true.

There is less doubt about Barney Peterson's photo. It was obviously staged. Peterson's job was to illustrate Dourghty's story so he needed a drunken lout on a bike. The lout they found was Eddie Davenport and the transcript of what happened after they found Eddie is the succession of shots Barney Peterson staged to accompany Dourghty's scribbles.

"Can we get the Johnny's Bar and Grill sign in the frame? Can we stand up some beer bottles around this guy's feet? More beer bottles. Eddie, drape your jacket over your shoulder. No, no, put it back on. More bottles. Knock them over."

Dourghty had written, "San Benito street, the main thoroughfare through the town, was littered with the wreckage of thousands of beer bottles, and other debris" so Peterson's snapshot had to illustrate that.

"Eddie, hold this bottle in your other hand like you're drinking from two bottles at once. Careful Eddie! Don't fall down yet!"

The *Chronicle* never ran any of Peterson's shots but the now fading paper will sell you a print of one of them. You can buy a copy of the photo that ran on page 31 of the July 21, 1947, edition of *Life* magazine. In that photo the front wheel of Eddie Davenport's motorcycle and his feet are lapped by a pond of empty bottles.

The photo accompanied a *Life* story about the "Hollister Motorcycle Riots" and the caption under the photo read, "Cyclist's Holiday: He and his friends terrorize a town."

Barney Peterson's snapshot and the events it was intended to represent mortified all of the respectable motorcycling world – especially the staid American Motorcyclist Association which, since 1924, had been the official sanctioning body of American motorcycle clubs; dedicated to "protecting the future of motorcycling, and promoting the motorcycle lifestyle of 'freedom on two wheels.'" The AMA washed its hands of these hoodlums. They were, a spokesman explained, "outlaws" and they represented at most only "one percent" of the motorcycling community. What the AMA proclaimed was a little different from what people heard.

The original meaning of the "outlaw" label was to describe unofficial motorcycle races and events, which is to say events that were not sanctioned by the AMA. But, when the loafing young veterans heard the comment they replied grinning, over and over, "Yeah. We're one percenter outlaws. Yeah." For young men, it was a very appealing idea.

Barney Peterson's photo stimulated other imaginations. A writer named Frank Rooney was inspired by the photo to write a short story called "Cyclists Raid." It was the original prose portrayal of outlaw bikers – the beginning of everything since, and Rooney's words describe a flaw in post-war America that was only coincidentally about thugs on motorcycles.

"I'm Gar Simpson and this is troop B of the Angeleno Motorcycle Club," Rooney's "tall, spare" and "coldly courteous" anti-hero introduced himself. "Like all the others he was dressed in a brown windbreaker, khaki shirt, khaki pants" and "dark calf-length boots."

"Where do you go after this," Rooney's host asked the frighteningly disciplined young pack.

"North."

"What are you interested in mainly?"

"Roads. Naturally, being a motorcycle club – you'd be surprised at the rate we're expanding – we'd like to have as much of California as possible opened up to us."

Rooney's tale was a frightening and thoughtful interpretation of the "Hollister Riot." America, a country and a dream built on endless expansion, had sent young men off to conquer the Pacific and Europe. They succeeded. They returned changed with blood on their hands. America had blood on its hands. Then, with no other worlds left to conquer, Rooney's young men in mufti threatened to conquer all the rest of us.

Harpers ran Rooney's story in the January 1951 issue. It was anthologized in *The Best American Short Stories 1952* and on the last weekend in 1953 it was released in its theatrical incarnation – as a movie called *The Wild One* starring a sullen and rebellious actor named Marlon Brando and a very edgy, ex-Marine sniper named Lee Marvin. The anti-hero's name was changed from Gar to Johnny. And, the movie, as movies always do, alchemized Rooney's story into something entirely different and new. *The Wild One* became one of three classic films – along with *Rebel Without A Cause* and *Blackboard Jungle* – to dramatize the emerging threat of "juvenile delinquency."

"Hey Johnny," a puzzled and innocent girl with an obviously pre-atomic-age mind asked the leader of the pack. "What are you rebelling against?"

And Johnny sneered, "What've you got?" It was a line that struck a chord deep in the American soul.

It rang so true the chord still sounds. *The Wild One* created an image of bikers America was eager to embrace. So Johnny the rebellious punk, not Eddie the happy drunk or Gar the lost soldier became the official image of the outlaw biker. The image became more important than the reality. The image mattered most of all to policemen who embraced the idea of being the brave sheriffs who faced down gangs of outlaws. Less than a year after Hollister a Sheriff in Riverside, California coined the phrase "Outlaw Motorcycle Gang." Four years before The Wild One premiered, cops were already writing reports about "OMGs."

A decade after *The Wild One*, Hunter Thompson wrote a quasi-novel about motorcycle outlaws called

Hell's Angels. Starting with the title, the book was an obvious compromise between what Thompson learned and what Random House wanted to sell. Thompson's editor, the now sainted James H. Silberman, insisted that the title must be spelled with an apostrophe on the assumption that the Angels were too stupid to know how to spell their own name. And maybe they were but now, after a half century of reflection, any Angel will tell you there are many hells. Silberman had edited James Jones and James Baldwin. At the time he started working with Thompson, Silberman had just edited Richard Farina's *Been Down So Long It Looks Like Up To Me* which, in most editions, ends with a postscript explaining that the author died in a motorcycle accident shortly after the publication of his book. Thomas Pynchon, another of Silberman's authors, would later claim that Farina's last words were "I soon must quit the scene" and that the bike was going 90 miles per hour. So, Hunter Thompson needed to at least top that.

Before he met Silberman and mutated into Gonzo Super Freak, Thompson had been heavily influenced by the postwar, social novelist Nelson Algren. Early in *Hell's Angels*, Thompson describes the outlaws he met as "Linkhorns" after the dope smoking, brawling, white trash family in Algren's novel *A Walk On The Wild Side*. Algren probably considered *A Walk On The Wild Side* to be his masterpiece. He described it as a parable about suffering, compassion and "the human basis of our democracy." It was a book about what should matter in America — about what was noble in the least of Americans. It is not too great a stretch to say it is about the kind of yeoman who once ran off to the frontier. And, Thompson seems to have intended to explore something close to Algren's theme when he began his tale about bikers.

"It would not be fair to say that all motorcycle outlaws carry Linkhorn genes," Thompson explained, "but nobody who has ever spent time among the inbred Anglo-Saxon tribes of Appalachia would need more than a few hours with the Hells Angels to work up a very strong sense of *déjà vu*."

Hell's Angels, of course, turned out not to be very much about the Hells Angels because Thompson never really found much to say about them. He discovered that the outlaw world was "pathetically mundane." He reported that almost everything everyone said about the Hells Angels was, "to a large extent untrue" because the United States was under the influence of "a national rape mania" and a "need for mythic villains; and the press has been more than willing to satisfy both."

Then Thompson and Silberman, the consort dancing together or taking turns, transformed *Hell's Angels* into something sensational that would sell. It became a funny and frightening caricature of its author. Tragically or ironically it became the suit Thompson had to wear the rest of his days until he blew his brains out in February 2005.

Big chunks of his biker book are extravagant lies. The most dramatic of those lies is the invention that Thompson was the moth who flew too close to the flame; that he lived on the edge of a cliff; that he danced with danger for just a few minutes too long and danger made him pay. His immortal legacy in the outlaw world is his lie that even to write about motorcycle outlaws is dangerous. Most of the idiots who concoct think pieces about outlaws quote Thompson directly or indirectly. His bravery is routinely celebrated and *Hell's Angels* is widely considered a primary source. One editorialist recently commented that, "much of what we know comes from this classic" as if the motorcycle outlaw frontier is the far side of the moon instead of a bar on the outskirts of town.

Thompson ends his *Strange And Terrible Saga Of The Outlaw Motorcycle Gangs* by claiming, "On Labor Day

1966, I pushed my luck a little too far and got badly stomped by four or five Angels who seemed to feel I was taking advantage of them. A minor disagreement suddenly become very serious."

The Angels tell a different story. Thompson was a flawed man; an alcoholic who liked to play nasty practical jokes; and he was just the sort of orphan who gets adopted by a motorcycle club. But, he kept his distance from the Oakland Angels and he lied – which is considered a more terrible sin among young boys and motorcycle outlaws than among politicians, publishers or television producers. Thompson promised the Angels beer and eventually it became obvious that he had lied. It was not the beer that mattered. It was the lie.

Thompson also made sure the Angels knew he didn't want to become one of them. Then after a year of getting on everybody's nerves, he interjected himself into a domestic dispute. Whether he was morally right to do so or not is beside the point. Most people know better than to try to rescue a woman from her husband. Thompson, for whatever it reveals about him and however dangerous he actually found the Angels to be, did not.

What happened was that an Angel named "Junkie George" was slapping his wife around. Of course, George should not have beaten his wife. He should have nurtured and treasured her but sometimes in the course of human events men beat their wives. No one now seems to remember why George hit his wife. Maybe she confessed to turning tricks. Maybe she confessed to turning tricks and not giving any of the money to him. Maybe she burned the pork chops – again.

Thompson was about ten yards away when Junkie George exploded in rage. George's dog was closer. The dog took the wife's side and bit his master. So, George kicked his dog. Which was precisely the moment when Thompson chose to counsel George that, "Only a punk beats his wife and kicks his dog."

George punched Thompson and, as is the custom in motorcycle clubs, "three or four" other club brothers were honor bound to punch Thompson, too. "We let them beat him up for a minute," Sonny Barger, the most famous Hells Angel, has said "then we broke it up and told him to get out of here and he left and got in his car."

The incident was not as good as actually dying in a motorcycle accident as Farina had done but it still provided exactly the dramatically satisfying conclusion Thompson and Silberman had been searching for. "My face looked like it had been jammed into the spokes of a speeding Harley, and the only thing keeping me awake was a broken rib," Thompson wrote at the conclusion of his book. Then he quoted the most famous line from Joseph Conrad's *Heart of Darkness*. "The horror! The horror! ... Exterminate all the brutes!"

Barger dismisses that last bit as "malarkey" and deconstructs the memorable image of Thompson's badly beaten face as "his style of writing."

Despite their grumblings, Thompson succeeded in making the Hells Angels and almost everything they did famous. It was an age of rebellion. Upper-middle class children throughout the 1950s had been ordered by their parents not to succumb to conformity and they obeyed. "This monstrous falsehood taught by many of our social agencies –you must adjust—has become the eleventh commandment in our society," a psychoanalyst named Robert Lindner lamented in the New York *Times* in the Spring of 1955. Adlai Stevenson warned a Vassar graduating class about the "hazard" of conformity.

That first generation of outlaw bikers heeded Stevenson's warning. And, since part of being a biker involves putting on a kind of costume they easily fit into the next decade as well. Hippies also liked costumes.

Bikers and hippies also shared an interest in intoxication. Halfway through the sixties, as Hunter Thompson was engaged in his perilous adventure, the late novelist Ken Kesey introduced the Oakland Angels to LSD. Simultaneously, the Angels resented their fame and found it opened many doors.

The similarities between the Hells Angels and hippies were superficial but it was easy for social conservatives to lump the two categories together. Bikers and hippies. Hippie bikers.

Looked at through a telescope, the Bay Area Hells Angels of the late 1960s seem to have been the most interesting men who ever lived. They were celebrities and they were real. They were dangerous and kind, anti-authoritarian and deeply patriotic. They gangbanged Neal Cassady's slight, pretty, ponytailed mistress Anne Murphy one night and by Murphy's own account she loved it. Afterwards one of them gave her a business card with the printed message, "You have just been assisted by a member of the Hells Angels." Afterward, that gangbang became one of the most compelling scenes in Thompson's book.

When the drug scene in the Haight-Ashbury turned vicious and ugly after the Summer of Love the Oakland and Frisco Angels took over the drug business and cleaned it up. All Angels still have a rule that stipulates, "No drug burns" and some old members still wear a patch that proclaims, "You can trust me. I'm a Hells Angel."

The Oakland Angels stole guns and explosives from radicals and sold them to the police. "Mr. Barger would load them in the back of my car," a former Oakland cop named Ted Hilliard once testified. "Automatic rifles and dynamite, for example."

The Oakland Angels were whole-heartedly patriotic. In 1964, Barger visited a writer for the Oakland *Tribune* and asked him to help the Angels enlist to fight in Vietnam. "Our oath of allegiance is to the United States of America," the President of the Angels said. "If there should be trouble we would jump to enlist and fight. More than 90 percent of our members are veterans. We don't want no slackers." They supported the troops in Vietnam. At one point the Oakland Police stopped an anti-war parade at the city line, then looked the other way when the Angels waded into the crowd with flying fists.

They inspired dozens of low budget biker films. Most of them were produced by American International Pictures. A couple of them featured Jack Nicholson. One of them, called *Hell's Angels '69* starred Barger and the original Oakland Angels. It was Barger's only dramatic role until late in 2010 when he played a pimp in an episode of *Sons of Anarchy*. *Hell's Angels '69* was not a good movie but the same can now probably be said of *A Hard Day's Night*. Arguably, the truest scene in *Angels '69* is the one in which an Angel named Terry the Tramp sells his woman for a pack of cigarettes, discovers that the pack is almost empty and still thinks he got the best of the deal.

These biker movies also reinforced a misconception that began with Hunter Thompson and that persists to this day. Thompson left the impression that the Hells Angels, and by inference all motorcycle clubs, were monolithic – like an army. The idea was that the criminality of some motorcycle outlaws represented the criminality of all. In fact, chapters, or as the Angels call them "charters," are connected to one another about the way fried chicken franchises are connected. And, what connects all the inhabitants of the outlaw frontier is a shared culture.

All outlaw motorcycle clubs are closed, masculine tribes. Members are friends in a way that most modern men can no longer be friends after

54

childhood. They are gangs in the way that Tom Sawyer had a "gang."

"'Now we'll start this band of robbers and call it Tom Sawyer's Gang,'" Twain wrote. "'Everybody that wants to join has got to take an oath, and write his name in blood.' Everybody was willing.

"So Tom gave out a sheet of paper that he had wrote the oath on, and read it. It swore every boy to stick to the band, and never tell any of the secrets; and if anybody done anything to any boy in the band, whichever boy was ordered to kill that person and his family must do it, and he musn't sleep till he had killed them and hacked a cross in their breasts, which was the sign of the band. And nobody that didn't belong to the band could use that mark, and if he did he must be sued, and if he done it again he must be killed. And if anybody that belonged to the band told the secrets, he must have his throat cut, and then have his carcass burnt up and the ashes scattered all around, and his name blotted off the list with blood and never mentioned again by the gang, but have a curse put on it and be forgot, for ever.

"Everybody said it was a real beautiful oath, and asked Tom if he got it out of his own head. He said, some of it, but the rest was out of pirate books, and robber books, and every gang that was high-toned had it."

The most obvious trait of men who join outlaw motorcycle clubs is that they are "old boys" and, like professional athletes and coaches, they cling to a set of ideas and ideals that, increasingly, modern men must abandon as part of growing up. This simple world view embodies exactly the same set of ideas and ideals to which men are expected to adhere when they must fight a war. Anyone can see this who actually looks at motorcycle outlaws with his own eyes. It is both the most interesting and the most important thing about them. They are, at once, who men are expected to be when they are boys and who men were expected to be before America declined, when America was still full of youthful hope and possibility, before the frontier died.

Sometimes, objective observers stumble into the fact of this boyishness but they rarely consider it to be important. For example, a reporter for the London (Ontario) *Free Press* named Jane Sims once said some Canadian Bandidos "sounded like the He-Man Woman Haters Club from the old *Little Rascals* television series." But Sims did not think her observation was astute enough to pursue.

Like boys from long ago, motorcycle outlaws can be truthfully generalized as anti-materialistic, anti-authoritarian, honor obsessed, violent and stubbornly loyal. The United States and the Western World have become increasingly ambivalent about this whole combination of traits since the end of Second World War and particularly when these traits are exhibited by outlaw bikers.

Yet for some reason there are now more motorcycle outlaws than there have ever been. Outlaws are everywhere. In Bremen Kurds who call themselves Mongols fight Germans who call themselves Hells Angels. In Australia, Shia outlaw bikers fight Sunni outlaw bikers. The Bandidos have a chapter in Japan.

Gary Kamiya, the co-founder and former executive editor of *Salon*, writing about the Mongols a few years ago, explained away what he called "the myth of the romantic outlaw" by evoking the tired image of the drunken Eddie Davenport about to pass out on his bike. "In some uptight small town of our collective imagination the outlaws are perennially facing off against the squares, and we want the outlaws, if not to win, then at least to go down in a blaze of defiant glory."

Sons of Anarchy creator Kurt Sutter explained his fascination with outlaws as "Vicarious badassary. I'm just a shy, fat kid from Jersey who always wanted to be a badass and have brothers who would stand up for me. Most of my work…has always spun a tale of the dangerous antihero whom we love and fear. That's what I want to be." Sutter went on to say that his television show is meant as an "homage" to modern outlaws.

There have been several of these tributes. The most influential was a film released in July 1969.

When Dennis Hopper and Peter Fonda wrote the script for *Easy Rider* they intended to make just another quick and dirty biker film. Then American International turned them down. American International made *Hells Angels '69* instead. So Hopper and Fonda took their script to Columbia. Columbia let them make the film but with such a limited budget that the shooting schedule was rushed and they had no money for a musical score.

The happy result of that was many scenes, as the late critic Vincent Canby poetically described them, of men on motorcycles, moving in "isolation, against the magnificent Southwestern landscapes of beige and green and pale blue. They roll down macadam highways that look like black velvet ribbons, under skies of incredible purity, and the soundtrack rocks with the oddly counterpointed emotions of Steppenwolf, the Byrds, the Electric Prunes – dark and smoky cries for liberation."

Easy Rider was a very important movie the summer it was new. Hopper won an award for directing it at the Cannes Film Festival. Jack Nicholson won an award for best supporting actor from the New York Film Critics Circle. It was advertised as: "A man went looking for America. And couldn't find it anywhere."

The film was sold as tale of happy nonconformity crushed by cruel repression.

In 1998 the American Film Institute named *Easy Rider* one of the 100 greatest American movies ever which is a very long stretch. It is certainly one of the most iconic movies. Along with Thompson's book and Brando's film it is part of the foundation for what people like Gary Kamiya think they know about motorcycle outlaws.

The film tells the unlikely story of two bikers named Wyatt (as in Earp) and Billy (as in The Kid) who score two kilos of cocaine in the Andes, sell it to Phil Spector at the end of a runway in Los Angeles and then, for some reason, decide to smuggle the money in their gas tanks to New Orleans. Maybe they just don't trust banks. Along the way they meet an interesting hippie who takes them to his commune, gets them laid and gives them a magic pill – a tab of acid that is so potent that they must promise to consume it only if they first split it four ways.

After practically begging to get arrested by disrupting a patriotic parade they meet a stupid and drunken lawyer named George Hanson who tags along with them. In the finished film Hanson is played by Jack Nicholson but he was not the first actor in that role. The part originally went to Rip Torn but according to Hopper, Torn was fired after he and Hopper got into a knife fight on the set. Torn later stated that he never had a knife.

Eventually Wyatt and Billy make it to New Orleans, go to a whorehouse and split the tab of acid with two easy women in a cemetery. The acid trip is portrayed in such a way as to suggest that maybe Wyatt and Billy should have split that tab of acid eight ways.

Then Wyatt and Billy are murdered by Rednecks, not because they are bikers but because they are nonconformists, because they are hippies with long hair. The film is an artifact from a timeless moment when the most admirable and morally superior subculture was called "Hippie." And, in July 1969, when the film debuted, many people liked bikers because they thought they were hippies. That sentiment didn't last long.

Easy Rider was still playing in theaters a month later as both the Manson murders and Woodstock unfolded. It was no longer in distribution four months after that when the free concert at the Altamont Speedway became something less than a total love fest.

Inspired by the good vibrations of Woodstock, the Rolling Stones gave a free concert at the Altamont Speedway in Alameda County, California. The Stones advertised the concert as their way of saying "thank you" to America for the $1.5 million they earned from the un-free portion of their American tour. They called it a "Christmas and Chanukah rite for American youth."

The rock group contracted for a concert film by "direct cinema" auteurs David and Albert Maysles and Charlotte Zwerin. The profits from the film were supposed to offset the costs of the free concert. One of those costs was "security." Emmett Grogan who founded a hippie community action group called the Diggers and Rock Scully who used to manage the Grateful Dead recommend the Oakland Angels. The Angels agreed to take the job for $500 worth of beer and with the understanding that thousands of Stones fans would be eager to buy drugs from dealers they could trust.

It did not then look like quite so half-assed an idea as it does now. Most politicians and police thought Woodstock had been a disaster and wanted to discourage imitations. Rock entrepreneurs saw Woodstock-like concerts as great profit opportunities. When off-duty policemen in Orange County, Florida refused to provide security for a concert there the job went to the Brethren Motorcycle Club who later patched over to the Outlaws. Two years after Woodstock and 20 months after Altamont the Galloping Goose Motorcycle Club provided security for another huge concert in McCrea, Louisiana until state police finally moved in. The bikers were the first people the police ran off.

In 1969 the Angels seemed like a logical choice to guard the stage for the Rolling Stones. The Stones were infatuated with the Angels and not merely some chapter of the Hells Angels but all of them – the whole idea of Hells Angels. They hung out with Angels in London. Angels were very visible at a memorial concert for Brian Jones in Hyde Park.

Three hundred thousand people showed up at Altamont. Four of them died. One of them drowned. Two of them died in a car accident. The fourth one died in the concert movie, *Gimme Shelter*, twice.

That last victim was an 18-year-old named Meredith Hunter and he was stabbed by a 22-year-old Hells Angels prospect named Alan Passaro. Hunter was black. Passaro was white. By most accounts Hunter was obnoxious and kept blocking other peoples view of the stage. That led to a fight with several concert goers at the front of the stage. He was a very tall young man who towered over his opponents. When he began to lose the fight he pulled a gun and fired what was probably meant to be a warning shot. The gun is clearly visible in the film. The Angels took it as an attempted murder.

Passaro said that was when he pulled his knife and swung. "I don't know if I stabbed him," Passaro testified at his trial. "I didn't have no intention of killing." Passaro was acquitted but the moment of Meredith Hunter's death persists to this day as one of the images that flashes through people's minds when they think of motorcycle outlaws. The Maysles and

Zwerin edited their film around the stabbing. The movie dramatically succeeds mostly because Hunter dies in it. Any success *Gimme Shelter* enjoyed was not because of the Stones music but because of Meredith Hunter's homicide. Four decades later the killing infuses every play of the song "Gimme Shelter" which was not even the song the Stones were performing when Hunter died. They were playing "Under My Thumb."

Albert Goldman, writing in the New York *Times* later portrayed Hunter as "a young man with no criminal record (as opposed to his assailant Alan Passaro, who had already been jailed for dope dealing and theft when he was arraigned for the murder)." In Goldman's version, Hunter was only trying to escape the villainous "Angels' fists and leaded pool cues when suddenly he turned around, pulled out his weapon and came back toward his tormentors." According to Goldman, Passaro took that opportunity to stab Hunter in the back just because he was in the mood to kill.

Goldman's version was the story that stuck. By the end of 1971 two kinds of hippies had cytokinesed in the American imagination. There were good hippies and bad hippies. The Manson family and outlaw bikers were how bad hippies looked. It was a stunning public transformation.

Mongols And Angels

After Altamont, almost touchingly, all Angels everywhere publically and humbly demonstrated their distress that America didn't love them anymore. The Mother charter in Oakland hired a public relations firm to tell them where they had gone wrong. They began to invite reporters along on their runs and on at least one occasion to one of their weddings. They helped organize an alternative to the hopelessly square American Motorcyclist Association, which they called the Modified Motorcycle Association. Angels appeared in schools to lecture young children on the dangers of drugs. Angels went on television to talk about their love of motorcycles.

They invented something called "The Toy Run." The San Fernando Valley charter of the Angels enlisted the help of a television star named Art Linkletter – who had written a best selling book called *Kids Say the Darnedest Things*. The Angels filled two trucks with toys and 200 motorcycles escorted the trucks from Griffith Park in Los Angeles to City Hall where the toys were presented to Linkletter. Then, on their own, to prove what good citizens they were, the Valley Angels organized their own "holiday blood drive." It didn't help. "I suppose Hitler did some good things, too," one anonymous cop told the Los Angeles *Times*.

The Angels became political activists. They found a cause in the mandatory helmet law. Bikers had always ridden without helmets until Ralph Nader's book *Unsafe At Any Speed* inspired the National Highway Safety Act. The act ordered states to make bikers wear helmets. Most bikers at the time enjoyed the wind in their hair and the Angels jumped to champion their cause. Along with a magazine called *Easyriders*, named after the movie, the Angels helped organize an advocacy group called ABATE, for "A Brotherhood Against Totalitarian Enactments." When Burbank passed its own helmet law in 1973 the Angels threatened to jam a City Council meeting "with 500 bikers," which in hindsight might have been counterproductive. The helmet law in California was actually repealed and proponents of the law accused politicians who voted for the repeal of "caving in to the pressure of outlaw motorcyclists."

The Hells Angels whole-hearted efforts to try to at least partially integrate themselves into mainstream society were damned from the start.

Exactly as many veterans had returned home from World War II and started their own motorcycle clubs waves of profoundly alienated combat veterans returned home from Vietnam and founded or joined new motorcycle clubs.

The Bandidos, Warlocks, Vagos, and Sons of Silence were all invented during Vietnam. All of these clubs and many older clubs quickly overflowed with highly disciplined, profoundly alienated, Vietnam Veterans who had been inoculated with violence, calloused against mere materialism and greeted upon their return with contempt and scorn. None of them were afraid of the Hells Angels. Some of them became Hells Angels. All outlaw bikers in America today are a legacy of Vietnam. There is an outlaw motorcycle club called the Vietnam Vets. There is an affiliated club called the Legacy Vets that draws it core membership from veterans of Iraq and Afghanistan. Many of the Legacy Vets are the sons of Vietnam Vets patch holders.

One of the clubs those veterans formed was the Mongols, in December 1969 in a town called Montebello, which is just East of Los Angeles. It is common for biker authorities, like NPRs Mandalit del Barco, to say that the Mongols were founded by *Xicano* veterans who were denied entry into the Hells Angels because of their ethnicity but the Mongols always had both white and *Xicano* members. One of the white members who patched into the club in 1973 was a Navy diver named "Dirty" Jim Janos who later changed his name, for professional reasons, to Jesse Ventura and eventually became Governor of Minnesota. Because Ventura sounds Mexican, the former professional wrestler is often cited as an example of the Latin veterans against whom the Angels discriminated.

The Mongols in the early 70s were clearly hell raisers while the Hells Angels at the same time collectively aspired to something more than that. Some of the Angels wanted to be small businessmen. Some of them wanted to be drug lords. Barger has called the period "our gangster years."

In California, various Hells Angels virtually controlled the manufacture and distribution of LSD and methamphetamine. In the 1970s federal and local cops began to draw an analogy between the drug business of the Angels and other outlaws and bootlegging gangsters in the 1920s. Even in the "gangster years" it wasn't quite true. One organized crime investigator hit the nail on the head when he wrote: "The (Hells Angels) organization does not reap large profits from the illegal activities of its individual members.... The profits made by one member or several members in concert is theirs to keep. Other than the $20 local dues and the $10 state dues, the members are not required to share their profits with the organization."

That is still true. Outlaw bikers, like many Americans, consider selling drugs to be a victimless crime. A Mongol explains, "I didn't want to sell drugs. I don't use drugs. I have never done coke or meth in my life. But it's an easy way to make money. And, I liked hanging out with my club brothers so much I didn't have time to work. So I sold drugs."

The outlaw frontier is Darwinian. In the new millennium, most Hells Angels still believe that their club brothers hold the exclusive franchise to sell "drugs, guns and women." Hells Angels who are as law abiding as nuns are still honor bound to support and fight for club brothers who are as dirty as politicians. Hells Angels, individually and collectively, up to and including the eminently grey Sonny Barger, believe that as the senior and preeminent motorcycle club in the world the Hells Angels has the right to say which motorcycle clubs may exist and under what terms and which may not. These are all, at their core, matters of honor that are only coincidently about illicit business. Preeminence is a vital concept in the feudalism that organizes the outlaw frontier. The Angels are very stubborn about this. And, this jostling for preeminence has led to more violence, tragedy and inconvenience than most policemen can begin to comprehend – let alone most television producers.

From inside this subculture violence is a given. Outlaw bikers must live their lives like heroes. They must suffer no insult to their honor. They must be respected. Their clubs must be respected. They are the last Americans to fight duels. In order to belong to this subculture you must be willing to fight and die at any instant. Outlaws seek their moment as Beowulf sought his. Most modern Americans consider this kind of behavior to be pathological – which indicates something that has changed in America since the disappearance of the frontier. A century ago this violence would have been considered tragic.

The feud between the Mongols and the Hells Angels illustrates this tragedy. In the beginning, in the early seventies, the Mongols were just one of several clubs in Southern California that found themselves under the Angels thumb. At the same time that the Angels as a whole were trying to clean up their club's image with toy runs and blood drives individual Angels and Angels charters were stuffing bodies down wells, throwing hand grenades at the mothers of witnesses and strangling snitches. It was a public relations nightmare but most of this havoc happened out of the public view just as almost all biker violence is private today.

In the 1970s, the last thing the Angels, the self appointed top rung on the outlaw ladder, needed was for a minor, half-breed club like the Mongols to start busting up bars, terrifying citizens and competing for the Angels' drug business. It was important to many Angels that prospective, middle class, drug users not be afraid of their dealers. All most of these dealers were really after was a car and enough cash to buy a small business.

The Angels have a rule about territoriality which elaborates their rules about selling contraband. Most simply stated (probably too simply stated) the rule is that if the Hells Angels are in a state they own it. The Hells Angels started in Southern California, in San Bernardino, but after Barger joined the club the Angels' center of power and influence moved north to Oakland. In the late 70s the Angels had four chapters from Los Angeles south – the San Fernando Valley, Berdoo, Orange County and San Diego. By 1975 the Mongols outnumbered the Angels in that part of the Golden State.

Until that year the Mongols had always worn a bottom rocker on their vests that claimed a particular city or area like Montebello, Long Beach or South Bay. That manner of claiming territory followed the protocol on which the Angels insisted. Even outnumbered, the Angels were still the preeminent club in Southern California.

In 1975 the Angels acknowledged the right of a club called Satan's Slaves to exist in the San Fernando Valley, north of the Los Angeles basin. When the Mongols established a chapter in the Valley they began to fight with the Satan's Slaves over which club had the right to be there. When the Satan's Slaves began to lose they invited a friendly takeover, a patch over, by the Hells Angels. So by the first Christmas toy run and blood drive, the Mongols were no longer at war with the Satan's Slaves. They were fighting the Hells Angels and the Angels had their hands full.

The Mongols noticed they were winning and swapped their city name bottom rockers for a bottom rocker that read "California." The Angels took that as a Mongol challenge over the right of the Angels to exist so the Mongols offered a compromise. They started wearing a second small patch above their California bottom rockers that read "Southern."

That compromise did not last through the summer. The Angels, who obtained most of their drugs from Southern California and Mexican drug labs, demanded that the Mongols stay out of the drug business. It was a year when America, and especially Los Angeles, was awash with drugs. Many of the Mongols of that era abused drugs and there was a very faint line between users and suppliers. The Mongols decided that there was plenty of business for everybody.

And then, on top of everything else, there was a woman. A stripper at a bar near Los Angeles International Airport began sleeping with a Mongol and a Hells Angel simultaneously. She was apparently the kind of woman to let both of them know. She was the kind of woman to unflatteringly compare them to each other. The two men ran into each other at a motorcycle parts swap meet in July, 1976. They both were accompanied by friends. A huge brawl ensued and the two clubs have been fighting each other most of the time since.

The San Diego Mongols and Angels, who both smuggled weed and whites over the line from Mexico, particularly hated each other.

Thirteen months after the swap meet brawl, on September 5, 1977 the President of the Mongols, a man named Emerson "Redbeard" Morris and a another Mongol named Raymond "Jingles" Smith were machine gunned off their bikes on the Golden State Freeway north of Escondido on their way home from a Mongols Labor Day party in San Diego County. Redbeard Morris' wife Delores was riding on the back of his bike. She was also shot and paralyzed.

Any doubt that the shooting was a message from the Hells Angels disappeared four days later. At a viewing for Morris and Smith at the Conrad Mortuary in Lemon Grove a mourner no one knew arrived in a white, 1962 Rambler. He left a bouquet of carnations. The flowers were red and white, which are the colors the Angels claim. He walked away and three minutes later the Rambler exploded. No one was killed but two Mongols and the father of a Mongol were severely injured.

Two and half weeks later a biker brought a tire to be repaired into the Frame-Up motorcycle shop on Figueroa Street in the Highland Park section of Los Angeles. The shop was owned by two Mongols. One of them, Henry Jimenez and a 15-year-old boy named Raymond Hernandez who worked part time at the shop were killed when the tire exploded.

A few days after that, the President of the San Fernando Valley chapter of the Mongols, a man named Luis Gutierrez, escaped death when he opened the door to his van and it blew up. That summer was very long ago but the Mongols remember these timeless moments as if they happened yesterday.

Los Angeles newspapers called the freeway murders of Morris and Smith "the Labor Day murders." They changed everything in the biker world.

The day after Labor Day, 1977, every cop and every motorcycle outlaw on the West Coast knew who killed Morris and Smith. A San Diego Sheriff's Department uncover detective was making drug buys from various Angels when the Mongols died. The undercover cop asked the President of the Angels Dago charter, a man named Tom "Crunch" Renzulli, if the Angels could use some help blowing up a Mongols car and Renzulli said, in effect, "Yes. Thank you. Please. That would be very considerate of you." A federal and a San Diego Grand Jury returned indictments against 39 people on a variety of charges on October 5. The state charges included all the accusations for which outlaw bikers are routinely charged: Possession and sale of drugs, receiving stolen property, being an ex-felon in possession of a firearm, possession of explosives and assault. The federal charges included separate counts of being an ex-felon in possession of a firearm, receipt of a firearm by an ex-felon, and failure to register the possession and transfer of a sawed off shotgun.

Raids were carried out, as usual before dawn, on October 7. Twenty-one of the accused were members of the Angels Dago charter and the stated objective of the arrests was to shut down the Hells Angels there. "There are 23 known Hells Angels members in San

69

Diego County and two of them are already in jail" a San Diego District Attorney's spokesman said. If the other 21 are all arrested it will certainly put this chapter out of business for a while." Then he went on to claim that the raids "were not linked" to the Labor Day murders. The truth was, the cops wanted to stop a biker war but they could not actually prove the Angels were behind the murders and the bombings that started it.

The murder case went cold. Then, almost five years later, on June 17, 1981 the law changed. Congress did not write a new law. The United States Supreme Court did. In a case called *United States v Turkette*, the Supreme Court changed the meaning of an existing law, called the Racketeer Influenced Corrupt Organizations law, or RICO. The decision wasn't even close. Conservatives and liberals agreed. Justices White, Burger, Brennan, Marshall, Blackmun, Powell, Rehnquist and Stevens all agreed, in essence, to make being a criminal a federal crime punishable by 20 years in prison. Only Justice Stewart dissented.

Turkette opened a philosophical and legal Pandora's Box that redefined the meaning of words like "crime" and "racket;" and redefined whatever separation or connection might once have existed or not existed between local, state and federal crimes. Today a federal prosecutor can federalize virtually any crime he wants federalized. Under federal law punching somebody in the nose can be a "predicate crime." This evolution of federal law also created a special circumstance under which defendants can be denied a presumption of innocence.

Until *Turkette*, the Labor Day murders and the bombings had been California crimes prosecutable under state law in several jurisdictions. *Turkette* allowed all these incidents of, what was essentially, tribal warfare by the some Hells Angels to be tied together and tried all at once as the federal crime of racketeering.

70

The Federal prosecutors had to rush. The statute of limitations for all federal crimes is five years which meant the Hells Angels could no longer be prosecuted for the murders of Morris and Smith under RICO after midnight on Sunday, September 4, 1982. The federal grand jury returned the secret, thirteen-count indictment on Friday afternoon. Five Hells Angels were charged with racketeering on the basis of several predicate crimes. Predicates are state crimes or, in some cases, non-criminal acts like wearing outlaw insignia or legally owning a firearm, committed during a ten-year-period that indicate that a criminal conspiracy exists. In the case of motorcycle clubs, prosecutors must only prove that a defendant is a member of a club and that he committed some crime, say marijuana possession, in under to charge him with racketeering which Turkette had redefined as the crime of being a criminal. Two of the defendants, Crunch Renzulli and David Harbridge were arrested a week later. Another indictee was already in jail in New York and two more were in the wind.

The indictment charged the defendants with waging "war" on the Mongols. "The purpose of the war was to prevent Mongols club members from wearing the word 'California' as the bottom line...on the Mongol Club jackets because the Hell's (sic) Angels claimed an exclusive right to use the word 'California' as a 'bottom rocker.'" The indictment never mentioned the stripper. The war probably sounded stupid enough as it was.

News coverage of this prosecution and the federal indictment itself repeatedly referenced the Labor Day Murders and the bombing at the Conrad Mortuary and the red and white flowers but the Angels were never charged with any of that. The accused Angels were charged with *conspiring* to machine gun Morris and Smith and *conspiring* to bomb the mortuary. A number of other

71

charges were also thrown in, in order to force these Angels to defend themselves against as much as possible and exhaust whatever financial resources they might have. It is a tactic that is commonly called "running wild the charges." It is the precise model for prosecuting outlaw bikers that is used to this day.

The one thing this prosecutorial model cannot do is actually stop biker violence because the cause of this violence is a quaint adherence to a set of heroic ideals. Righteous and proper outlaws refuse to ignore their duty to fight and if necessary die just to avoid breaking some state or federal law. Outlaws who usually do not have careers to which they may devote themselves and who feel alienated from their governments devote themselves to their clubs instead. Outlaws, from their own perspective, must obey a higher set of laws: For example an eye for an eye, a tooth for a tooth and one for all and all for one. Prosecutors don't really want to stop the violence anyway. In fact, federal police encourage violence between outlaw motorcycle club members in hopes that the bikers will accomplish what the Department of Justice cannot, which is the extermination of outlaw bikers. So far, that tactic has not worked.

In fact it is the violence that fascinates outsiders, from which people cannot look away. Motorcycle outlaws are the you that you bind in chains. They are the chaos to which civilization must never be allowed to descend. They are the you that you wish you were when you are humiliated or overwhelmed or bullied or condescended to or made to admit that you are small. The violence on the outlaw frontier is virtually revolutionary. In a nation comprised of increasingly powerless citizens this small group of outsiders finds reasons to live, die and kill. It is the same mentality that caused Andrew Jackson to fight at least three duels. It is the same mentality that caused Aaron Burr to kill

Alexander Hamilton. It is the same set of heroic ideals that sent Wyatt Earp to the O.K. Corral and then on his vengeance ride.

This violence happens in the country that invented the hip pocket – as a place to carry one's pistol. It happens in a country that recently idealized and still romanticizes Billy the Kid, Doc Holliday, Bat Masterson, John Wesley Hardin, Ben Thompson and Wild Bill Hickok. In a nationally televised speech in 1953, the most mundane of all our Presidents, Dwight David Eisenhower described his boyhood hero, Hickok, as a paragon of courage all Americans should emulate.

Americans have always been violent. Around the time of the Revolution, an Anglican minister named Charles Woodmason besought his rural congregation, "I would advise you when you do fight not to act like tigers and bears as these Virginians do – biting one another's lips and noses off, thrusting out one another's eyes, and kicking one another on the cods, to the great damage of many a poor woman."

An unfairly forgotten historian with a flair for words named H. C. Brearley once called "the South, that part of the United States lying below the Smith and Wesson line."

H. Rap Brown understood that "violence is as American as cherry pie."

"The essential American soul," D. H. Lawrence thought, "is hard, isolate, stoic, and a killer." All of these observers would probably agree that on the long lost frontier each man, guided by his conscience and his own self interest, was a law unto himself. On the motorcycle outlaw frontier these men join into clubs that are laws unto themselves.

The America of the new millennium is increasingly focused on transforming the souls of its citizens into something less dangerous and more materialistic than they once were. And, it is almost taken

73

for granted that the agents of this perfection of the American soul should be the police. In an interview John Ciccone, the ATF Agent who is probably the Bureau's leading authority on motorcycle outlaws, said he pursued investigations against outlaws bikers because he wanted to "stop the violence."

So by that standard, the ATF mission is a failure.

In August 2008, two months before Hitman Martin was killed, in Sturgis, South Dakota, near Deadwood in the ruins of the old frontier, two Hells Angels and five members of an outlaw club called the Iron Pigs fought a duel with fists and guns in a bar called The Loud American Roadhouse. Local news media described the fight as an unprovoked attack. The five Iron Pigs described themselves as being surrounded and attacked by two Angels.

The Iron Pigs Motorcycle Club is an outlaw motorcycle club comprised of sworn piece officers, prison guards, security guards and fire fighters. The club was founded in Oroville, California in December 2000 by disgruntled members of another "cop club" called the Wild Pigs.

One of the Iron Pigs, a Seattle police union official and Pawn Shop Unit detective named Ron Smith had been trying to pick fights all day. According to witnesses, the five Iron Pigs surrounded the two Angels. Smith insulted one of them and when the man punched Smith in the face and knocked him down Smith shot the Angel twice in the stomach. At the time, Smith was 43.

The outlaw frontier is infested with cop clubs like the Iron Pigs, the Untouchables, the Renegades, the Blue Steel and the City Heat. The Chosen Sons Motorcycle Club, for example, comprised of cops, bounty hunters, private detectives and prison guards, wears a bottom rocker that claims Baltimore.

That club was founded in 1969 by Baltimore policemen and has four chapters in Maryland. A fictionalized and somewhat sanitized portrayal of the Chosen Sons appeared in a 1995 episode of a television series called *Homicide: Life on the Streets*. The dramatized Chosen Sons were called the Deacons. But most of the Deacons were played by actual members of the Chosen Sons

The ATF was actively investigating the Chosen Sons in he Spring of 2009 after the arrest of a former bounty hunter and member of the club named Michael Papantonakis for selling guns to members of the Crips and Bloods street gangs and to Hells Angels.

A year earlier one of the founders of the club, a former cop named Norman Stamp, was killed by a uniformed Baltimore policeman outside a strip club. Stamp was at the stripper bar for the initiation, or patching-in ceremony, of a new member named Michael Privett. Witnesses said the Chosen Sons and other patrons got into a fight over a woman. When the fight spilled outside, Stamp spilled outside with it. He was wearing brass knuckles which are illegal in Maryland and when a uniformed officer named John Torres saw the brass knuckles he ordered Stamp to freeze. When Stamp ignored him Torres shot Stamp with a TASER. Stamp fell to the ground. Then he pulled a gun and aimed it at Torres and Torres reacted by shooting Stamp twice in the chest. Stamp was given a full, bag pipe funeral attended by numerous Baltimore cops and members of the Chosen Sons. Baltimore Police Commissioner Frederick H. Bealefeld III gave his eulogy. Stamp was 65.

Many outlaw clubs, like the Hells Angels, refuse to consider current or former
peace officers for membership. But at least partly because of their proximity to the Chosen Sons, the

Pagans Motorcycle Club does allow former, and in some cases current, law enforcement officers to join.

The Pagans are generally considered to be the preeminent outlaw club in Maryland, Pennsylvania, New Jersey and Delaware. The most celebrated ex-cop among the Pagans is a former Philadelphia patrolman named Steven "Gorilla" Montevergine. Montevergine is widely credited with chasing both the Hells Angels and the Mafia out of Philadelphia. Law enforcement sources allege that the Mafia was effectively replaced in Philadelphia by the Tenth and Oregon Avenues Gang. Around the turn of the millennium, a member of the "Tenth and O" tried to kill Montevergine by shooting him nine times. But, as his road name suggests, Gorilla is a robust man, he survived, and he is widely believed to have gunned down his attacker on a South Philly street corner in broad daylight. The feud between those two groups was still going on in March 2009 when members of the two groups fought it out in a Philadelphia bar.

About a week after the Pagans fought the Tenth and O a man unaffiliated with any club, what outlaws call a "civilian," named Albert Kolano walked into the wrong bar at the wrong time. It was a place near Pittsburgh called the Longview Lounge and Kolano soon found himself engaged in a spirited debate with a reported fifteen or twenty Pagans over which musical genre is the most beautiful: Country or Heavy Metal Rock?

A few minutes later Kolano called his brother and told him he needed help. Someone at the bar also called the police who did not come. After his brother arrived, with no police in sight, Kolano tried to escape. Four to six Pagans followed the pair outside. Kolano found himself nose to nose with a Pagan named Bryan Perun. Perun is a former Pittsburgh cop who had been investigated for killing a motorist in October 2001 but authorities ruled that shooting to be a justifiable homicide. Perun left the police force in 2004.

When Kolano's brother tried to drive away Perun pulled a knife, stabbed a tire and said, "You ain't going nowhere." Perun then pulled a gun and fired one shot into the ground and another shot at Kolano's brother but missed. That distraction gave Kolano just enough time to scramble into his own car and try to drive away. More shots were fired. Kolano was hit. He crashed and after police finally arrived he was pronounced dead at the scene.

On November 7, 2008, a month after Hitman Martin was murdered, a Hells Angel named Robert Daniel Thompson got into a fight with four Mongols outside a bar called The Shanty in Eureka in Northern California. Shots were exchanged. Thompson, who had just been released from jail that day, was found lying in a pool of his own blood with a revolver by his side. He denied any knowledge of the gun and refused to testify against his attackers. Thompson was 43. The four Mongols later pled guilty to relatively minor charges.

Three and a half months later a 30-year-old Mongols club officer and mixed martial arts fighter named Ezra Sanders was found dead in front of his trailer in McKinleyville, in Humboldt County, California. Sanders body had both cash and drugs on it when it was found. A spokesman for the Humboldt County Sherriff's Office would only say, "We have heard mention that our victim may have been involved in a biker gang and, certainly, that is something we will continue to investigate. Whether or not that has anything to do with his murder has yet to be determined."

On December 20, 2008 eleven Hells Angels and two friends of the club attacked three Mongols at the Special Memory Wedding Chapel in downtown Las Vegas after the chapel manager inadvertently scheduled a Mongols wedding right after a Hells Angels wedding. The Mongols groom was stabbed three times in the stomach. The best man was also stabbed. The bride was chased from the chapel and one of the Angels threw a bottle at her.

And, as is almost always the case with outlaws, Las Vegas Metro Police would only confirm that a fight had in fact occurred but then refused to release even the most basic details of the brawl including the names of the two clubs involved, or even that the fight involved motorcycle clubs, or the names of the combatants or the extent of their injuries.

"We have some video that we are reviewing," Metro Police Lieutenant Richard Fletcher reluctantly admitted. "It won't be released at this time. It has been turned over to detectives." The relevant portion of the secret video is about one minute and twenty seconds long. It shows a very large Hells Angel, dressed in black and followed by three other men walk over to a Mongol whose back was turned and start pummeling him in the wedding chapel lobby, decorated for Christmas, amongst glass counters filled with last minute wedding supplies, while eleven adults and five children watch. The spectators continue to watch as Angels pour into the lobby and divide up to attack the two Mongols. The spectators don't begin to run away until after Angels are already stomping one victim curled up in a fetal position as other Angels grab the other Mongol, stretch out his arms and start stabbing him in the stomach. Even then, one pretty woman with a baby on her hip cannot tear herself away from the spectacle until the fight spills within three feet of her.

In March 2010, Fernando Fernandez, a member of the Dago chapter of the Mongols Motorcycle Club was stabbed to death by an Dago Angel named Michael Ottinger. Fernandez was on a date with his girlfriend. He was just 30-years-old.

In August 2011 in Sturgis, a hundred feet from the Loud American, two Mongols got into a knife fight with an unknown number of Hells Angels.

In September 2011 approximately 60 Vagos and a dozen Angels got into a fight in John Ascuaga's Nugget Casino in Sparks, Nevada during the annual Street Vibrations Rally. Two Vagos were shot and wounded. Jeffrey "Jethro" Pettigrew, the President of the Angels San Jose charter was shot and killed. The next day a third Vago was shot as he rode his motorcycle through Sparks. Pettigrew was 51. The man who shot him was 53.

Two weeks later, at Pettigrew's funeral, Steve Tausan a close friend of Pettigrew's and the Sergeant-at-Arms for the Angels Santa Cruz chapter got into a fist fight with a San Jose Angel named Steve Joseph Ruiz. Tausan, who had a limited career as a professional boxer, knocked Ruiz on his ass. They were fighting over a matter of honor. They were fighting over whether every Angel in the Sparks casino had fought as hard as possible to keep Pettigrew alive. Tausan, a peacemaker among Angels, thought that none of the Angels in the casino had been cowards. Ruiz thought some of them had been. After he fell to the ground, Ruiz pulled a gun and shot Tausan twice in the chest. Tausan was 54. Sonny Barger was at the funeral. He had just turned 73.

A dozen other Angels disarmed Ruiz and threw him out bad on the spot. They stripped off his colors, put a baseball cap on his head, threw him into a car and he disappeared. This happened at a funeral attended by 4,000 bikers and totally surrounded by police. Other Angels carried Tausan out of the cemetery. According to witnesses, once he reached the street police refused to allow the Angels to put Tausan in an ambulance. One cop said drily, "let him bleed out."

The catalog of violence on the motorcycle outlaw frontier since Hitman Martin was shot off his bike could easily fill several books. The ages of the combatants in the few examples cited above may undermine fatuous sociological arguments about the origins of violence and who is likely to be violent and how violence may be prevented or controlled. No one, particularly in the Department of Justice or the ATF, actually wants this violence to stop. Despite John Ciccone's specious words, the ongoing federal war to halt the biker menace is actually about government careers, fat paychecks, neurotic malice, headlines, celebrity, book and movie deals, television ratings and adventure. The rest of this book may convince even skeptics of that.

Ciccone

John Ciccone is the primary source, either directly or at some remove, for virtually everything every cop and every crime reporter knows about motorcycle outlaws. Ciccone has worked for the ATF for 20 years. For the last fifteen years, he has testified, "all I've worked is outlaw motorcycle gangs." Before bikers he was involved in a handful of mundane cases and, with Dan McMullen of the FBI, he led the racketeering investigation of gangsta mogul Suge Knight and Death Row Records.

He used to play second base. He looks like a shortstop. He went to Grand Valley State University in Michigan. The ATF was the only police force that would hire him after he graduated. And, he is very private. He won't say if he is related to Madonna. He has no opinions about Dave Foley, the cynical ATF Agent in George V. Higgins *The Friends of Eddie Coyle*. He never read the book. There is no reason why he should. He deserves a thinly veiled role in a novel by James Patterson or a movie by Tony Scott. Ciccone is more important and more new millennium than anybody Higgins could have made up.

His wife is Vietnamese. He is short and he is self-conscious about his height. He is about five-seven in boots with very thick soles. Men who have been interrogated by him, Mongols and Hells Angels, think

81

he is about five-four. He has described himself a "midget." He is lean, muscular, handsome, fair and he hangs a little, hipster goatee from the end of his chin. He makes great eye contact, has a firm handshake and he speaks bluntly. He has an inviting quality that is difficult to answer with suspicion or reserve. He may be the most professional policeman in the country.

Which is to say he lies as other men breathe. He lies easily and convincingly to grand juries, judges, informants and to the men he arrests. Lies pour over Ciccone's lips and out of his fingertips. Police lie continually to the people but it is a crime to lie to a policeman. Ciccone may not know when he lies. He may simply believe what he hears himself say. He told a Grand Jury in Las Vegas in 2004 that he had been working biker cases for eight years.

The same day, March 25, he told that Jury what he thought were differences between the Hells Angels and the Mongols. About the Angels he said: "Well, you know a lot of them, you know, are involved in legal, legitimate businesses, and a lot of them are involved in, you know, illegal businesses. They do a lot of, they have a lot of prostitution rings that they run, they are involved in extortions, they're involved in thefts of stolen motorcycles, they're involved in different, you know, murders, assaults, narcotics trafficking, firearms trafficking. A lot of these members don't have any jobs. But on the other hand there are some people that do have some legitimate businesses that they operate, tattoo shops and different things like that. So, you know, it's kind of a mix with the different members but they accept whatever you're involved in."

Then he said: "The Mongols are primarily a Southern California street gang. A lot of the members were former street gang members that have elevated up through street

82

gangs into a motorcycle gang and ninety-five percent of their membership is out of Los Angeles. There is approximately thirty-nine chapters in the city of Los Angeles in and of itself and about ninety-five percent of them are Hispanic, Hispanic gang members. They do have chapters in Oklahoma and Colorado, and they do have chapters in Mexico. They're not nearly as large as the Hells Angels with the world-wide perspective of the club, but they're primarily based out of Los Angeles."

Maybe he was telling the truth as he saw it. Around the same time he told a Los Angeles Commission he had been working biker cases for nine years. He was a founding member of a joint Los Angeles Sheriff's Department – ATF special unit called the One Percenter Task Force in 1997. So, pick your favorite date. He began stalking bikers in '95, '96 or '97. He will not admit to cynicism about his job. He says, "Oh, I believe.

Professional policemen do not see the world other men see. When John Ciccone looks at the motorcycle outlaw frontier he becomes a man studying Jackson Pollock's *Full Fathom Five*. He stares intently into its mottled green depths. He misses some things. He sees other things most men would miss. He takes it all in. A smile widens over his little goatee. He washes his hands with air. Then, like a good policeman, he can't resist the impulse to grab some solvent and a putty knife and clean up all that spilled paint.

According to former ATF Agent William Queen, Ciccone began "targeting the growing outlaw motorcycle gang problem in Southern California" in 1998. Queen says Ciccone "developed a 'gang' of his own; ATF Special Agents John Carr, Eric Harden, and Darrin Kozlowski, fondly referred to as Koz, were the core. They'd all started with the Bureau together."

In 1999, Ciccone and Carr spent seven months trying to get something on the Sundowners Motorcycle

Club. "The Sundowners," Ciccone has written, "is a documented outlaw motorcycle organization which has close ties with the Hells Angels and whose members are involved in narcotics and firearms trafficking." The ATF Agents enlisted a paid "confidential informant," a CI which is what the ATF calls a professional snitch, to try to entrap the bikers. As a result of all that effort, "a total of three federal search/arrest warrants were executed at the clubhouse and members' residences" and "a total of 14 firearms, approximately three pounds of methamphetamine, and one stolen Harley-Davidson motorcycle were recovered from various members of the organization. Two members were charged with federal firearms and narcotics violations." Ciccone called the Sundowners a "heinous group."

The same year, Kozlowski made a botched attempt to infiltrate the Hollywood chapter of the Vagos. Ciccone sweet-talked a disgruntled prospect. The prospect introduced Kozlowski as a hang around – an informal friend of the club, like Porno Ron. Then the prospect died and his club brothers discovered that his bike was registered to the ATF. The official version of this episode, recounted by William Queen, states that the Vagos "went to the deceased CI's wife and threatened her, demanding to know why her husband had been on a bike owned by the federal government. The terrorized woman gave up everything – that her husband was working as an informant for the ATF and that Koz was in fact an undercover Agent.

"With his cover blown while deep inside an outlaw biker gang, Darrin Kozlowski should be dead today."

"But Koz was no one to mess with. A tall, strapping, Midwestern boy with a quick smile, an easy laugh, and an affable demeanor, Koz refused to relocate or cower."

84

Actually Kozlowski simply walked away. Only the infiltration was ruined – temporarily.

Beginning in April 2000 Carr stepped into the ongoing Vagos investigation. The attempt to catch the Vagos at something went on for a full three years. During that time, a paid, full time, ATF confidential informant managed to make "15 undercover purchases of evidence, which included firearms and narcotics."

Simultaneously, Queen reports, "For months Ciccone, Carr, Hardin and Kozlowski strategized about the Mongol problem in Southern California." And, also simultaneously Ciccone, or his ATF supervisor began giving these investigations military sounding names. The investigation Ciccone "strategized about the Mongol problem" was called Operation Ivan; because Ivan the Great rid Russia of the Mongols.

That investigation began with the courtship of Sources of Information, or SOIs, to try to determine the names of some Mongols and where they might be and what they might be doing. Ciccone convinced two of those sources, a man and a woman, to introduce an ardent motorcyclist named Billy "Slow Brain" St. John to the Mongols. Slow Brain's real name was William Queen. Queen was a former ATF SWAT partner of Ciccone's: And a Vietnam veteran, a graduate of Guilford College, a former local cop and Border Patrol Agent from High Point, North Carolina. He was experienced at working undercover. He had already established a false identity during the Sundowners investigation which spilled over into surveillance of the Valley charter of the Hells Angels. And, although Ciccone later described him as "only average as an undercover agent," he had the most important qualities motorcycle clubs seek in prospective members. He was likable. He can be humble although the New York *Times* described him as "roosterish." He was physically and

85

mentally tough. And he had the personal quality that is most difficult to fake – Queen was becoming lost. He was near the end of his ATF career and he was becoming increasingly estranged from his wife and his children. Queen later blamed Operation Ivan for contributing to that estrangement. Nevertheless, outlaw motorcycle clubs are magnets for lost men and Queen was eventually drawn to the Mongols in more than simply a professional way.

Ciccone and the ATF seemed to be genuinely concerned for Queen's safety so he was surveilled and backed up at all times during the next two years by Ciccone, Carr, Kozlowski and a couple of undercover Los Angeles Sheriffs named Michael "Bubba" Williams and David Luther. Their concerns were reasonable. At the time the Mongols Motorcycle Club was at its nadir.

The long war with the Angels had reduced the club to no more than 100 members. A methamphetamine epidemic swept through the Mongols and that resulted in numerous random, senseless bar fights and other assaults. On top of that some Mongols had actually started to chase prospective members away for profit.

The President at the time was a short, powerfully built, thickly mustachioed man named Scott "Junior" Erickson. Erickson was a Mongols hero. In 1982, the same year the President of the San Diego charter of the Angels confessed to racketeering for the Labor Day murders, Erickson, with the alleged assistance of four other Mongols, fought, beat, shot and killed the next top Dago Angel, a man named Ray "Fat Ray" Piltz, in a bar called the Horseshoe Tavern. Erickson was convicted of manslaughter and when he got out he became President of the Mongols. By 2000 he was addicted to crank. The National sergeant at Arms at the time was another crank addict, a tough, formidable man named Donald "Red Dog" Jarvis.

In many outlaw clubs, including the Mongols at the time, prospective members must sign over title to their motorcycles to the club. At its most idealistic, this is a way of helping a member protect his asset. Usually, it is a way to keep a member from quitting and is a way to punish members voted out bad. New members must also pay an initiation fee and purchase their patches. The profits from at least some of that went to Erickson and Jarvis.

Doc Cavazos, Mongols President until shortly before Hitman Martin was killed, later wrote that most of profits went to those two men. Cavazos also alleged that Erickson and Jarvis were harassing members into quitting just so they could steal their motorcycles. Jarvis, as a national officer, was a member of the Mongols Mother Chapter but he spent most of his time with the San Fernando Valley chapter – the same chapter that had started a fight with the Satan's Slaves that soon became a war with the Hells Angels. At least partly because of Red Dog's penchant for running off prospects, the Valley chapter was very small and always looking for new members.

In Operation Ivan, William Queen joined the Valley chapter. It was the easiest chapter to hang around and prospect and, because of Red Dog, it was one of the tougher chapters to actually join. Queen claims he was assaulted and punched on numerous occasions by Jarvis. He calls Jarvis a "loose cannon." The Mongols and other motorcycle clubs were still echoing Vietnam. During Vietnam, Army and Marine Corps recruits in Boot Camp or Basic Combat Training were routinely punched, kicked, slapped and hit with rifle butts. Prospecting an outlaw club is a version of Boot Camp. The Mongols enacted a rule in 1998 that prohibited "beating on" prospects. Red Dog ignored that. "I didn't know what I was getting into," Queen told a television interviewer a decade after the fact. "I walked right into a swimming pool full of sharks."

Red Dog later said he was as hard on Queen as he was, not because he was trying to run him off and make him forfeit his motorcycle, but because, "I was suspecting him of being a cop from the very beginning. I just knew it."

According to Queen, the way Red Dog said hello was, "Billy, if you turn out to be a problem, I'll cut your motherfuckin' throat," In another incident that so unnerved Queen that he put it in his memoir twice, Red Dog and some other Mongols took the ATF Agent out target shooting and fired a round past his head. In Queen's numerous accounts of his infiltration, he has always maintained ""If they would have found out I was an ATF agent they would have killed me."

"We're not stupid people," Red Dog replied in 2005 when Random House, Hunter Thompson old publisher, released Queen's book. "We have rules, you know, we have...we have policies. Especially about killing."

The investigation, putatively, started because of a perceived public threat of biker violence. "They're about violence," Queen said about the Mongols. "John Ciccone wanted to stop them." And that sounds very reasonable. It also almost sounds reasonable that in order to win the trust of the Mongols Queen had to become even more violent than they were supposed to be. Queen picked and fought in numerous brawls. His mentor in this tactic was ATF Agent Darrin Kozlowski. "I'd done my homework," Queen wrote. "I'd studied the way Koz had improvised...when he was undercover with the Vagos." In another self-admitted episode Queen got into a knife fight, feared that he would be killed and begged another Mongol to kill his opponent. "Shoot him, Rocky! For fuck's sake, shoot him!" The menacing Mongols did not shoot to save the ATF Agent but simply disarmed the other man.

Queen also blithely recounts several incidents in his investigation when he did not do drugs. Technically, ATF Agents are not allowed to ingest drugs or commit other crimes during an investigation. One of the principal reasons the ATF uses paid, confidential informants is because those contract employees can ingest drugs and are protected against prosecution for virtually any offense during their employment.

It all took a toll on Queen. He was losing much of his life when he began to infiltrate the club. To replace what he had had, Queen found them. Like many modern Americans, Queen dreamed "about riding away with them."

"I couldn't help myself," he wrote. "I felt overwhelmed by a shameful guilt, like lusting after your best friend's wife. I watched the Mongols hugging and high-fiving, laughing and toasting the new year with beer. They exchanged war stories and put their tattooed arms tightly around one another. They put their arms around me. They freely and sincerely expressed their love for one another and for me. It was sincere. I knew that they honestly loved Billy St. John. And at that moment I desperately wanted to be Billy St. John."

The Mongols, with the exception of the cartoonish Red Dog were clueless. "Yeah, looking back at it, there were little things he did like leaving bars too early and wearing long-sleeve shirts in summer that now seem like giveaways," J.R. "Hoss" MacDonald said years later. "But at the time, he was just Billy. He rode with us. He partied with us. He was our treasurer. Nobody ever thought twice about it."

And, despite all that effort and anguish, the investigation, like prior Ciccone investigations, was more sizzle than steak. The problem was that the Mongols were deeply alienated social outsiders who were violent as schoolboys but they just weren't that criminal. They broke drug, gun and traffic laws. They were often oafish and rude. Ordinary people had to walk on eggshells around them. They were often very aggressive with women and when they beat somebody up they usually put him in the hospital. They engaged in a terrible, murderous feud with the Hells Angels. Daffy as it seems, the Mongols were, and can still probably be understood as a violent poltergeist from the American frontier. They may be anachronistic. But they are not very much more criminal than college students.

Queen's federal investigation bore little fruit because they were not a racket. Part of the intelligence Queen gathered was the Mongols "Five Commandments." Commandment Five is, "A Mongol never uses his patch for personal gain."

"What we were hoping to do," Queen said about what he understood the original goal of Operation Ivan to be, "was get next to the club where we could buy guns from guys in the club. Where we could buy dope from guys in the club. Where we could identify or maybe even see some of the assaults that were occurring there."

The idea of investigating bikers was not entirely Ciccone's idea but it had become his mission. He had inherited this mission from an Agent named Steve Martin who had infiltrated and subverted the Warlocks in Florida in the early 90s. Martin became friends with the Warlocks, patched in, told his new friends that he would be "murdered by Columbians" unless the Warlocks sold him guns, then started a whole chapter of the Warlocks comprised entirely of cops. Martin went on to become the Special Agent in Charge of the ATF office in San Francisco. When Queen infiltrated the Mongols, he was riding Martin's old motorcycle. Outlaw bikers like guns and they like to get loaded so from the inside evidence of criminality is easy to witness. Bikers are extremely loyal to one another so after they accept you as a friend they are easy to entrap.

But in the Spring of 1998 the ATF still almost shut Operation Ivan down. The few gun buys and incidents of drug use and assault and the intelligence was just not enough to justify the cost. To be successful, a biker investigation must gather tremendous amounts of information and then try to pick out the pieces that make a pattern. To be successful, Operation Ivan had to prove, in Queen's words, that "contemporary biker gangs aren't simply hard charging, heavy-drinking, 'wild child' Americans, a version of the James Gang on Iron horses. Today's biker organizations are sophisticated, calculating, extremely violent – nothing less than the insidious new face of global organized crime." Gathering enough information to be able to suggest that to a jury required lots of wiretaps, video surveillances, money for drug and gun buys and lots of agents and paid informants. The ATF looked at what Ciccone had accomplished in his previous investigations into the Vagos and the Sundowners and decided Operation Ivan just wasn't worth what it would cost to make it work.

If the ATF had shut down that investigation much of what follows in this book and most of Ciccone's career would never have happened. But for some brief time in the Spring of 1998 Ciccone simply refused to follow a direct order from the Special Agent in Charge in Los Angeles. The ATF might not have known that Ciccone could eventually prove the Mongols were a racket but Ciccone did. Because the Supreme Court, a decade after *Turkette*, had just changed the definition of racketeering once again.

Most of the nonsense that is written about motorcycle outlaws, that they are "international crime empires" and all of that, is based on an amalgamation of sixty years of American history and on a conflation of what most people understand to be the definition of racketeering with the technical, legal definition of racketeering. Most people understand racketeering, a term coined in the 1920s, to refer to something like "protection rackets" or corrupt labor unions, fixed horse races, loan sharking or the Countrywide Home Loan racket. But the *Scheidler* decision four years before had made it possible to convict almost any fringe group of racketeering.

National Organization of Women, Inc. v Scheidler was a civil RICO case brought on behalf of abortion providers against a political organization called Operation Rescue. Joseph Scheidler, for whom the decision is named was one of the leaders of Operation Rescue. Members believed that first-term abortion was morally wrong and should be legally prohibited. They protested outside abortion clinics and harassed and intimidated the women who tried to enter. There was a national consensus that members of Operation Rescue were loutish, cruel and unreasonable. The National Organization of Women accused them of being a racket.

"'We cannot tolerate the use of threats and force by one group to impose its views on others,'" NOW's lawyer. Fay Clayton explained.

A Federal District judge, dismissed the case on the grounds that RICO could only be applied to "enterprises" motivated by financial gain. The Supreme Court overruled him. A racket could then be any group who members were contemptuous of the law. It was a great victory for federal policemen and prosecutors.

Professor G. Robert Blakely, who wrote the RICO Act and gave it its ironic name, lamented that he had never meant for his law to be applied to political and fraternal groups. He said he was "concerned" that after *Scheidler* RICO might be used against labor unions and other fringe groups like gay rights activists. Since

Scheidler, RICO has been most commonly used a basis for the prosecution of outlaw motorcycle clubs.

In 2009 Ciccone, who sometimes refers to himself in the third person, said, "John Ciccone was not nearly as smart and wily as he is now and the Mongols escaped relatively unscathed.... John Ciccone has chosen the lifestyle he believes is for him, he is committed to it and works hard towards what he believes is the greater good and appears to have maintained some integrity."

As a result of Operation Ivan, a massive and videogenic raid was made possible. forty-two Mongols were arrested. Seven hundred policeman raided scores of homes and searched for evidence of illegality. Often they found dope and guns and brass knuckles and Mongols paraphernalia. They seized motorcycles and wrecked homes. Fifty-four men were indicted and fifty-three of them were convicted of something. "Most of them," Queen wrote, "opted for guilty pleas." What Queen neglected to mention is that when you are federally indicted, you always take the plea. A Swat Team escorted Queen out of town.

The ATF encouraged Queen to write about his experiences in Operation Ivan. That became *Under And Alone*. Queen was assisted with the book by the author Doug Century who later said, "I did not write the book. Billy Queen did." Ciccone was prominently and sympathetically featured throughout that book.

A *Vanity Fair* correspondent name Ned Zeman and his writing partner Daniel Barnz wrote the film script of *Under And Alone* and sold it to Mel Gibson's Icon Productions. Gibson intended to star as Queen. Icon refused multiple requests to discuss the project or who might play Ciccone or Red Dog. Antoine Fuqua, whose credits include the lurid and hyperbolic *Training Day*, was signed to direct. ATF street Agents love *Training Day*. One Agent explained how clean an ATF undercover biker investigation had been by describing it as "not *Training Day*."

Ivan was a real breakthrough for Ciccone. He almost failed, he almost ruined his career, but instead by luck and pluck and disobeying orders he pulled victory from the jaws of defeat.

After Operation Ivan Ciccone had all the pieces to the Mongols puzzle and he knew how to fit them together. After Operation Ivan Ciccone got it. He is smart enough to see the big picture. The publication of Queen's book and Hollywood's appetite for demonstrate to all of the ATF the vital component needed to create a war against the biker menace is propaganda. Ciccone got that. And, he also understood that he had found his calling and that he would eventually have another go at the Mongols.

So it was and remains vital to Ciccone that he find ways to demonize the Mongols as much as possible. He has repeatedly cited three examples of intolerable violence that justify ridding the world of these outlaws.

One is the murder of a man named Daniel Herrera in 1999. One November night some Mongols rolled into a bar called The Place in a dreary Los Angeles suburb named Commerce. A woman named Sandra Herrera and a friend were drinking in The Place when the Mongols arrived. Some women like outlaws. Sandra Herrera flirted with one of the Mongols. He bought her drinks. Then her husband, Daniel walked in. He told his wife to come home. She said she wanted to stay where she was. A Mongol named Adrian "Panhead" Gutierrez told the husband something like, "She doesn't want to go home with you."

The husband said something like, "You have two kids at home and you need to get out of here."

She said some version of "No."

Daniel Herrera said, "Well, fuck you bitch. And, fuck the Mongols." The Mongols beat him savagely for that insult. Herrera escaped the bar. He ran out to the street and the Mongols followed him and began to beat him again. He fought back and when he did Panhead Gutierrez stabbed him and Herrera died. Later, Gutierrez was awarded a special patch reserved for Mongols who have fought for the club. After Operation Ivan ended, Gutierrez was convicted of murder with a "gang enhancement."

The Herrera murder is one of the most dramatic elements described in William Queen's book and it has been dramatized in two television shows,

The second atrocity was a nasty brawl at an Indian Casino named Morongo in Cabazon, California near Palm Springs. A Mongol named Rick "Bad Boy" Slayton was fighting there in a mixed marshal arts bout in March, 2002. A hundred Mongols were there, in colors, to cheer Slayton on. Slayton kneed his opponent in the groin and the referee called a foul. There are Mongol and Ciccone versions of what happened next.

In Ciccone's version the Mongols became so upset with the foul call that they started throwing cups of beer at the ring. A ringside spectator retaliated by throwing his cup of beer at the Mongols. Which by the peculiar, inexcusable but still comprehensible logic of the outlaw world led to a massive brawl.

Ciccone later told a state grand jury: "A Mongol named Lucifer pointed his finger at Alex, approached him, and said, 'You.'"

The spectator said, "'Forget about it,' grinned, and exchanged words with the Mongols, Marco Antonio Reyes and another man, presumably defendant (Fernandez.) (The victim's brother) told the two men he did not want any trouble.

"Defendant hit (the victim) behind the head. While on the floor, someone hit him with a chair and stomped on his face with a biker's boot. Mario was also hit numerous times but could not see who was attacking him because he was on the floor trying to cover up.

"This led to other fights breaking out and chaos, resulting in a melee and riot situation, with over 100 officers responding to the scene. A group of Mongols rushed toward the ring. Mongols fought with other spectators and threw chairs."

By Ciccone's account six people were stabbed. In the same grand jury testimony, in July 2004, Ciccone explained why he thought the Mongols had reacted with such over the top violence. He did not blame profits, guns, drugs, women or mental illness. He blamed the infuriation of the kind of powerless men who join motorcycle clubs.

Ciccone said, "That is really what the Mongols are about. They are involved in numerous assaults, stabbings, and required to assist one another. And that is why you rarely see

a one-on-one fight. It is always 12 on one, 13 on one. And they just send the message: 'That is how we are.' And it is just the fear thing and intimidation thing."

The State Attorney asked, "How does respect play into the Mongols? I mean, the term 'respect for the gang' and 'respect for other members of the gang?' And, if they are disrespected, how does that play all into the gang mentality?

Ciccone answered, "Well, it is a big thing for the Mongols. Like I said, they are not in it to make money. They are in it just for that one thing alone, fear and intimidation. And they want the respect. And that's how they get it."

The brawl was all caught on surveillance video. Ciccone looked at the footage and identified the Mongols for the Riverside County Sheriff's Department. Ten members of the club were arrested and convicted of assault with a knife. And Ciccone has shown the video to several judges since in order to prove his point that the Mongols must be a racket because they present a clear and ongoing public danger.

The third incident that outrages Ciccone happened in a casino town called Laughlin.

Laughlin

There are now, and probably for a little longer, two kinds of outlaw identities. One is mostly a commodity and the other is not. One is an identity that anybody – your dentist, a television producer, Vladimir Putin – can buy. The other is an identity that can only be earned after a terrible quest. What the two identities share is a particular kind of motorcycle.

Harley-Davidsons are American machines, made in American factories by American workers who feed American children. The motor company almost succumbed in the late 1970s and there would be no Harley-Davidson today if it were not for the loyalty of motorcycle outlaws. Every outlaw club requires members to own an "American motorcycle" and dealers frequently give patch-holders discounts. Outlaws do not own Harleys because they think Harleys are still good motorcycles. Outlaws buy them out of reverence for tradition and out of patriotism. Then they usually rebuild them.

The central act of being a motorcycle outlaw is not fighting, drinking, wenching or stealing but riding a big loud motorcycle. All outlaws are "brothers in the wind." The wind is all you feel on a stripped down Harley when you get much above 80 or 90. It buffets, batters and tries to knock you over. In the Mojave in summer when the black top reaches 150 degrees the wind mummifies. The hot wind sucks you dry and thickens your blood until your heart must pound to pump oxygen to your brain. Your vision narrows and blurs. You start to pant. Your balance goes. The last thing you see is the road. Then you live or you die.

In Alamogordo in Spring when the roses bloom the wind smells like an easy woman. In Oxnard and Yuma in autumn it smells of fresh, corn tortillas. Half the year in Kansas and Missouri the wind carries apparently drunken and suicidal jays. In Wyoming the flies are big as hummingbirds. In all places at all times the wind carries the ringing of the long haulers. In the Four Corners the wind is *Katsinam* whispering secrets in a forgotten language.

Wah was hot sos lop wuh wuh is is is.

You smell the weather in the wind. The wind is your brother at your back. For the last fifty years, fugitive outlaws have been described by their accomplices and their pursuers as being "in the wind."

The outlaw life is lived in a hurricane and to ride a motorcycle on the 605 in El Lay, across the plains in a hail storm or through the mountains in a forest fire is to hold hands with one's mortality. Cops, authorities and social engineers refuse to understand. It is what's up with bikers and all the skulls. The skeletons and skulls recall the 14th Century *danse macabre*. Bare bones unite all of us. Motorcycles remind us that we are fragile. This is why combat veterans join motorcycle clubs. This is one of the ways bikers frighten people. This is one of the things the frightened people think is wrong with outlaws.

The men who live in the hurricane now are survivors of the genocide of the American laboring class. They are Eric Hoffer without a truck to load or a ditch to dig. They are the voiceless and all seeing phantom Tom Joad. They are the inheritors and caretakers of an obviously irresistible notion. The scholars who define the frontier as an ideology describe only half of the deconstruction. In "post-frontier" and "post industrial" America the most lucrative commodities are romantic ideas.

Now, and for a little longer, to throw your leg over an overpriced and underperforming Harley-Davidson motorcycle is to ride off to discover America again. To simply climb on a Harley and ride around the block is to transform oneself into an iconic image and to travel back in time at least as far as the great, lost age of tail fins. The lone, grey wolf on his vision quest is now a costume you can buy. And that is why prosperous, aging men buy overpriced motorcycles they hardly ever ride – because they grieve for their squandered, lonely lives.

The voice over narration in a 150 second, 2006, Harley-promotional film called "Live By It" brilliantly summarized this commodity.

"We believe in going our own way, no matter which way the rest of the world is going. We believe in bucking the system that's built to smash individuals like bugs on a windshield. Some of us believe in the man upstairs. All of us believe in sticking it to the man down here. We believe in the sky and we don't believe in the sun roof. We believe in freedom. We believe in dust, tumbleweeds, buffalo, mountain ranges and riding off into the sunset. We believe in saddlebags and we believe that cowboys had it right. We believe in refusing to knuckle under to anyone. We believe in wearing black because it doesn't show any dirt. Or, weakness. We believe the world is going soft and we're not going along with it. We believe in motorcycle rallies that last a week. We believe in roadside attractions, gas station

100

hotdogs and finding out what's over the next hill. We believe in rumbling engines, pistons the size of garbage cans, fuel tanks designed in 1936, freight train sized headlights, chrome and custom paint. We believe in flames and skulls. We believe life is what you make it. And, we make it one hell of a ride. We believe the machine you sit on can tell the world exactly where you stand. We don't care what everyone else believes. Amen"

The other outlaw identity was summarized by Stephen Crane four years after the U.S. Census declared that the old frontier was gone forever.

> *I stood upon a high place,*
> *And saw, below, many devils*
> *Running, leaping,*
> *And carousing in sin.*
> *One looked up, grinning,*
> *And said, "Comrade! Brother!"*

In 1983, the newly rejuvenated Harley-Davidson Company understood how much of its business depended on the loyalty of motorcycle outlaws, how small that core clientele was and how seductive the outlaw image was to a big international market. So Harley started its own motorcycle club. The company called it HOG, which is an acronym for the Harley Owners Group and the club house was your local Harley dealer. HOG harkened back to the original motorcycle clubs formed during the Great Depression and at its beginning nobody quite knew what consumers got out of HOG after they joined.

A Harley dealer in Los Angeles named Dale Marschke decided to take his HOG chapter on a ride across the state to the Colorado River. Once there they could take a "Laughlin to Oatman River Run." (Oatman is a largely abandoned town near Laughlin in Northern Arizona.) Laughlin, Nevada was where the biker rally was reinvented as a costume party for consumers. And, it was where the biker world split in two.

Marschke knew an entrepreneur named Don Laughlin who had bought a boarded up, dirt road diner in 1966 and turned it into his own gambling town. By 1983, Laughlin, Nevada had 350 hotel rooms to rent on a paved road and 100 fulltime residents. Marschke also knew Joe O'Day, who had an events company called Dal-Con Promotions. The three of them put together a motorcycle event that sold out Don Laughlin's hotel.

The River Run immediately became the biggest event in Laughlin's town every year. By 1987 the town was practically civilized with 1600 hotel rooms, a school and a new bridge across the river right at the end of the end of the gambling strip. The far shore of the river was a town called Bullhead City and Don Laughlin owned most of that, too. Laughlin became Nevada's third gambling city, after Vegas and Reno. It also became the place where the two outlaw identities met. The success of the run was based on the affluence of rich, part-time bikers who admired, as Harley did, the outlaw way.

Until the mid-nineties the River Run was a sloppy, rude, biker party with few rules and it became a model for how to get rich off a new, broad market of outlaw admirers. Other runs came and went as the baby boomer biker fad waxed and waned. Starting in 1993, the Four Corners Iron Horse Rally coalesced every Labor Day weekend on the Southern Ute reservation near Durango, Colorado. Hollister invited the mellower, more upscale bikers to a "Fiftieth Anniversary Rally" to commemorate the original "motorcycle riot." Local innkeepers, saloons and tee shirt vendors anticipated a windfall. Police gravely warned that dangerous outlaws might show up along with the poseurs who towed their

Harleys to their motels then rode into town from there. When there was no second Hollister riot police explained that, thanks to outstanding police work, a bullet had been dodged but next time would be worse unless more money was spent on overtime for the underappreciated and overworked cops.

Real, live outlaws became one of the main attractions at these rallies. In the early years of the new millennium, one of the Laughlin tourists told a local reporter about spotting a dozen Hells Angels at a convenience store. "It just spellbound everybody on the lot," he said. "Nobody would go and talk to them, maybe out of fear. They were just sitting back and letting them do their thing…. That'll probably be one of the top three things I got to see."

Billy Queen was accepted by the Mongols after he rode across the desert with them to Laughlin. All the major clubs in the West went to Laughlin every spring, particularly the clubs with a major presence in California, Nevada and Arizona. They kept peace among themselves.

Sixty thousand bikers representing the full outlaw spectrum, from poseurs to scooter trash, jammed into Laughlin in 2002. The Angels occupied the Flamingo at one end of the hotel strip, Casino Drive, where they entertained their admirers with burnout contests every night. Throughout most of the history of the Run, the Mongols had always stayed at the original hotel, the Riverside Resort, right next door to the Flamingo. Eventually Don Laughlin banned them. "They were fighting," Laughlin said. "We just kicked them out and told them we didn't want their business."

So in 2002 the Mongols stayed as far away from the Hells Angels as they could get. They checked into Harrah's at the opposite end of the strip. Harrah's welcomed them with open arms. "Basically we had the run of the hotel," Roger Pinney, who was President of the Mongols at the time, said. "Whether we wanted to go upstairs and go to sleep or go to the bar outside and gamble."

That was the year Laughlin became famous for the most notorious biker brawl in American history. Afterward the press was encouraged to call it the "Laughlin Riot."

Sixteen hours or so before that fight began the head of Harrah's security politely requested that the Mongols not dangle knives on their hips. "He was very pleasant and we were very pleasant back," Pinney said. "There was no problems. He just asked if some of the brothers, you could see their knives hanging, and he asked us if we could remove any weapons because they are not allowed in Harrah's. I said, 'Yes, there's no problem.' We're here to have a good time. We don't want no confrontation."

The President of the Mongols was an edgy, bright, articulate, charming, prosperous, often drunken, Vietnam Vet. "I just started riding with some friends of mine. And, then one of them joined, I believe. And, it's just like it wasn't too many people looking for veterans, Vietnam veterans, in those days. So I had a friendship with them," Pinney said. "In those days it was basically just run around acting stupid, fetching beers and cigarettes and just a bunch of kids' stuff."

Pinney had a criminal record. He served a two-year sentence for involuntary manslaughter in the late 1970s but he hardly fit the description of a career criminal or a racketeer. Unfortunately, Pinney was not entirely in charge of the Mongols that day. No club president is ever actually in charge of a motorcycle club because motorcycle clubs are heroically democratic. And, that April the Mongols was actually splitting in two.

The Hells Angels was and remains fiercely territorial about Arizona. Sonny Barger did time in

Arizona. He liked the climate so he returned there to live. The Angels patched over a ferocious club called The Dirty Dozen and occupied the state. There were Bandidos to the East in New Mexico, Vagos, Mongols and Bandidos in Nevada, Utah and California and Bandidos, Mongols and Sons of Silence in Colorado but as far as the Angels were concerned Arizona belonged to them. It was their new homeland. Sonny Barger had chosen it.

Through a succession of club Presidents the Mongols challenged then conceded the Angels right to Arizona. The Mongols had a chapter in Phoenix then gave it up. It was the sort of move an old outlaw like Pinney would understand. The Golden Rule of motorcycle outlaws is "Give respect, get respect." One Hells Angel who was in Laughlin that year said, "Before the fight in Laughlin we actually got along pretty well with the Mongols. We used to party together sometimes. Doc changed that."

Another Angel said, "We got along very well. Partied with each other when we saw one another. A lot of the Southern California members of both clubs hung out with each other all the time. In 2000 I stayed at Don Laughlin's Riverside, where the majority of the Mongols used to stay and I had absolutely no problems. That was the same year Billy Slow Brain says 'They made their big stand at the Flamingo.' That wasn't a big deal. I was there when that happened too."

Pinney had a rival for control of the club. The long feud with the Angels had greatly depleted the Mongols and, to keep their numbers up, the club had begun to recruit members it might have rejected a few years before. One of those new Mongols was the ATF Agent who called himself Billy Slow Brain. Another was a former member of The Avenues street clique in East Los Angeles named Ruben Cavazos.

Cavazos was a tough guy with a rough past. He enjoyed the company of other tough guys but he was too old to be a gang banger and he didn't want to be a gangster. He had been riding a motorcycle for less than six years that Spring in Laughlin but he had greatly admired outlaw bikers for longer than that. Multiple sources, speaking years after the fact, claim his name in the Avenues was "Disco Bunny." Because he was an X-ray technician his road name in the Mongols became "Doc." Doc would later assert that at the time he joined the club, the Mongols was down to 27 members.

And because the Mongols numbers were depleted Doc was encouraged to help recruit new members. So, Doc did and most of the new Mongols he found were also former members of Mexican street cliques. From its founding in East LA, the Mongols had always been one of the most *Xicano* of all clubs. After Doc began to recruit reinforcements for what he intended to be a renaissance of the war against the Angels, the club became even more so. The new members were attracted to the outlaw mystique exactly as most of Harley-Davidson's new customer base was. Old members were happy to have the reinforcements and flattered that so many young men wanted to join their club. The problem was that many of the older members did not consider the new members to be "proper outlaws." Instead they were seen as instant outlaws.

A power struggle began to develop between the old and new Mongols in the ranks and between old time Mongols like Red Dog Jarvis and Doc Cavazos at the top. Where Pinney had thought that cooling it with the Angels was wise Doc thought abandoning Arizona was a sign of weakness. Cavazos, largely on his own initiative, began to establish Mongols chapters in Northern California which the Angels also considered to be exclusively theirs. Many of the ex-gang banger

Mongols were more loyal to Doc than to anyone else in the club. By April 2002 Doc Cavazos had Red Dog Jarvis' old job – he became the Mongols Mother Chapter Sergeant at Arms. Pinney who, even at 60, was always more interested in raising hell than transforming his club was aware of Doc's growing influence. At the time Pinney became President, Doc was ineligible for the job because he had only been a Mongol for four years. According to Doc and other sources, Cavazos agreed to back Pinney for President if Pinney agreed to step down after a year and cede leadership to him.

When the security chief at Harrah's asked Pinney to have his Mongols disarm it was because Harrah's had been told by John Ciccone that trouble was brewing. Harrah's knew something Roger Pinney did not in the hours leading up to the fight. "Intelligence reports indicated the Mongols intended to bolster their status by attacking members of the Hells Angels," a Las Vegas police memo written after the fight stated. Sonny Barger, who knew about the split in the Mongols, anticipated the potential trouble. He tried to organize a "peace powwow" for the next week. The ATF, through local police, warned Hells Angels the day before the fight that the Mongols were planning to attack them. The Angels told the messengers that they could "handle any problems themselves."

The Angels increased security and some of them holed up at a rundown motel called Gretchen's Inn across the river in Bullhead City. The ATF knew. The Bureau had a paid confidential informant staying there. The ATF was everywhere and knew everything.

The actual trouble started when several Hells Angels from San Francisco who had always stayed at Harrah's, checked in. According to Ciccone, some Mongols thought they were spies. When the Angels tried to catch a cab they were surrounded and harassed by Mongols. This may have been instigated by either

Cavazos or Pinney. Pinney was at least a little drunk all day and when he drank he had a reputation for starting fights.

By mid-afternoon Friday, the Mongols were on the move. When Roger Pinney partied, everybody partied. When Pinney decided to ride down to the Golden Nugget for a drink fifty Mongols rode with him. When they arrived at the Golden Nugget they discovered a handful of Hells Angels selling tee-shirts in the parking lot. The Mongols surrounded the tee-shirt stand and discouraged the non-outlaw tourists from buying the Angels' souvenirs. Allegedly, a Hells Angels associate, who might simply have been a tourist in a Hells Angels tee-shirt, was "beaten." More than 100 cops, including a SWAT team responded immediately. What is most notable about this incident is that the police knew what had happened almost instantly and arrived within three minutes.

"It was a very friendly conversation," Pinney later said. "We made it very plain that…we were going to stay there or go back to the Harrah's and we don't want any problems." The Mongols abandoned their revels and rode back to Harrah's.

An attorney representing a Hells Angel would later charge that "the ATF," which should be understood to mean John Ciccone, knew something bad was coming and did nothing to prevent it. Police were, "present and aware that this attack was brewing and imminent and did nothing to defuse it," the lawyer, Louis Palazzo, said. Palazzo charged "law enforcement" with channeling "resources to monitor and infiltrate the clubs with undercover agents and cooperating informants, and created a general atmosphere designed to make the confrontation more likely to occur, rather than to take active, protective measures to defuse an otherwise volatile set of circumstances."

Laughlin was crawling with undercover police. Most of the federal undercovers drifted in and out of a safe house in Bullhead City. Some occupants of the house that week described it as a "party."

Some Mongols and some Angels think that somehow the ATF provoked the confrontation. There is no evidence of that but the charge is more plausible than you might now think. The ATF predicted the fight and did nothing to prevent it. The ATF had two, paid confidential informants in the Mongols the night of the fight. Confidential informants in biker investigations always behave as *agents provocateur*. Both informants witnessed the confrontation and immediately after the fight they were both taken by uniformed, local cops to a secure area for debriefing. But their role, if any, in provoking the fight is now completely obscured.

All week long, federal agents operated the cameras in the surveillance rooms at both the Flamingo and Harrah's. According to a source who has examined the tapes, the cameras "would follow Mongols, Hells Angels or Brother Speed (Motorcycle Club) members, regardless of their activities. Usually in a casino, security will only take the cameras off of their money for something else that also involves their money."

The brawl took at least 45 minutes to build and much of this prelude sounds like high school. Sometime before 1:30 Saturday morning a group of seven Frisco Angels sat drinking at the Rosa's Cantina bar in Harrah's. Biker brawls always start like this – with one club disrespecting the sanctity of another club's territory. Sometimes the disrespect is intentional and sometimes it is accidental. As far as the most militant Mongols were concerned, they had stayed out of the Flamingo and the Angels should have stayed out of Harrah's. Federal agents, sitting in the surveillance room, watched all of this as it occurred.

When three of the Angels at the bar got up to go to the bathroom a dozen Mongols followed them and waited for them outside the door. A few minutes later twenty Mongols in single file squeezed past the seated Angels bumping into them as they walked by.

Two undercover ATF Agents were drinking with Angels Donald "Smitty" Smith and "Ramona Pete" at the Flamingo around the time this was happening. One of the agents at the bar was Darrin Kozlowski. John Carr, arguably the least principled of all the ATF undercover agents who would later participate in Operation Black Rain, was somewhere loose in Laughlin gathering "intelligence."

The Agents at the Flamingo reported that Smith got a call from one of the Frisco Angels at Harrah's. Smith left, then came back and left again. This was later reported in ATF documents as, "the Angels sent spies to the Mongols hotel."

About quarter to two, a group of Hells Angels did enter Harrah's. More than to spy, they came to support the Frisco brothers who were staying at the hotel. They were sick of the Mongols pushing their weight around. They were there to prove that they were the toughest motorcycle club in the world and they could go anywhere they wanted. And, they were also there to emphasize the absolute inviolability of the state of Arizona, just a hundred yards away across the river.

The two clubs coexisted in Rosa's Cantina for another 15 minutes before some of the Mongols intimidated some of the Angels into phoning for more reinforcements. If the Flamingo ATF Agents' comments have any truth to them at all, and they may not, this would have been when Smith reappeared at the Flamingo.

Then about two dozen Angels rushed out of the Flamingo like busy commuters catching a train. They formed into a very loose pack and rode their bikes up the strip. It is less than two miles but during River Run the distance can take motorcyclists almost as long to traverse as it takes a symphony orchestra to play Ravel's Bolero. Police with sirens can cover the distance much more quickly.

There were at least six hundred police within a mile of Harrah's at the time. Police helicopters circled overhead. A Vegas Metro Police Sergeant and an officer counted 29 Angels in the pack. They followed the Angels bikes into the Harrah's lot. No one had set up a checkpoint at the entrance to the hotel complex. John Ciccone stood in the Harrah's lot and watched.

The Angels parked illegally around the Vegas police jeep. The Police Sergeant activated his light bar and whooped his siren. The Angels ignored him. The sergeant reported later that many of them had "weapons" in their hands. Of all the things the two cops might have done at that moment, they chose to radio for "assistance." Later a government lawyer explained, "The officer had radioed for assistance, which quickly arrived, but the Hells Angels' plan for confrontation with the Mongols moved too quickly...." There was, the U.S. government would argue over and over, no way to anticipate that a fight was about to occur and no way to prevent it even if it could have been predicted. Not even by the agents watching it unfold in the surveillance room. A Mongol who was in Rosa's cantina at the time claims that another pack of Angels had parked at the back of the hotel and that the Angels were attempting to come at the Mongols from two sides at once. If that was the case, the Angels at the back of the hotel never made it inside.

There were, according to multiple participants on both sides, 42 Angels in Harrah's after the pack arrived. At the same time there were about 115 Mongols on the casino floor.

The first Angel from the pack in the Harrah's door was Ray Foakes, the Sergeant at Arms for the Sonoma County charter of the Angels. Foakes was not armed. A security guard asked another Angel to remove the Buck knife he was wearing on his belt. He complied. Another of the Angels in that pack was Sohn Rigas from Reno. Rigas had a license to carry a concealed firearm in Nevada and he had two handguns in his saddlebags. He left them there and walked into Harrah's with two Angels named Jeramie Bell and Robert Tumelty. As they strode into Harrah's the Angels warned civilians to run away. The ATF, and the press, would later report Mongols left their rooms in the hotel and headed down to the bar. No Angel or Mongol who was there that night can remember a single case of that.

What did happen in the next minutes is remembered by members of both clubs as a tragedy.

Some of the Angels and some of the Mongols started, as a witness later put it, "mad-dogging each other." Roger Pinney, who has great and justified faith in his own considerable charm, decided to try to take charge of the situation. "I noticed the Hells Angels were congregated to the left side of the bar coming in, and I just sensed there was trouble brewing," Pinney said. "I told the brothers who were at the bar, 'Prepare yourself, I think something's about to happen.'" All told, there were about 150 potential combatants.

Pinney walked over to a bank of slot machines and to a senior Angel named Maurice "Pete" Eunice and said, "We need to defuse this bomb before it gets out of hand." The accuracy of Pinney's recollection is debatable. At the time the President of the Mongols was drunk enough to stagger and sway.

Another Angel told Pinney the Angels had been "disrespected. I don't want to talk that shit."

Seconds later, at 2:16 a.m., a Mongol told Foakes "We're going to fuck you up," which was the point where the confrontation got much more serious than high school. Foakes karate kicked the Mongol in the chest. On the other side of the room, an Angel from Alaska named Dale Leedom punched Pinney in the face and dragged him to the ground. During the fight, Leedom was shot. As Pinney went down another Angel named James Hannigan repeatedly stabbed Pinney in the right side and back. "Basically, they were just holding me ... stabbing me from the back," Pinney later testified. "The next thing I remember, I was gushing blood." Pinney managed to struggle to his feet.

Another Mongol got Pinney out the door and into a courtesy cab from another hotel. The cab took Pinney to a hospital in Bullhead City where he was evacuated by helicopter to a trauma center. While he was in the hospital someone sent him a bouquet of red and white flowers. The flowers were, of course, a blatant reminder of the bombing at the Conrad Mortuary in 1977 and a taunt. Not a single Angel seems to think their club sent Pinney the flowers. Most of them, and at least some Mongols, think the flowers were a gift from Ciccone.

Later, after he was released, Pinney was charged under RICO with murder. Numerous participants in and spectators to the brawl were charged with racketeering and murder.

A Hells Angel named Ron Arnone, was videotaped crouching against a wall during the fight. He was charged with racketeering and murder. "Arnone exercised his right to free association," his lawyer complained. "He also chose to crouch in a public place."

Despite what has been widely reported, most of the Angels and most of the Mongols did not fight. One Hells Angel who was there, and who did fight, and who was later charged with racketeering said, "A majority of both clubs didn't fight at all. Most of the Mongols ran.

Doc was one of the first. Don't take what I am saying as being offensive toward anyone. There wasn't a reason to fight. Besides, I have no problem with people running or ducking."

The lone Mongol killed in the fight, Anthony Salvador "Bronson" Barrera, 43-years-old and one of Doc's Cavazos' recruits, was wielding a flashlight as a weapon when he was stabbed in the heart. He was probably killed by either Jeramie Dean Bell or Robert Emmet Tumelty. Bell was just 27. Tumelty was 50. They were the two Hells Angels who entered Harrah's with Sohn Rigas and they were the two Angels killed in the fight. They were killed by shots from a .45 caliber pistol fired by a Mongol named Alexander Alcantar who was also severely injured in the fight. Alacantar was probably trying to defend or avenge Bronson Barrera.

There is a primal, wacky logic to violence on the motorcycle outlaw frontier that is both infuriating and touching to see. None of it is as wacky or as callous as the ATF's reaction to it.

Sohn Rigas saw Bell and Tumelty die. Rigas is a tough, nice man with an open face and years later he still wept for his two dead friends. Rigas seems to still regret not taking his guns inside instead of leaving them in his saddlebags. If he had, it is possible that Bell and Tumelty would still be alive and Alexander Alcantar would have died instead. Rigas' actual participation in the fight was confined to tackling a Mongol who tried to hit him with a sign. Then, under RICO, Rigas was charged with nine counts of attempted murder and 12 counts of carrying a concealed weapon.

The brawl was not stopped. It spent itself like a angry lover. Not only did hundreds of police do nothing to stop what they saw coming but once it started the cops ran like alley cats just as most of the Mongols and most of the Angels ran. John Ciccone, by his own account, continued to wait in the parking lot until the

114

two clubs had done a maximum amount of damage to each other then he "entered the Casino afterward to assist Las Vegas Metro Police Department at the crime scene...."

Ciccone would eventually testify under oath that there was no way he could have predicted what happened in Rosa's Cantina. The presence of the federal agents in the surveillance room has never been acknowledged. "It could have happened anywhere at any time," Ciccone said. The clear implication was that the sympathizers and poseurs who comprised most of the crowd at Laughlin were in constant danger from the Mongols, the Angels and the rest of the biker menace. Certainly, if the menace was to be stopped or controlled, the task would have to be accomplished by brave men like John Ciccone.

A Las Vegas homicide cop named Kevin Manning later told reporters, "This didn't just fester that weekend. This stuff has been going on for a long time and it happened to boil over."

An attorney later said what most of the survivors thought. "It's almost as if they," by which he meant the police in general, "wanted it to happen."

The whole fight was, of course, recorded by multiple video surveillance cameras. The brawl lasted just over a minute and it led most American newscasts the next day. It was a marvelous news story. Americans love biker stories although they rarely question that affection. It was only a tragedy if you were there or if you knew any of the people involved. News anchors clucked their tongues, rolled their eyes and wagged their heads.

About two dozen outlaws in Rosa's Cantina were stabbed, shot or otherwise seriously injured. The official government account claims more than 100 casualties. Most of the wounded were carried off by their club brothers. Fifty minutes later, the body of a

Hells Angel named Christian H. Tate was found next to Interstate 40 near Ludlow, a desert gas stop 100 miles west of Laughlin. He had been riding his motorcycle away from Laughlin and toward home to California when he was shot multiple times in his upper back and torso.

The next day, news outlets in Las Vegas reported Tate's murder was what had set off the brawl. "This event was going to come off without incident until the body was found," an anonymous source said. Tate's body was not discovered until almost 3 am but fourteen months later a "deep background" federal source told a reporter in Las Vegas that "Tate's killing in San Bernardino County, California may have ended up sparking a deadly biker riot at the Laughlin River Run. Within roughly an hour of Tate's shooting, Hells Angels members clashed with members of their rival motorcycle gang, the Mongols, in a crowded casino at Harrah's Laughlin."

Most Hells Angels still assume that Tate was murdered by Mongols. In the months after the fight in Harrah's a federal wiretap recorded a conversation in which two members of the Angels San Diego charter blamed the Mongols San Diego chapter President Michael Bill "Mike" Munz for Tate's murder. The ATF spent millions of dollars and more than a decade trying to implicate Munz in the murders of other Hells Angels. Undercover Agent William Queen tried and failed to get Munz to brag about those murders. So, it is plausible that Munz might have been involved in Tate's murder.

But, at least some Mongols believe Tate was murdered by the ATF. Munz has been in federal custody since October 2008 and since January 2009 the ATF has had the means to prove whether Tate was murdered by Mongols or not. Despite that, Tate's murder continues to remain unsolved.

The fallout from the brawl was significant. By daylight, Doc Cavazos was fully in control of the Mongols Motorcycle Club. And, John Ciccone was able to point to Rosa's Cantina as proof that outlaw bikers were as dangerous to the general public as he had been saying they were all along. He was still saying it at least as late as 2010. Multiple, federal criminal cases and at least two ATF undercover investigations grew out of the fight in Rosa's Cantina.

The first of those to become public was an investigation of the Hells Angels in Arizona that was given the public relations name Operation Black Biscuit. The name was invented for television. As most men know, a black biscuit is a hockey puck. And, even though Phoenix has a professional ice hockey team calling an undercover operation in the Arizona desert Black Biscuit seemed like the height of wit to whoever names operations for the ATF.

The lead undercover agent in Black Biscuit was one of the dozens of undercover cops in Laughlin the weekend of the fight. He was one of the two undercover agents, along with Darrin Kozlowski, who was drinking with Smitty Smith, and Ramona Pete at the Flamingo just before the brawl at Harrah's. The agent was already posing as an unlicensed gun dealer and he lived in the safe house in Bullhead City. He was a former University of Arizona wide receiver named Jay Anthony "Bird" Dobyns.

Bird

John Ciccone has never gone undercover and his regard for the ATF Agents who have may be ambivalent. It is impossible for a mere observer to actually know because it is so hard to tell when Ciccone is investigating – which is to say when he is lying – and when he speaking from his heart. From one side of his mouth he dismisses William Queen who gave him his first bureaucratic triumph as "only average as an undercover agent." From the other he sounds like a guilt stricken armchair warrior when he says that after undercover agents return from the terrors of the motorcycle outlaw frontier, "They should get anything they want!"

ATF undercovers tend to be self-involved, theatrical men. When the public hears about them, their investigations are usually described as adventures. And, since they are polished tellings of recollections of chains of events that were all contrived in the first place, those adventure stories always follow the same hackneyed plot.

First these agents are like Amish youth during *Rumspringa*, the time when pious adolescents are allowed to live among the "English" and experiment with drugs, alcohol and sex. On our behalf, for the good of all, repugnant though their necessary actions may be, ATF undercover agents are compelled by their roles to start fights, beat up civilians and sometimes provoke biker wars. "Tone your shit down," one Hells Angel advised Jay Bird Dobyns early in the investigation that made him a *Fox News Channel* celebrity. For some agents like Blake Boteler who investigated the Sons of Silence in Colorado Springs or Darrin Kozlowski there is only this adventure.

This is how Jay Dobyns describes Darrin Kozlowski. "Koz was a crazy, improvisational UC who *always* looked scary. He was famous for joking, 'If I die on this job, I sure as fuck don't want it to be in a traffic accident or because I had a heart attack at my desk. I don't want to get hit by a bus on my motorcycle. I want to be duct-taped to a chair and shot gunned in the face. I want those motherfuckers to cut my head off. I want the boys to say, "Did you hear? They cut Koz's head off!"'"

But, some of these agents begin to remember themselves as Joseph Campbell's *Hero With A Thousand Faces*. Two or three years after the fact they become men who descended into a netherworld that none of the rest of us who are not ATF heroes can ever really know. Simultaneously, they may begin to feel real remorse for what they have done: Not so much for the drugs they have consumed, their sexual indiscretions or the laws they have broken but for the men they victimized and betrayed. Steve Martin, the agent who betrayed the Warlocks, was vilified by some factions in the ATF for the regret he eventually expressed over what he had done.

The most flamboyant undercovers begin to see themselves as not merely underappreciated but actually betrayed. In at least three instances, these recovering undercovers imagine themselves to be Donnie Brasco: A tortured hero who must live in two worlds and then betray one of them. And then the tortured hero is betrayed in turn by the ungrateful world for which he has sacrificed so much. Jay Anthony Bird Dobyns is arguably the craziest of all these self-dramatizing jackasses.

The night of the "Laughlin Riot," the night he and Kozlowski were drinking with Smitty Smith, and Ramona Pete at the Flamingo, Jay Dobyns was, as he put it, "running some game" across the river in Bullhead City. He picked Bullhead City because: "It's a broken-down town full of semi-employed mechanics who've shacked up with women who are – or were – 'dancers.' It's a meth capital teeming with high school dropouts, and it's all set down in a brown and tan valley that looks more like Mars than Earth."

America no longer gives a damn about places like Bullhead City or the far more "broken down" Golden Valley on the other side of the of the jagged mountains that line the Colorado River Valley. If the nation did, more citizens would know that Bullhead City is a beautiful place, really, particularly at twilight when those mile-high rocks turn deep purple and pink streaks glow in the sky. But Bullhead City is increasingly impoverished and that is not a story most journalists care to recount.

America would rather see anything about almost any celebrity than see the dispossessed families running to or from places like Bullhead City. From a motorcycle the families are impossible to miss on the highways of Southern Nevada and Northern Arizona: Driving the rent-a-truck, towing the car, the adults grimfaced and ashamed, the kids laughing and waving at the bikers as they roar past as if this road of flight is just a passage in an adventure and they have just seen real, iron horse cowboys. Dobyns rode a motorcycle here and somehow never saw that.

Much of this part of this part of flyover America looks like a refugee camp in central Asia. Bullhead City, with its steady supply of cheap lots and pre-owned trailer homes is one the places those families go when they are down to their last dream. This is the America from which motorcycle outlaws come.

Dobyns went there because he makes $185,000 a year to hurt those people. He went because America no longer trusts that if you give free people a chance, they will work things out for themselves. He went because, "Bullhead was ripe for the picking, and…getting evidence up there would be like shooting fish in a barrel."

Ciccone had already started an investigation of the Arizona Hells Angels before the fight at Rosa's Cantina. Ciccone had turned a Hells Angel named "Mesa" Mike Kramer into a paid confidential informant. Kramer, handled by Ciccone, became the key informant in what was then called "Operation Dequiallo." Eventually Dequiallo and other investigations became called Operation Black Biscuit. The ATF is so Byzantine an institution that it is impossible to know when the Bureau and Ciccone began to regard Dobyns as an asset in the new investigation. What is clear is that Ciccone started paying Mesa Mike before the River Run and that as the showdown between the Mongols and Angels loomed Dobyns was already occupying a safe house all the other undercover agents could use.

Few Angels become paid informants. Kramer did so because he had murdered a woman named Cynthia Garcia on October 25, 2001. Her body was found on October 31 and Mesa Mike started talking to Ciccone on November 26 – five months before the Laughlin brawl.

Like the Herrera murder by the Mongols, the murder of Cynthia Garcia has been cited numerous

121

times to illustrate the depravity of the sort of men who become Hells Angels and, by inference, outlaw bikers in general. It has also been exploited to illustrate why the ATF should be encouraged to stop these biker brutes at all costs. The ATF friendly *Fox* show *America's Most Wanted* described the crime like this: "A group of HAs" was hanging out at the Mesa clubhouse "when they decided to send somebody out to scour the streets for some women to bring back for the party. Cynthia Garcia, was a 44-year-old mother of six who happened to be out and about that night when she got the invite to party with the bikers back at their clubhouse. Cynthia, a mother of six, had been through some rough times. She had been in abusive relationships with men, and had struggled with alcohol problems. But, by all accounts from her family, she was a sweet person at heart.... As the party continued inside the club house that night, an inebriated Cynthia started 'mouthing off' to some of the Hells Angels. Police say the bikers warned her to keep quiet. When Cynthia kept talking, one of the Hells Angels allegedly knocked her off of a barstool. Then, a confidential informant told police that he, (Hells Angel Paul) Eischeid and another biker began beating and kicking Cynthia until she was bleeding and unconscious. Then, police report, they tossed the woman into a car trunk, and drove out to the desert where they took turns stabbing the woman until she was nearly decapitated. The gang left their victim's corpse to rot in the desert."

The confidential informant this account mentions was Mesa Mike Kramer. The Angel who knocked her off the bar stool was Kramer. He was the most senior Angel there. The crime exhibits the earmarks of methamphetamine rage. Mesa Mike Kramer was a methamphetamine addict.

An ATF friendly "biker authority" and "investigative journalist" named Julian Sher later wrote:

"For me, it brought back memories of an equally disturbing scene from my recent biker investigations. I was standing in a patch of desert outside Phoenix with two police officers as they pointed out where a woman named Cynthia Garcia had been left to die, stabbed more than 40 times for daring to talk back to Hells Angels in their clubhouse. One of her killers – who eventually squealed to the police and turned in his alleged accomplices – remembered how, with her life and blood draining out of her, she grasped his pant leg and then collapsed." The Angel who squealed to police was Mesa Mike.

By his own admission, Mesa Mike orchestrated the murder. He punched the woman and knocked her down. Mesa Mike kicked her and ordered three other patched Angels and two prospects to kick her too. The three patched members were named Kevin Augustiniak, Paul Eischeid and Richard Hyder. The prospects were named Dennis Gilliard and David LeMoine. Kramer ordered the other patched members to bring around a car and throw her in the trunk. Mesa Mike slashed Garcia's throat and gruesomely tried to decapitate her. He ordered the car driven to his house where he tore the carpet out of the trunk and attempted to clean up the evidence. Kramer got rid of the murder weapons.

In May 2002, the month after Laughlin, one of the men present at the murder, and a witness who could contradict Mesa Mike's version of events, Richard Hyder was killed in a motorcycle accident in California. The driver of the truck which killed Hyder was Mesa Mike and at least one attorney familiar with the case said "the circumstances of the 'accident' are suspicious."

Ciccone remained Mike Kramer's handler throughout Jay Dobyn's investigation of the Arizona Angels. Kramer confessed his insatiable meth addiction to Ciccone on multiple occasions. Kramer had been addicted to crank most of his adult life. When he was

17, his mother had him committed to rehab for crank addiction. Kramer is also an alcoholic. Multiple times during the investigation Ciccone officially reported, "The CI (Mesa Mike Kramer) has never used methamphetamine in the past while working on behalf of the ATF, does not have a drug history and has never been convicted of a drug offense."

Mesa Mike was guilty of numerous assaults while he was working for Ciccone. Kramer beat one man with a baseball bat for "disrespecting" him. He dragged another victim outside a bar and stomped him while the victim begged for his life. "He was screaming like a little bitch," Kramer said. During his career with the ATF Kramer bought and sold drugs and explained that because he was an ATF informant, "the rules did not apply," to him. Kramer epitomized the men who actually make cases for the ATF against motorcycle outlaws.

An ATF report praises Kramer. "He did what he could to make John happy." He had "daily" contact with Ciccone and "he learned by trial and error."

In return for making Ciccone happy Kramer entered into a plea and bargaining agreement in which he admitted he was guilty of manslaughter and was sentenced to five years probation. During 2002 and 2003 the ATF paid Mesa Mike Kramer approximately $135,000. Mesa Mike was also allowed to keep any profits from drug dealing and other illicit business transactions while he was working for the ATF. At the conclusion of Operation Black Biscuit he was paid an unspecified bonus and enrolled in the US Marshall's Federal Witness Relocation Program.

Before or after the Laughlin Run and riot, Ciccone sent Kramer to see Dobyns. Dobyns, who fears and detests motorcycles, was already riding one in Bullhead City although the official narrative is that he was not there to investigate motorcycle outlaws.

Dobyns had previously participated in the dirty and overblown ATF investigation of the Sons of Silence. His field office in Phoenix was already trying to contrive a paper RICO case against the Arizona Angels by tying crimes committed by individual Angels to other crimes using public documents and tax records.

Kramer introduced Dobyns to Augustiniak, Eischeid and an Angel named Calvin Schaefer. During the brawl at Rosa's Cantina Schaefer attacked two Mongols with a ball peen hammer, shot at and probably hit a Mongol named Richard Nolan and shot and severely wounded another Mongol named Benjamin Levya while Levya was fighting two other Angels at once. According to public records, Kramer also identified Donald Smitty Smith, with whom Dobyns and Kozlowski had been chatting and drinking as the Laughlin brawl brewed in the early morning hours of April 27. According to the ATF account, Dobyns was assigned by the Phoenix ATF Field office to start investigating the Arizona Hells Angels in the first week in May, 2002.

Operation Black Biscuit, for which Dobyns has taken most of the credit, lasted for more than two years and was as perversely corrupt as the participation of Mesa Mike Kramer would suggest. There were actually five, simultaneous investigations. One of them was Operation Dequiallo. Three of them were identified by numbers rather than media friendly names: Phoenix ATF 7805040-02-0049; California LA ATF 784015-02-0006; and Laughlin ATF 784015-03-0054. A fifth investigation was named for a defendant named Daniel Fabricant. Most of those five investigations remain secret. To a certain extent, they remain secret so no one will know how much all these investigations cost. There is really only one ongoing biker investigation. And, the reason that one ongoing investigation is fragmented is so that ATF bureaucrats can control the print and broadcast narrative of the ATF's secret war on the biker menace.

For the most part, motorcycle club investigations are the work of paid contractors. Sometimes these informants, like Mesa Mike, go to work for the ATF as a way of beating a criminal charge. Rudy Kramer, was another one of those. Kramer was a crank cook known as "the pharmacist," because of the high quality of the methamphetamine he produced. He was a member of saloon society and he was acquainted with many Hells Angels. He even claimed to know Sonny Barger. It was Rudy Kramer's notion that Dobyns present himself to the Angels as a member of a small cross border outlaw club with its mother chapter in Tijuana, the Solo Angeles CM. The Pharmacist introduced Dobyns to most of the Angels Dobyns would later try to entrap. Rudy Kramer made numerous "controlled" drug transactions with members of the Angels.

In Rudy Kramer's case, "controlled" meant that when he reported each alleged transaction he also supplied a set of handwritten notes which were then used to draft an ATF Report of Investigation which could be used as evidence in a criminal case. The process is analogous to the miracle of transubstantiation. Before the notes are transformed into an ROI they are only hearsay. Once they are blessed by the ATF and transcribed, they are magically transformed into truth.

Kramer claimed to have wrested an agreement from the Angels to allow the Solo Angeles to operate and sell drugs in Arizona. It is more likely that Rudy Kramer assumed the Angels, as the preeminent club in Arizona, would acknowledge the right of the Solo Angeles to establish a presence in Arizona. In fact, there is wiretap evidence of senior Angels stating they are not in the drug business in Arizona let alone in a position to "allow" it. Rudy Kramer dropped out of the case after he was arrested with two ounces of methamphetamine by Arizona police while working for the ATF. He was charged after the local police determined that he was a methamphetamine addict.

Very often, the paid contractors the ATF uses are professional informants. The ATF sometimes refers to them as "proactive informants." The one who featured most prominently in Dobyns investigation was a sometime meth addict named James Daniel "Pops" Blankenship. Sometimes Blankenship calls himself "Bad Company." The government rationale behind using contractors like Blankenship is to protect Agents like Dobyns from breaking the law – for example committing assaults or blatant drug use – by letting the informant break the law instead. In actual practice, when an ATF undercover agent breaks the law the paid contractor takes the rap. Blankenship was Dobyns right hand man during "Phoenix ATF 7805040-02-0049" before parts of that were consolidated with parts of the other investigations and named "Operation Black Biscuit."

Blankenship, according to one skeptical account, "poses as a freewheeling, drug using associate of ATF Special Agent Jay Dobyns in the business of debt collection, drug purchasing, gun dealing, bounty hunting, and contract murder for the Phoenix HAMC ATF investigation, 7805040-02-0049. Blankenship's role was to locate and contact possible targets and attempt to involve these targets in criminal activity. Blankenship most often let it be known that he was seeking personal use drugs and he would purchase small quantities for his own use usually recording the transaction on a recording device."

Most of the predicate charges eventually elaborated in the RICO indictment against the Angels that followed the public announcement of Black Biscuit were for very small drug transactions. Sometimes Blankenship merely reported that he had ingested drugs or that he had seen drugs at a location where he had also observed a gun – an accusation that would make the alleged possessor of the gun a felon. Blankenship had a cash incentive for this "intelligence" beyond his standard informant's pay of about $2,200 a month. The more criminal offenses he could witness the more money he would earn. While wearing a body wire on February 11, 2003, Pops began with: "2/11/03 the time is 6:50 hours. I'm Pops. I'm going to the Inferno Bar in Bullhead City where HA Dennis is, Hang around Bob is, hang around Billy is supposed to be coming, HA Smitty, and HA Steve, all Nomads from Flagstaff. We are having a little get together for my birthday, gonna try and broker some guns from Smitty and some crystal methamphetamine from Dennis. I'll also try to get another bag of weed from Steve...."

After leaving the bar, the same body wire caught Pops saying to Dobyns on the phone, "...You know I got Steve done so. Oh fucking outstanding, outstanding. Right. We're going to make, we're going to make our quota, between the three of us, we'll make it. Right. Yeah we're looking good, yeah...."

"We were much worse than the Hells Angels," Blankenship later told a television producer for the *National Geographic Channel.*

Because there was so much to hide, the RICO prosecution that followed the investigation largely fell apart. The Angels hired competent and aggressive lawyers who demanded to see all the evidence and the ATF simply refused. A federal judge in Las Vegas disallowed the testimony of one key witness when he found out Ciccone was paying the man to testify. But, these cases are all so cynically calculated that after Operation Ivan they stopped actually being about securing convictions. They only had to look like good police work.

Biker cases are most about ATF Agents, professional informants and prosecutors getting famous and getting paid. All of "criminal justice" is about getting paid. It is almost a yawn to huff about the land of the free and the home of the brave locking up five times as many of its citizens per capita as Britain, nine times as many as Germany and 12 times as many as Japan. America's rate of incarceration has quadrupled since Nixon. There is an industry in America called "corrections" that profits from human flesh.

An organization called the American Legislative Exchange Council largely sets the agenda each year for the passage of new laws. ALEC invents model legislation behind closed doors. About a third of all state legislators belong to ALEC as do about 200 corporate "private sector members." About one in fifteen of those corporate members are involved in either the corrections or law enforcement business or both. One of the largest, Corrections Corporation of America, holds a seat in ALEC's Criminal Justice Task Force which writes the Council's model bills on crime and punishment. Those model bills include numerous example of "get tough on crime" legislation including mandatory minimum sentences, three strikes laws, and so called "truth in sentencing" laws that limit the possibility of parole.

The ATF in particular gets paid. The Bureau's 2009 budget included $1.028 billion for 4,942 positions, which works out to about $208,000 per ATF employee. "As a full partner in the President's Project Safe Neighborhoods (PSN), which was initiated in FY2001, ATF has joined with DOJ attorneys and other federal law enforcement agencies, along with state, local, and tribal authorities, to investigate and prosecute offenders, with a particular focus on armed violent and career criminals," the ATF explained in its budget request. By that the ATF means it keeps American streets safe by "infiltrating criminal groups through undercover operations and confidential informants."

Big biker cases are also about using federal prosecution as a form of punishment for people who fundamentally challenge authority and can easily be demonized. And, to keep getting paid and punish people the ATF does not need convictions. What the ATF needs most is good press. Before William Queen's book about Operation Ivan even hit bookstores, the ATF was ready to take manipulation of public opinion to a whole new level.

Before any of the cases that resulted from Operation Black Biscuit were tried, the ATF was promoting Jay Dobyns as a real American hero. The promotion was a joint effort between three ATF executives: W. Larry Ford, Assistant Director for Public and Governmental Affairs; Deputy Assistant Director Virginia O'Brien; and the Special Agent in Charge of the Undercover Branch, Kim Balog. In September 2004 Ford arranged for Dobyns to appear on the season premier of *America's Most Wanted*. It was actually the moment when pieces of the five ATF investigations including "Phoenix ATF 7805040-02-0049" were plucked, washed and packaged as "Operation Black Biscuit." The name Black Biscuit was invented for *America's Most Wanted*. It was the name of the episode in which Dobyns appeared.

According to a statement by Dobyns lawyer, "The Fox Media 'family' includes 20th Century Fox, the major motion picture arm of Fox Entertainment…. Accordingly, ATF…promoted Agent Dobyns to a television production company that is a subsidiary-related company to 20th Century Fox film studios. ATF introduced Agent Dobyns to FOX Entertainment and encouraged his involvement with the media family."

130

The ATF promoted Dobyns for the National Association of Police Officers "Top Cop" award, videotaped the award and an interview with Dobyns and then sold the resulting DVD to the general public.

Julian Sher, the investigative journalist and biker authority, saw Dobyns' *America's Most Wanted* appearance and contacted Larry Ford. Ford "approved, promoted and arranged" for Dobyns, Kozlowski, Carr, Ciccone and others "to cooperate with Sher." Ford emailed Dobyns that Sher was "an outstanding opportunity for ATF" and that his book would "be good for ATF." Sher's book, written with William Marsden and titled *Angels of Death: Inside The Biker Gang's Crime Empire*, contained the first lengthy prose account – about 220 pages – of Dobyns' perilous adventure among the brutes. The book is shameless ATF propaganda. Sher's "biker investigations" included the insights a psychologist at Folsom Prison named Stephanie Wagner. The psychologist explained, "I don't believe that I have ever recommended a Hells Angel to be released. I consider them psychopaths." She also called the club a "psychopathic organization" and, for his readers without a dictionary, Sher explained that what she meant was that Hells Angels, "don't have a conscience."

Sher later taught a joint seminar with Ciccone for police officers titled "Behind the Cuts." The course was intended to provide uninformed cops expertise in "OMG trends, officer safety information, investigative and intelligence gathering techniques, and other skills that are imperative for OMG operations." The course cost $125 to attend and, "Due to security concerns, the exact class location will only be given out with paid registration."

In a written interview, Sher explained his book's subtitle with a very generous quote.

The Hells Angels are a biker gang crime empire by, "Their own words and their own actions. The biker gangs themselves proudly display their "1%" patches and tattoos. They are the ones who are proud to call themselves outlaws, different than the other 99%. They openly say they govern themselves, live by their own rules and don't respect 'the man' or the cops or the law. Fine. Everyone is free to make choices – but you have to live with those choices. At least have the courage of your convictions. The American revolutionaries fighting the British were proud to be rebels; same with 'outlaws' and revolutionaries the world over. Even the mythical outlaw Robin Hood didn't complain the sheriff's men were hunting him because he saw the official powers as evil. But the bikers proudly boast they are outlaws and a law onto themselves when it suits them – and then when they are accused of being outlaws they complain like a bunch of cry-babies. 'We're just fun-loving, misunderstood rebels,' they and their apologists insist."

Sher's book was the first of three book length tributes to Dobyns' investigation.
An author, prosecutor and poet named Kerrie Droban published a book about Dobyns called *Running With The Devil.* The title alludes to a threat a Hells Angel named Robert McKay allegedly made against Dobyns in a Tucson bar. Dobyns' witness to this threat was Darrin Kozlowski and according to Droban McKay told them that Dobyns was "a marked man" who was "going to spend the rest of his life on the run." McKay was arrested the next day for threatening a federal agent. According to Droban, McKay's exact words were, "We'll find you. We'll get you. For the rest of your life you'll be running from the devil."

No one, including Dobyns, seems able to confirm Droban's quote but the author stands by it. She describes herself as "the female Woodward and Bernstein." Her publicity photo shows her wearing jeans and a black, leather jacket. Droban has stated publically that she was asked by "a mutual friend" in 2004 if she "would be interested in writing about the ATF sting against the Hells Angels, code named, Operation Black Biscuit. I was familiar with the case," she said, "since it had received some national coverage on *America's Most Wanted*, and I knew several of the participants involved in the investigation."

Droban replied to an inquiry about her sources by stating that her "material came from the horses' mouths and not the horses' asses if you get my drift? I researched the old fashioned way, getting in the trenches, interviewing the players, reviewing highly sensitive and confidential material. I can't reveal how I got my hands on that."

Droban has described her book about Operation Black Biscuit as an attempt to give readers the vicarious experience of being Hells Angels. She has since published *Prodigal Father, Pagan Son: Growing Up Inside the Dangerous World of the Pagans Motorcycle Club*.

Dobyns said, "*Running with the Devil* was written by someone with no access to the biker world and relied exclusively on her interpretation of public documents."

"In 2005," Dobyns said through his lawyer, "after becoming acquainted with Fox entertainment through ATF's introduction of Agent Dobyns with the *America's Most Wanted* feature, a film researcher for FOX and film director Tony Scott contacted Agent Dobyns. Fox and Scott were developing a film about the Hells Angels. A relationship was struck, based on the researcher's stated admiration for Agent Dobyns' work, dedication and honesty. The researcher asked Agent Dobyns to consult on two film projects, one for Fox and the other for Universal Studios."

Tony Scott has been collecting the film rights to properties about the Hells Angels for decades. He owns the film rights to Hunter Thompson's *Hell's Angels* and

Sonny Barger's autobiography. The one major book about the Hells Angels Scott does not own is *Chain of Evidence* by an author who used the pseudonym Michael Detroit. The book recounts the mostly true story of a female detective who was part of a 1980s infiltration of the Angels in Orange County, south of Los Angeles. The actress Jennifer Anniston bought the rights to that one.

According to Dobyns, he declined the consulting job so ATF Assistant Director Larry Ford was able to moonlight as a consultant for the movies *Déjà Vu* and *Miami Vice*. Dobyns is, however, a fan of the old *Miami Vice* television show. He told the Tucson *Citizen*, he had joined the ATF in the first place because "I thought I could be the next Sonny Crockett!"

Dobyns returned to television in 2007, in documentaries for *The National Geographic Channel* and *The History Channel.* He embraced his role. He dressed in biker costume for interviews and appeared in other segments, slowly and carefully, riding his motorcycle. Around the same time, Dobyns agreed to write a book with co-author Nils Johnson-Shelton, about his adventures for Random House. The working title was *Almost Angels: The True Story of the First Cop to Infiltrate the Hells Angels—the World's Most Infamous and Impenetrable Motorcycle Gang.* When it was published the book became *No Angel: My Harrowing Undercover Journey To The Inner Circle Of The Hells Angels.*

No Angel was a commercial success. Since its publication, Dobyns has regularly referred to himself as a New York *Times* bestselling author. Steve Gaghan, who directed *Syriana* and won an Oscar for the screenplay of *Traffic*, wrote the top frontis page blurb for Dobyns book. "If you want to understand the harrowing emotional realities of long-term undercover work," Gaghan wrote, "the balls out courage and insanity of a multi-year infiltration, or just plain read a great story with an original American voice, then buy this book, read it, and wonder at every page if you'd have the stuff to pull it off yourself."

Julian Sher said Dobyns, "reveals the true, violent face of outlaw bikers – but also the tortured souls of the undercover cops who dare to infiltrate them."

William Queen wrote, "Jay Dobyns is a hero. Out of a sense of duty, he closed his eyes and made a journey into hell. For two years he walked through the valley of the shadow of death, but thankfully, he lived to tell this riveting story."

Joe Pistone, "aka Donnie Brasco," wrote "Fughedaboudit! Moving and frightening. The most informative and authoritative book on undercover since *Donnie Brasco*."

What readers learn is that over and over Dobyns was able to make gun and drug transactions with men who trusted him because bikers are stupid and he is smart and because Hells Angels are evil and he is good. In one scene, Bird buys guns from a Hells Angel who won two Silver Stars in Vietnam. Over and over Dobyns describes Hells Angels trying to help him: Help him do his slightly shady business, earn a living, find a girlfriend, get loaded, have some fun and stay safe in the nasty world of the white, American underclass. And, many of the gun buys Dobyns made were actually legal transactions under Arizona and Nevada law. Their importance to the investigation was not to show the Angels breaking the law but to show a "pattern of racketeering activity."

At one point in his book, Dobyns has sudden, blinding *satori* while listening to Lynyrd Skynard, "I'm just like the guy in 'Freebird,'" he confesses, "who cannot stay, who cannot change, and whose Lord knows he cannot change."

Dobyns brags of riding through the Phoenix rush hour at 95 miles an hour in a pack of motorcycles with the bikes just 18 inches apart. An actual outlaw might discretely raise his eyebrows. An actual Phoenix commuter may politely clear his throat.

The book is stitched together with a thousand little lies and distortions and obvious fabrications that make the story sound cogent and that one cannot correct without seeming petty. Distances between points on a map are routinely doubled. The difficulty of certain motorcycle rides is grossly exaggerated. The way men conduct themselves in the outlaw world is distorted for dramatic effect. Whole chains of restaurants are described as lousy. Whole categories of men are described as phonies. The features of individual men and women are distorted to make them seem grotesque. Everywhere he goes Dobyns is terrified. Everywhere he goes other men are terrified of him. There is not a single passage about what the wind feels like on a Harley.

He describes riding off to fight an imminent war with the Bandidos. The truth is that as a prospect with the Angels he was given mundane chores. And one of those was standing guard at a Nevada Confederation of Clubs meeting at which both Angels and Bandidos were present. There was never any threat of violence at the meeting by anyone.

Real bikers go to biker events that are as banal, in their own way, as fantasy football or band camp. Dobyns on the other hand is the most confidant man who ever lived and he goes to biker events with disco balls, where professional announcers proclaim:

"'This is Good Time Charlie the Outlaw DeeJay here to tell you we got more Heeeeeellllllsssss Angeeeeeelllllllsssss in the Housssssssssssse-ah!' Spotlights hit the entrance as we walked in. 'Baaaaaaad Bahhhhhhhhhhb!   And his Angels brooooooohhhhhhhhssss!!!!!!' The crowd, which was respectable but not enormous, parted like the Red Sea for Moses."

In another movie ready scene, in front of at least 100 witnesses: "…in a fluid motion, Joby turned on her, unholstered a hip-belt .380 semiauto, and pushed it into her forehead. She stopped talking and went cross-eyed. Joby barked in a sudden, deep tenor, 'Bitch, I will kill you if you do not leave me and my brothers alone right now!'"

In Dobyns' own words, his account is "the best of my memory, but where my memory failed, Nils's (sic) creative and descriptive abilities filled the void." Virtually none of the book is filled with anything approaching truth – let alone artistic truth. For anyone wise enough to tell dollar bills from beans, Dobyns quasi-novel is so puzzling and unrealistic that it is sometimes to difficult to understand what he was trying to say. Dobyns' book, like Droban's invites readers to pretend that they are Hells Angels. "Here I was," Dobyns has said several times, "living the ultimate bad boy fantasy." That assertion may be all there is to the book.

There is, for example, a scene about a quarter of the way through Dobyns' book that is at once cinematic, fatuous and blatantly prevented. Dobyns goes to buy a gun at a run down house in Apache Junction, a crumbling suburb on the Eastern edge of the Phoenix sprawl. And, the people Dobyns meets there are loathsome, white trash, meth addicts—stupid, oafish, and unlike the self-congratulatory Dobyns undeserving of compassion or respect.

One of them is a little boy named Dale and Dale's only toy is a used tire. It could be a fine scene. It will make a memorable image if Tony Scott ever makes the movie. And, it might be the truest snapshot in all of Dobyns' book. Everybody who has ever actually strolled through the outlaw world knows the romance is overrated and they have met this white trash kid. Some fraction of bikers were that kid and they all know that kid does next. That kid gets a hammer, or a club or a stick, and he starts to beat that tire, over and over until his hands bleed, and he never stops pounding until he dies.

That little, white trash boy has been the dark angel of an imperfect America since before the Civil War. Mark Twain called him Huckleberry. Steven Crane, Jack London, Frank Norris, Theodore Dreiser, Sinclair Lewis and John Steinbeck all wrote movingly, hopefully and truthfully about that child.

A friend of Robert Frost, a suffragette with a name that now sounds ridiculous, Sarah Norcliffe Cleghorn, wrote four perfect lines about that little boy's great-grandfather and his great-grandfather's sister and cousin:

The golf links lie so near the mill
That almost every day
The laboring children can look out
And see the men at play.

Jay Dobyns and his writer collaborator let it go with: "I added myself to the long list of people who had abandoned him." And then Dobyns spends thousands more words talking about Jay Dobyns, about Bird's bravery, his virtue, his truthfulness and the clever way he can get men to believe his lies.

Hollywood could find no fault with Dobyns' book. Hollywood thought the tale was superb. Before the book was published Dobyns also agreed "to sell his life story rights to 20th Century Fox film studios."

The myth of Dobyns snowballed. "Overwhelming positive public response," Dobyns lawyer said, "caused ATF to seek additional public relations attention from the networks. Based on the success of the television programs and the notoriety ATF received from Agent Dobyns' documentaries, ATF subsequently promoted other investigations and ATF agents to the networks resulting in documentaries…."

Documentaries on *The National Geographic Channel* and *The History Channel* told the official ATF version of William Queen's infiltration of the Mongols, Operation Ivan. Over and over again Queen told a blatantly ridiculous story about how he had fooled a Mongol into thinking he had ingested methamphetamine when he really had not. Over and over, basic cable ran one of the reenactments of the Daniel Herrera murder.

Other "documentaries" were episodes of a *History Channel* "reality" series called *Gangland*. By the time Dobyns book was published in January 2009, undercover ATF Agents were everywhere. Steve Martin relived his infiltration of the Warlocks and bragged about how he engineered a mass arrest to coincide with a Warlocks funeral. Like Queen, Martin expressed the emotional ordeal he went through when he betrayed his friends. Blake "Bo" Boteler recounted his infiltration of the Sons of Silence for a television audience. Boteler told a story almost as ridiculous as Queen's drug tale. Boteler said the time two dozen witnesses saw him beat up a man was only an illusion, because, actually the man had slipped.

And, thanks in large part to the adoring press Dobyns had found, the ATF also "promoted…Agents John Ciccone, Darrin Kozlowski, John Carr, Paul D'Angelo and Greg Giaoni" in a *Gangland* episode about the Mongols Motorcycle Club. Kozlowski later entered portions of the episode into evidence. He testified: "On May 15, 2008 a nationally televised episode of the series *Gangland* aired on *The History Channel*. During the episode, several Mongols were interviewed, including some of the defendants in *US v Cavazos et al*. At one point, Ruben Cavazos (a.k.a. Doc), the National President of the Mongols said the following in reference to Mongols members and the Mongols patch: 'We dictate what you're allowed to wear on your vest and what you're not. We dictate the type of shoes you can wear, the way you stand, the way you act in public, even your face. We used to have what was called a "war" face. And that was your face in public. The meaner or harder you looked, the less chance there was of somebody making a violent move on you.'"

In that same case Ciccone later introduced as evidence, "video footage obtained by ATF from the producers of the television show *Gangland* who produced an episode concerning the Mongols. The footage included in the clip includes some footage that was broadcast, as well as some that was not. Many of the defendants in *United States v. Cavazos*, including Ruben Cavazos, are featured in the clip."

Curiously, the more famous a hero he became, the more Dobyns found himself at odds with the ATF. Dobyns began to argue that the Hells Angels were going to get him and his family. He claimed that the Hells Angels "intended to sue" him "in civil court with the intention of getting him fired." Once he was "outside of ATF protection" the motorcycle club was going to murder him. And, according to Dobyns' version, before the unnamed Angels murdered him they were going to "arrange and videotape the gang rape" of his wife.

In general, no one at the ATF thought these were real, credible threats. The sources of the threats are secret. Some of the threats seem to have originated with Rudy The Pharmacist Kramer in an attempt to lie his way out of jail. All of what Dobyns feared were embellishments on stories told by snitches to please the ATF. Dobyns emerged from the Hells Angels investigation as, he says, the ATF "golden boy."

But in June 2006, around the time he was being proclaimed a national hero, his supervisor in Los Angeles told him that he "had worn out his welcome with ATF. If I have my way," the supervisor continued, "you'll spend the rest of your career in Headquarters or Guam. I am familiar with Anderson Air Force Base there. It is a postage stamp in the middle of nowhere. A perfect place for you to finish your career." As Dobyns describes it, he was not surprised. Not only had he concluded that the Hells Angels were out to get him. He had already concluded the ATF was out to get him, too.

Dobyns, like all undercover agents and like Ciccone, is an enormously likable man. He is also the undercover *agent provocateur* who told Julian Sher, "I know I can get over on people." Dobyns also very much enjoys being rich and famous.

He began complaining publically that the ATF was refusing to protect him from credible threats. As he became a celebrity his voice grew louder. Dobyns also took the position that he would be safer if he was richer. In September 2007 he reached a settlement with the Bureau. The ATF agreed to pay him $373,000 if he would just shut up.

Nothing was settled. The ATF was late on its payments and subjected Dobyns to "internal affairs investigations ... on over eleven different occasions." Dobyns did not get along with his supervisors in Los Angeles, and eventually he moved back to Tucson where, he said, his enemies the Arizona Angels were.

In August 2008 somebody set fire to Dobyns' house. The fire apparently caused about $30,000 damage although in Dobyns' version it caused ten times that amount. Dobyns asserts that his insurance company, State Farm, determined the destruction to his home and contents "to be a near total loss." Someone had tossed a small amount of flammable liquid on Dobyns back porch and set a match. Dobyns was "verifiably out of

141

town" at the time. His cell phone was turned on so its location was traceable and the phone proved that at the time of the fire Dobyns was actually travelling away from Tucson. Or, at least his phone was taking a trip. But, his wife and children were home and they were forced out into the night dressed only for bed. Within days, a "senior ATF Phoenix supervisor" named Dobyns as a suspect in the arson. Dobyns called that accusation a "malicious reprisal."

Many of Dobyns defenders assumed that the fire was set by the Hells Angels. For example, in July 2009 Shepard Smith greeted Dobyns to his *Fox News* show with: "Jay Dobyns joins us now live and we're not going to tell you where he is. (Dobyns was actually in Washington.) Jay, thanks for being with us. The Hells Angels burned down your house with your family inside. Fortunately they, uh, escaped. They put a contract on your head."

Dobyns did not bother to correct Smith. He walks a fine line with truth. He later said "I have never said to anyone publicly or privately that the Hells Angels burned my house down. Find where I have. I have said that ATF let someone get away with it and in the process also get away with attempting to murder my family. Believe it or not but my beef is not with the Hells Angels. They are in my rear view mirror. My beef is with ATF."

In September 2009, Dobyns sued the ATF again for slightly more than $4 million. He wanted $1.6 million to compensate him for his "suffering;" $600 thousand to compensate his wife and children for their "suffering;" $200 thousand for his lawyer; and he also asked for ten years pay at the rate of $185,000 per year. The ATF seemed to think that Dobyns was crazy.

Public documents assert that an ATF supervisor "stated in front of multiple witnesses on multiple occasions" that "Dobyns is mentally unfit for duty," and

"Dobyns is broken." The supervisor has been quoted as saying, "it is my duty to see that Dobyns is removed from…this agency."

Allegedly, an ATF Internal Affairs Investigator classified Dobyns as "certifiable," by which he meant crazy.

The ATF retained a psychiatrist named Daniel Blumberg who allegedly betrayed his conclusions about Dobyns' mental health to ATF officials after "privileged and confidential sessions with Dobyns." According to Dobyns, the psychiatrist later apologized and explained that he had been "coerced and extorted" into disclosing the "privileged information" out of "fear that he would lose his ATF-funded retainer contract."

Dobyns accused the ATF of attempting to publish, release and expose his "medical records to defame, intimidate and coerce" him. And, according to Dobyns, these attempts to discredit him as crazy began in the autumn of 2006, the season when all the world was being told he was a hero.

Dobyns has formally accused the "senior Los Angeles ATF supervisor," whose name is John Torres, and who was one of the ATF officials who wanted John Ciccone to shut down William Queen's investigation, of trying to "defame Dobyns to his peers and other law enforcement agencies outside of ATF. The Los Angeles supervisor enlisted the support of ATF supervisors in Chicago and Seattle to obstruct justice by defaming Dobyns as a government witness. The Los Angeles supervisor also attempted to recruit ATF attorneys into his defamation scheme."

One obvious question to ask Dobyns is, "Are you mentally and emotionally fit?"

"Maybe," Dobyns replies. And, then he elaborates, "Going through what I have and am going through changes a person. In my case probably for the worse."

A decade after the Laughlin brawl, Dobyns still describes himself as a hero, a victim of ATF heartlessness and as a hunted man. He continues to claim he has been green lighted by the Hells Angels, the Mexican Mafia and Mara Salvatrucha. He makes these claims on television. There is an audience for him. During, arguably, the most surreal of his interviews, to ensure his personal "security," he appeared as a "Second Life" three dimensional virtual world character. Dobyns the cartoon was interviewed by an avatar for the British "poet, fictioner, editor, journalist" Adele Ward. "I've been living with the threats for five years," the crude Dobyns cartoon told the crude Ward cartoon.

A year after he published *No Angel*, the ATF sued Dobyns for an "accounting, restitution, and disgorgement of all money received, or to be received, by Mr. Dobyns" from his book *No Angel* and from "an agreement with 20th Century Fox regarding the sale of rights to the book for purposes of making a motion picture."

"After the conclusion of Operation Black Biscuit," the lawsuit self-righteously complains, "Mr. Dobyns sold the story of his official duties for his own private gain."

Late in 2010, Dobyns publically found Jesus and pledged to devote at least some of his life to saving African orphans. That year he began writing a second memoir, *Still Raising Hell*, about his many travails, insights, astounding accomplishments and good deeds.

In 2011, after Cheryl Atkinson of *CBS News* began reporting that that the ATF had been allowing American guns to be smuggled into Mexico, Dobyns further refined his brand. He became an "ATF whistleblower" who had tried to stop ATF corruption and had been punished for his efforts by the ATF. The ATF, the refined version went, had even ignored death threats by the Hells Angels to prevent Dobyns from exposing their lies. He has made a career of his dramas. He has been living quite openly most of the time since he signed his book deal. He spent Christmas 2010 in Bruges.

Black Biscuit made Dobyns a go to source for reporters writing a biker story. In November 2011, *Associated Press* reporter Paul Elias quoted Dobyns in a story about the Hells Angels. There has never been an accounting of how much Operation Black Biscuit cost – whatever Operation Black Biscuit was.

And Black Biscuit was only one of the two major investigations inspired by the brawl at Rosa's Cantina. The other one, combined with the subsequent prosecutions, cost at least $150 million. It was called Operation Black Rain. And, Black Rain would not have been possible were it not for the vanities and vulnerabilities of a man almost as interesting as Jay Dobyns. His name is Ruben Doc Cavazos.

Doc

For a few, golden months before the Mongols voted him out bad, Ruben Doc Cavazos shared an agent with Lauren Bacall, Rita Rudner, Kirk Douglas, Goldie Hawn, Marlee Matlin, Diane Keaton, Joan Collins, Henry Winkler, Dog the Bounty Hunter and the estate of Elia Kazan. "I do love memoirs by unique people," the agent, Alan Nevins, said.

At the end of May 2008, Doc attended Nevins' Book Expo Celebrity Dinner at Restaurant 208 in Beverly Hills. Doc never went anywhere alone. So while Doc enjoyed his steak and made small talk with Henry Winkler, the four Mongols who comprised his entourage, including his son Ruben "Lil Rubes" Cavazos, Jr. and future racketeering defendants Bouncer Soto and Daniel "Big Dog" Medel, waited patiently. Nevins, who has had years to consider that night, takes pains to "clarify" that he did not buy any of the other Mongols so much as a sandwich or a nice glass of wine. "Only Doc was invited to that dinner. We allowed him to bring some of the guys with the understanding that they would have to remain outside."

Nevins is a gracious man who looks like a 1950s movie star. He started his career working for a Hollywood legend named Irving "Swifty" Lazar. He is not particularly thrilled at the prospect of being mentioned in a book about motorcycle outlaws. He is man enough to talk anyway.

After that spring dinner, the celebrity authors demonstrated the "balls out courage" needed to make the "harrowing journey" out of their private dining room to mingle with "America's most violent motorcycle gang." Several wonderful photos of that adventure survive. One is of the gaminesque author Heidi Murkoff, who invented the *What to Expect When You're Expecting* publishing phenomena, surrounded by five Mongols including the ever glowering Bouncer Soto. Another photo shows Tony Curtis in the middle of the same group of outlaws. Doc has his arm around the old star's shoulder. Both men look formidable and proud. And behind them, the six four, 400 pound Bouncer, who might not have known or cared who Heidi Murkoff was, is laughing out loud – and looking exactly as if laughing out loud hurts.

"He was very decent to me and I liked him and the guys that were around him," Nevins said. "They were nothing but kind and, in fact gentlemanly, to me and Doc and I had several occasions to speak about some rather interesting subjects and it was quite invigorating. He was very good to me and I think he would say the same about me. We were very respectful of one another – our differences and our similarities."

In addition to selling Cavazos memoir, *Honor Few, Fear None: The Life and Times of a Mongol* to William Morrow, Nevins negotiated on Doc's behalf with the "major networks and HBO and Showtime." Nevins also arranged Doc's compensation for his appearance on the *History Channel* series *Gangland*. Nevins did not say how much that compensation was. Doc's principal competition in the entertainment industry that summer came from the debuting *FX* series, *Sons of Anarchy*. Ultimately, entertainment executives decided that a fictional *roman a clef* about the Hells Angels was more marketable to the masses, yearning to be free, than a reality based property about the Mongols.

Nevins is not inclined to consider how he became an asset in a clandestine investigation carried out by the ATF. "He wrote the book and someone recommended him to me," Nevins explained.

It is not how books like Doc's are usually published. "True crime" books must usually be "proposed" before they are written. It may not have been Doc's idea to write his outlaw memoir. The idea was suggested to him repeatedly by the three ATF undercovers who were "constantly up his ass."

The project began as a reply by Cavazos to William Queen's book about the Mongols. Later, as Doc's ego inflated, the book became more of a Valentine to Doc's Mongols from Doc than a rebuttal of Queen. Ciccone, who listened in on some of the wiretapped conversations between Cavazos and Nevins provably knew about the book but he won't admit to it.

Nevins is also slightly unforthcoming about the project. The one person who actually saw Cavazos working on the book was Doc's brother Al "The Suit." "Doc would sit out in the backyard and work on it," Al said. "The writer would ask Doc questions. Doc would answer him and the writer would take notes." Several authors, including Doug Century who collaborated on Queen's book, deny any involvement in the project.

There is disagreement among sources about whether the idea to encourage Doc Cavazos to write a memoir and become a media star originated with John Ciccone or was thrust on Ciccone from above. One source said that Ciccone thought too much publicity might place the undercovers – like Kozlowski whose ambitions include a spectacularly grotesque death – in danger and he resisted. On the other hand Ciccone did suggest that some of the paid snitches in the Mongols investigation also consider writing books.

Doc's book attracted interest from the entertainment industry. In the summer of 2008 Cavazos and other Mongols attended a meeting with representatives of the action movie star Vin Diesel. Diesel would have played the larger than life role of Doc but Ciccone and events intervened before that deal was struck.

Nevins' willingness to talk about Doc at all suggests that he was only a stooge who really did think Cavazos was an interesting man. Nevins hired a writer to work with Doc and he fully exploited Doc's notoriety – as any good agent would. William Morrow and its parent company Harper Collins, refuse to discuss Doc's book which remains in print and continues to provide income to the publisher and presumably to the ghost writer.

The book was very improper for a motorcycle outlaw. Motorcycle outlaws in all major clubs and most minor ones are forbidden from profiting from their association with their club. Sonny Barger wrote an autobiography, of course, titled *Hells Angel* that was also published by Harper Collins and acquired by Tony Scott. But, most of Barger's book recounts ancient history and after more than forty years of sensational headlines it was reasonable for him to tell his version of events after he retired.

Doc, on the other hand, chased fame like it was a recently divorced woman. "When pushed, Mongols join together to push back," the press release for his book brags. "Just ask the Hells Angels, the Ukrainian mafia, the Mexican mafia and the U.S. government. All have tested the Mongols resolve.

"In *Honor Few, Fear None*, Doc is ready, for the first time, to share the stories of the Mongols battle to survive and thrive against incredible odds and sometimes terrible violence. Doc takes you to the streets and into the bars, the secret meetings, the brawls, and the shootouts, all proof that if you live like a Mongol does you must *Honor Few, Fear None.*"

Doc's brother Al says Doc intended the book to be fiction and that all the crimes in the book are made up. Some of what Doc (putatively) wrote rings true.

"One of the hardest parts about being me, really, is that I have to sit there and listen. People talk about us on television and write about us in the newspaper and the police give their version of events, but I know the true story behind it all and I just have to live with it. I watch this Billy Queen talk, and I think to myself, what a crock of shit. Worse is that he says it and the public believes him, and the public gets an image of us. And the image snowballs as others pick up on the idea and the police feed the hunger for violent news. Then the same stories get rehashed and picked over, and everybody's record is pulled out for the world to see. Unfortunately, in trying to create a villain, they ruin people's lives. They create the monster and they add to it, like Billy still does to this day on TV."

And, although Doc would have missed it, as Billy Slow Brain sometimes does on National Public Radio – where the journalists report "legends" and the news stories are sweetened with sound effects.

Some of Doc's book is simply ridiculous. The ancient motorcycle outlaw tradition of telling tall tales to the squares has a long history of unfortunate consequences. The Oakland Angels told Hunter Thompson that new members were baptized with urine, feces and used motor oil. Thompson couldn't have believed it. All he had to do was look at the relatively clean patches of the men who told him this. But he wrote that lie down anyway and men like Ciccone and Julian Sher still tell it to cops who wish to become experts in the expanding police specialty of OMGs.

Expert cops still tell this lie to reporters on deadline, who have all already heard this lie before anyway. But it gives those reporters a reason to tell this lie to you. Again.

Nevins helped Doc turn his status as the President of the Mongols into money. "Doc was all about the money," Roger Pinney who was stabbed for the Mongols said. "Out for himself and not the brotherhood of the club."

"I heard on one run he made $900,000. That's a lot of money," a former Mongol named Tony "Snake" Vodnik told *The Associated Press*. Vodnik was one of many Mongols Doc forced out of the club. "He was stripping the club of money. That was the club's money not his money…No President is supposed to gain from the club. And he bought houses, bikes, cars for his son and his brother."

Al Cavazos calls Snake Vodnik "an idiot" and is incredulous that any reporter would believe anything Vodnik said.

Fiction or not, eventually portions of *Honor Few, Fear None* were entered into evidence in federal court. On at least one occasion, a federal prosecutor argued that a defendant must be a criminal because his photo appears in Cavazos' book.

Doc's decision to appear on *Gangland*, in an episode arranged by the ATF, struck most Mongols as stupid. One Mongol said, "I knew right then it was only a matter of months."

"Until what?"

"Until the ATF shut us down, man. Until something happened. I have always said any motorcycle club that goes on television is just asking for trouble. Was I right?"

The ethics of the ATF accessing raw footage shot by field producers working for Gangland LLC on behalf of *The History Channel* may trouble some journalists. In March 2010, almost two years after Doc made his initial television appearance, in a case titled *Tennessee versus Gutierrez*, both *Gangland* and *A&E Television Networks* made a brave show of refusing to turn outtakes over to prosecutors on grounds of journalistic privilege. The television show had interviewed a man named Jonathan Gutierrez who belonged to a street gang called Brown Pride. Gutierrez was subsequently charged with murder and a Nashville prosecutor wanted to see if he had confessed to a reporter and what other interesting things he might have said.

After the prosecutor subpoenaed outtakes from the *Gangland* episode right minded people said high minded things. Frank Gibson who is the Executive Director of the Tennessee Coalition for Open Government complained that, "Journalists should not become arms of the police department or the prosecution. Their job isn't to investigate things and then turn their notes over to law enforcement."

Thomas Steffus, who produced the episode warned, "If documentary reporters, producers, or production companies may be subject to subpoena…whenever there is a mere possibility that there may be some useful information or the district attorney is curious about what is on outtakes, the role of documentary reporters and producers will be changed from that of investigators and reporters to adjuncts of the trial process." Steffus seemed not to know that *Gangland* was already, in at least some cases, a component of the "trial process."

Then after proclaiming their journalistic bona fides, *Gangland* and *A&E* announced that they had "made a journalistic and editorial decision" that because of all the publicity the outtakes had, "become newsworthy." So as journalists they had a sacred duty not to withhold news. "We" are committed "to provide you, our viewers, with material which we deem to be newsworthy," an *A&E* press release read. "We believe that this case has become part of that national discussion about the reporter's privilege, and have made a determination that the interview of Jonathan Gutierrez has become newsworthy." So *Gangland* was courageous, independent, principled, practical and cooperative all at once – a paragon of all American virtues and great entertainment to boot.

Some other interested parties are blunter about *Gangland's* journalistic standing.

In a series of angry letters to and about the producers of *Gangland* a former member of the Outlaws named Kevin P. "Spike" O'Neill, writing from his prison cell, compares the ATF war on outlaws to COINTELPRO, the now largely discredited, covert FBI Counter Intelligence Program that spanned the years from McCarthy to the normalization of relations with China.

In high school, O'Neill ran track, cross country and was the captain of his high school basketball team. He attended the University of Wisconsin-La Crosse but quit and went to work in his father's auto body shop. One Outlaws attorney called him "the rich boy.

The Milwaukee *Journal Sentinel* said there is "an aura about him. Shackled in handcuffs, he stands with his feet wide apart, head swiveling slowly as he inspects the courtroom. There is a nod and a smile to relatives and friends, and then – as he takes in the faces of the others in court – the smile fades and a hint of menace emerges as his eyelids drop." Spike, who got his name in high school, is now serving a life sentence for racketeering, drug trafficking and murder.

After *Gangland's* producers contacted O'Neill about appearing in an episode that would dramatize the Outlaws the bright and tragically damned biker let loose. He called, "Gangland's 'promise' that it is 'committed to accuracy in its reporting,' and that 'stories will be presented respectfully and competently' merely boilerplate rhetoric." He accused Special Agent Christopher Bayless, the ATF Agent who appeared, with his face hidden, in the Outlaws episode, of facilitating "violent acts between targeted motorcycle clubs." He accused Bayless of being an accessory before the fact, with another agent named Ron Holmes, of the murder of a biker named LaMonte "Monty" Mathias who was President of the Hell's Henchmen Motorcycle Club in Rockford, Illinois in June, 1994. O'Neill blamed the murder on an ATF Confidential informant named David Wolf. He quoted a line from *No Angel* in which Jay Dobyns confesses that an undercover agent must "constantly trade his or her ethics for the greater good of a case." He described Darrin Kozlowski, who was also involved in the Outlaws investigation, as a "narcissistic psycho unleashed by his masters to wreak havoc on the public." He claimed the ATF "stirs the pot" to try to set off biker wars. Spike said this helps the ATF infiltrate outlaw clubs "by exploiting a common weakness among clubs engaged in a conflict with a so-called rival – that is – the overzealous need for allies and recruits." And, he sounded almost poignantly disappointed that "*Gangland* exemplifies partisan journalism and is a fraud on the American public."

Spike O'Neill's distress with American journalism is poignantly naïve. Sometimes journalism soars to the realm of literature. Most of the time journalism is more about "copy hunger" than truth. Increasingly, American journalism is blatant "infotainment." Horace Greeley may have invented infotainment. What has changed in the last century and a half are the subjects journalists select.

The disparate elements of American journalism no longer agree that they are obliged to inform American citizens about where their tax dollars go or to give those citizens fair warning about what the "narcissistic psychos" who work for our government do with that money. Among much else, Operation Black Rain demonstrates that whatever rot has infected modern journalism has spread to all of American arts and letters.

An attorney named Andrew Carlon, writing in the *Virginia Law Review* in May 2007, calls this blind and ignorant version of America "The Sadistic State."

"The sadistic state raises the specter of totalitarianism," Carlon said. "As Professor Hannah Arendt writes, the totalitarian criminal justice system is marked by, among other things, the 'replacement of the suspected offense by the possible crime.' Classical totalitarianism *predicts* possible crimes on the basis of one's status as an 'objective enemy.'"

"Reality is inside the skull," O'Brien the cop told Winston the outlaw in George Orwell's *1984* – a book that gradually lost its force as satire. "'The real power, the power we have to fight for night and day, is not power over things, but over men.' He paused, and for a moment assumed again his air of a schoolmaster questioning a promising pupil: 'How does one man assert his power over another, Winston?'

"Winston thought. 'By making him suffer,' he said.

"'Exactly. By making him suffer. Obedience is not enough. Unless he is suffering, how can you be sure that he is obeying your will and not his own? Power is in inflicting pain and humiliation."

The ATF is the American secret police. The Bureau, which many Americans assume mostly regulates fireworks and things like cigarette and alcohol taxes, may actually hide more secrets than the CIA. The point of Operation Black Rain and other biker investigations is not to solve or prevent crimes but to manipulate mass media in order to define motorcycle outlaws as an "objective enemy" and then make them suffer.

The press, publishers, television and film are all natural allies of the sadistic state. Because, it is interesting when people suffer. It is fun to watch the humiliation of the proud. Some days the sadistic state humiliates Mel Gibson – who abandoned his biker project after getting drunk one night in Malibu and unleashing an anti-Semitic tirade at a policeman. Sometimes the proud who must be made to pay are the men who have staked their claims on the motorcycle outlaw frontier. The German word for the joy that comes from watching these humiliations is *schadenfreude*.

Ultimately, the Bureau's corruption of the press – if the press actually needed to be corrupted – makes finding out what happened in investigations like Black Rain impossible for most reporters to accomplish. As far as the ATF is concerned, you can either write what they want you to write or you can go to hell. In the end, it is simply too easy for reporters to believe that the ATF is good, that outlaw bikers are bad and to then trust the "good guys" and do "the right thing." Authors like Julian Sher, or the Los Angeles television reporter Chip Yost, or the television personality John Walsh are simply doing the best that can with what they assume are the facts available to them.

One fact of which none of these journalists and "opinion makers" seems to be aware is that long before Doc had his picture taken with Tony Curtis the ATF was practically running the Mongols. An ATF Source of Information, named Robert Lawrence "Lars" Wilson III, and an ATF Confidential Informant, named Daniel "Coconut Dan" Horrigan, supervised by John Ciccone, controlled the distribution of Mongols patches and the chartering of new Mongols chapters outside of

California. One of those chapters, in Baltimore, provided the foundation for the next ATF investigation against the Outlaws. Another of those chapters, in Henderson, Nevada was encouraged from its foundation by Undercover Agent John Carr to behave criminally.

Wilson and Horrigan tried to provoke biker wars with the Outlaws and the Sons of Silence. At one point, Horrigan severely beat a Sons of Silence patch holder in a bar in Indianapolis, stole his patch, and reported the incident to Ciccone as an attempted murder. The incident later appeared in the indictment as one of the "predicate acts" that would prove the Mongols were a racketeering conspiracy. What the ATF has made impossible to know by its extreme institutional secrecy is whether the attempted murder was Ciccone's idea or Horrigan's or whether the attempted murder is an entirely fabricated incident that never happened at all.

Wilson created an investigation against the Pagans in West Virginia and promoted an alliance between the Mongols and the Pagans to try to provoke the Hells Angels. The three ATF Agents undercover in Los Angeles, Dirty Dan Kozlowski, Painter D'Angelo and Russo Giaoni became Doc's confidants at least partly because they were full time Mongols and most Mongols were not. Those federal agents suggested and helped arrange Doc's celebrity. At least one of them, according to several sources, made sure that Doc never ran out of cocaine.

Doc Cavazos, who assumed control after Laughlin, essentially transformed the Mongols Motorcycle Club. Whether Doc was always an ATF tool by which the Bureau exploited, as O'Neill put it, "a common weakness among clubs engaged in a conflict with a so-called rival – that is – the overzealous need for allies and recruits" is a matter of conjecture. If one stares at the ATF long enough one must conclude that the Bureau is capable of anything. If one stares at Operation Black Rain long enough, eventually it turns into a psychedelic butterfly.

"Doc never used drugs in his life," his brother insists. "Never!"

Factually, when Doc took over many members thought he was a breath of fresh air. Doc wanted to start a group health plan for members. He wanted to modernize the process by which prospective members join. He wanted to "grow" the club as entrepreneurs grow businesses. After hitting a low of (possibly) 80 members the club rebounded under Doc to at least six times that many. The Mongols, from the very beginning, had always been a heavily *Xicano* club. Under Doc the club became even more *Xicano* and the club may actually have been invigorated by it.

Every motorcycle club has a rough and sometimes charming personality. The Pagans, who roam over a wide swath of the Northeast all sound a lot like South Philadelphia – even when they speak with Southern accents. The Hells Angels, anyone who has ever been near them in the last 20 years will tell you, are bright, charming and ironic.

The Mongols have a unique personality, too. The brusque, formidable men all look like motorcycle outlaws. To glimpse them is to understand why people who don't know them are scared of them. They want people who don't know them to be scared of them. Once they know you, you find yourself surrounded by a big, tough, heartbreakingly sincere, family. Some of their women are pretty, some of them are plain and they all like to wear very tight jeans. Their children look like everybody else's kids except they are slightly better behaved.

And, another layer in, the family becomes almost Shakespearian. The tight knit Mongols family gossips. All outlaw motorcycle clubs gossip. It is one of the things the ATF undercovers and John Ciccone know and that outsiders do not. The outlaw frontier is such a small place and outlaw clubs are such small, tightly knit, closed societies that gossiping becomes inevitable. Bands of Apache probably gossiped mercilessly among themselves, too. The Mongols, in the wake of Doc Cavazos, gossip more viciously than most clubs. The gossip divides between those who liked Doc and those who did not. After a couple of years around the club even outsiders begin to hear conflicting versions of the internecine feuds. Doc lent one Mongol "$10,000 for Christmas." When Doc asked for the money back his club brother turned on him. Another Mongol lent a club brother $5,000 and was never paid back. Years ago, one Mongol refused to get out of bed to help a club brother who had been in a motorcycle accident and the incident remains ever fresh as the Labor Day massacre. A prominent Mongol was chastised by Doc for rape and for then "shooting up" his victim's apartment. One brother was "sharing his woman" with his club brothers and she got Hepatitis. While another brother was away in prison, his wife was sleeping with Lil Rubes. Doc made money from his book and other Mongols did not. It is impossible to decide whether Doc Cavazos created this squabbling family or if this family survived Doc.

No outlaw motorcycle club will officially tolerate drug addicts but lots of bikers burn the candle at both ends and develop a problem with "old school" or "new school," which is to say with methamphetamine and cocaine. In the summer of 2008 Doc appeared to have a problem. He might have developed this problem even without the assistance of the ATF or the government of the United States may have simply presented the apple to Doc and encouraged him to take a bite. Before he was ever suspected of abusing cocaine Doc started club paid rehab for members who did have drug problems. He tried to attract better prettier women to club functions by insisting that Mongols treat women better. Doc was charismatic and enormously likable. And, he always thought he was the smartest man in the room.

Doc's ambition was to surpass Sonny Barger in fame and his ambition for his motorcycle club was that it become more famous and respected than the Hells Angels. Doc recruited tough men to fight the Angels. Some of them were gangbangers which brought the club into conflict with the Mexican Mafia. The ATF version is that some of the new members stuck up a Mexican Mafia crank deal in a motel room and that was the moment the war with the Mexican Mafia started. Some of the new members certainly did not conduct themselves as proper outlaws. Motorcycle outlaws, in general, are the most polite people in the world because the consequences of rudeness can be so terrible. That rudeness contributed to the brawl in Harrah's.

The ATF so vigorously prosecuted the Mongols after Laughlin that the club had to raise hundreds of thousands to pay for the legal defense of its members. So Doc who once banged himself, the most popular Mongols' gossip goes, tolerated drug dealers who were willing to contribute generously to the club. Not even Doc thought he was turning the Mongols into a criminal organization. He thought he was being hardheaded and pragmatic.

In a wiretapped conversation from October 29, 2007, a year before the investigation ended, Cavazos said he thought the Mongols were "not going to get in trouble" as long as the club did not "actively recruit drug dealers." Doc winked at the problem by saying he could not "control personal use and abuse."

When Doc eventually pled guilty on January 23, 2009 to a racketeering conspiracy to distribute methamphetamine the judge asked him:

160

"Okay. Can you explain in your own words what you did that makes you guilty of these offenses?"

And Cavazos answered with his own question, like a nervous schoolboy, "Umm, I was the president of the Mongols Motorcycle Club while its members committed some of these crimes?"

Doc represented a new generation of motorcycle outlaws. He was exactly the kind of outlaw the ATF needed to make a case. Doc wanted to be rich and famous. Proper motorcycle outlaws do not aspire to be rich and famous. Proper outlaws wish to be esteemed by their peers – both by their friends and their enemies. Doc wanted power. He is a physically tough man but he seems never to have been a particularly angry one. He grew up poor but loved. More than being a Mongol, Doc loved being the boss of the Mongols.

And, after Roger Pinney was stabbed in Rosa's Cantina his only real rival for power in the club was an outlaw named Bill Michael "Mike" Munz. Munz has been the most respected Mongol and possibly the most feared man in the outlaw world for decades.

Munz, like many outlaws, was an abused child. He remembers he was loved by his mother and beaten by his father. He remembers lying in his bed after one beating when he was six, sobbing and telling himself over and over, "It doesn't matter. It doesn't matter." When he was seven, he came home crying after losing a fight. His father took him to the other boy's house and ordered Munz to fight again. The abuse continued until he left home. Then Munz found the Mongols.

Love heals all wounds but it does not necessarily turn abused boys into placid men. In 1980, Munz was arrested for possession of an unsecured firearm in a car. In 1982, in the most ferocious days of the Southern California biker wars, he was convicted of involuntary manslaughter in the death of San Diego Hells Angel "Fat Ray" Piltz. He was sentenced to six years, served three and was released in 1986. In April 1989, under the influence of methamphetamine, he committed a particularly ugly attack. Munz, who is about six foot two and weighs about 245 pounds pistol whipped a woman and her husband in front of their nine-year-old son. During the attack, according to prosecutors, Munz bragged about getting away with murder and "challenged the victim to play Russian Roulette."

Psychiatrists dueled at Munz' trial. Munz' psychiatrist testified that he suffered from temporal lobe – sometimes it is called psychomotor – epilepsy. This condition, which had only been recognized three years before, manifests as hallucinations, confusion, anxiety and blackouts. The defense argued that the condition caused Munz to black out when confronted with certain emotional or environmental triggers. In effect, the defense argued that Munz was innocent because he did not know what he did. The prosecution's expert testified that Munz was a poly-substance abuser with Intermittent Explosive Disorder – IED – and Adult Antisocial Behavior.

IED is comparatively common in men who have had violent childhoods. It may affect a fraction of motorcycle outlaws. The condition may have also affected numerous historically significant Americans. Andrew Jackson exhibited symptoms of Intermittent Explosive Disorder. John J. Bowie, the older brother of the man who invented the Bowie knife, said of his brother, "His anger was terrible, and frequently terminated in some tragic scene." IED is probably a learned behavior but may be caused by abnormalities in parts of the brain that control inhibition. Or, it may be a mealy-mouthed way of saying someone is a bad man.

The jury had to decide whether Munz was responsible for his actions or not. They found him guilty of mayhem, assault with a firearm and with being a convicted felon in possession of a firearm. He was sentenced to ten years in prison. As he entered prison he was said to have proclaimed, "I'm Mike Munz. If anyone has a problem with that, let's just get it over with now."

Ciccone believes Munz killed two Hells Angels for whose murders he has never been charged. William Queen described Munz as a manic-depressive who washed down lithium with beer and as a "scary guy." Doc Cavazos called him fearless and "level headed" in his book *Honor Few, Fear None.* But, Doc couldn't name his book "Respect Few, Fear None," which is what the Mongols actually say, because Mike Munz had already trademarked that phrase. Munz has been stabbed for the Mongols. And, despite his terrible sins, he had great moral authority in the Mongols because of his gallantry, generosity and humility.

Outlaws are usually considered to be loathsome and despicable and most prosecutors, cops and unbiased observers would agree that Mike Munz epitomizes that loathsomeness. Gary Kamiya of *Salon* described the Mongols as a "tangle of nasty freaks" for whom "few readers will shed tears." The police and many citizens believe there is a clear and glowing line between good and bad, evil and virtue, between us and them. Most Americans would agree that Munz' childhood and the strange and alien monsters that crawl between his ears might be sad but they don't matter. They don't matter. They don't matter. They don't matter. What matters is that Mike Munz is a brute.

Yet, in this same moment near the end of America, it is hard to imagine a current Congressman, Senator or a cabinet member who would go to prison for the United States. Or, who would kill with his own hands for something greater than himself. Or, who would willingly be shot or stabbed for his nation, or his

163

religion, or his family or almost anything except his own brilliant career. History is usually larded with irony. If the concept of "history" survives – and it may not, history may have less of a future than journalism – the contrast between the gallantry of this "tangle of nasty freaks" and the narcissism and avarice of America's "best and the brightest" might someday be seen as one of history's ironies.

Mike Munz was the Mongols' past. He was their Cincinnatus so he did not run for President of his motorcycle club.

Instead, the more thoroughly modern Doc Cavazos became king. Doc had Roger Pinney, many old Mongols and anyone else who opposed him expelled. Doc, most Mongols now believe, did not sacrifice for his club. Doc became prosperous and a little famous. Some Mongols still argue about Doc's prosperity. "He deserved what he got," one dissenting Mongol said. "He was the President of a major motorcycle club. He shouldn't be poor."

For whatever reason, Cavazos became embroiled in the war with the Mexican Mafia. Whether he did or not, most Mongols believe he used the club for his own gain. He put up with drug dealers. He embraced sycophants. He rekindled the war with the Angels. He became drunk with cocaine and power. He abandoned the outlaw credo of Mike Munz, which is "one for all." When Doc's successor as Mongols President, a man named Hector "Largo" Gonzalez, decided that Doc was ruining the Mongols Mike Munz helped lead the all members meeting that voted Doc Cavazos out bad. Then Munz sat down in the crowd again. By then Doc had already sealed Munz' fate. He had already sealed Largo's fate.

By then the ATF infiltration of the Mongols was so thorough that it might have been Ciccone who decided to get rid of Doc. Doc had asked Largo

Gonzalez to succeed him even though Largo had grown disgusted with Doc. After Largo became President one of his main supporters was ATF special agent Gregory "Russo" Giaoni.

Doc's greatest sin was allowing his club – his little nation on the edge of the once great nation – to be infiltrated and almost destroyed by ATF *agents provocateur*. That infiltration led to the imprisonment of dozens of men. A few of them were as bad as they were portrayed to be. Most of them were comparatively innocent. Some of them were completely innocent. None of them stood all on one side of any line.

An old fashioned and proper outlaw, a Hells Angel, replied to a question about Doc Cavazos by carefully composing his words for a day. Then he wrote:

"One can see why this downfall has transpired and also see how the Mongols were understandably conned. By his own admission their numbers had dwindled down to a small bottle neck of very few members, an easier target for him, when he came around with his snake oil for what ailed them. It's also plain to see how it was a ruse for his own financial gain and ego boost. He was an obvious snake oil salesman and Agent Ciccone saw it too. Doc is a cop's wet dream, a greedy, loud-mouthed moron who thought he could outsmart everyone. As proof, in his book and on *Gangland* he gave up crimes that his members committed just to make himself appear to be a force to be reckoned with. The timing was perfect for the ATF. They had Doc trapped. There wasn't a rock he could slither under – Mexican Mafia, Mongols and prison constricting his neck like the snake that he is. But, Doc being a snake will be allowed to slither his way out by Agent Ciccone. So, he can rot the body of the Mongols from the one time head down. I've dealt with Ciccone and he's a lot like Doc in that he's arrogant and greedy, his greed being the coin of fame and power. But unlike Doc, Ciccone's patient, methodical and a lot more intelligent.

"I've also learned from first hand experience and second hand accounts that when the police infiltrate a group that they have targeted they first try to entrap the members into committing crimes. And secondly, they try to get members to boast about past crimes – which are almost always exaggerated."

"It's a travesty really, the amount of harm Doc's folly is going to reap on not only the Mongols who are real bikers and motorcycle enthusiasts, but also the clubs and bikers not even affiliated with Mongols or Doc. After all, it's in law enforcement's best interest to vilify those groups because that's where their money is."

It is easy to put Doc Cavazos in a box with a label on the side. In the swirl of furious biker gossip there is an alternative narrative. "Drugs," a former Mongol who witnessed much of what is described in this book said, "had nothing to do with the war with La Eme. What happened was Weto from the Harbor City chapter had a problem with Bobby from Norwalk and it got out of hand."

"Doc never wanted to patch in the ATF agents. Doc thought there was something wrong with them from the start. Mike Munz wanted them in the club. Mike took them down to San Diego and gave them lie detector tests to prove they weren't cops. All the undercovers had been thoroughly trained in techniques to defeat lie detectors. Chief among those techniques were "getting in character" and clenching their rectums when they told the truth and unclenching and relaxing when they lied. They were the only Mongols who ever took lie detector tests. They all passed. Then Doc said, 'Okay.'"

Doc wasn't even President when he was becoming a multi-media star. "He stepped down as President in June and he wasn't voted out bad until the all members meeting at the end of August," the same source corrects. After Largo became President Giaoni kept talking in Largo's ear. He kept saying look at all the money Doc is making from his book. That should be the club's money. He kept saying that. But nobody cared that Mike Munz wanted to write a book."

"Doc didn't need to make money from the club. Doc made $100,000 a year working in a hospital. After Doc was voted out bad, you know what he said? He said, 'we're going to get hit by the ATF. We're divided in two. We don't stand a chance."

"What do you know about the murder of Hitman Martin?"

"Uh, yeah, yeah. Toonerville did that."

"Do you know why?"

"Yeah, yeah. Hitman was there with some brothers and they all started picking on this Toonerville guy. I don't know who the other brothers were. So afterward Toonerville waited for those guys to leave. The one they caught was Hitman. That's what happened that night."

Black Rain

Years after Operation Black Rain ended, Doc's brother Al Cavazos appears out of a cold night at the end of a pier in Los Angeles. Al, who did eight months for the crimes of being a Mongol and being Doc's brother, refuses to talk on the phone. "I know my phone is tapped." He turns down a drink at a nearby bar. "The ATF might have gotten there first." But Al wants to talk. "How can they do this to people?" He means the ATF and he means it enough to ask the question several times – like a prayer. "How can they?"

Doc's brother is a pleasant, grandfatherly man. He wants someone to listen and he wants his pound of revenge. He has a stack of documents in his car. He "can prove the ATF did" a murder. He has a list of "30 witnesses. If I can get this to somebody I got them. I got them." His voice cracks slightly. "How can they do this? This will shut down the ATF. How can they? Who can make something happen with this?"

It is a well known murder, conspicuous in the Mongols indictment by its absence. The obvious answers to Al the Suit's question are, "Cheryl Atkinson at *CBS* maybe. Greg Risling at the *AP*. Maybe Christine Pelisek at *The Daily Beast*."

"Who can really get these bastards?"

"Maybe somebody on (Congressmen) Darrell Issa's staff. New York *Times*? Tony Scott!"

"Can you help me get this to them?"

"No." Al's face falls. "Give me a couple of days. Maybe. Look, nobody cares. I'm sorry. Nobody cares."

"How can they do this to people?"

"Nobody cares."

Al shared a house with his brother and his nephew Lil Rubes who he always calls "Little Ruben," so after September 7, 2007 his every bowel movement and belch was electronic surveilled. According to Ciccone the "electronic surveillance was what cost so much."

Every word on Doc's cell phone and land line were recorded. Little Ruben's cell phone recorded every word he said. Ciccone was listening as Lars Wilson bragged on the phone that he planned to patch in 1,000 new Mongols at Daytona and take Florida away from the Warlocks and the Outlaws. Simultaneously, Little Ruben's girlfriend was having coffee with Ciccone.

As Lars Wilson was about to fly to Philadelphia to "promote the club" Cavazos complained that everyone was trying to "whack" him and that the club was full of "traitors." Wilson sympathized. A few months later, on February 8, 2008, Wilson and Shawn Monster Buss – who later that year would try to save Hitman Martin's life – discussed Wilson's plans to seize control of the club from Doc.

Ciccone was listening as Doc talked on the phone to an unnamed "reporter" about murders. That reporter has never surfaced. An obvious candidate is a local *Fox Television* reporter named Chris Blatchford who talked to Doc numerous times and who also has excellent sources in *La Eme*. Blatchford denies it was him.

"That March 11 phone conversation with Doc was not me," Blatchford said. "I can't remember specifically what I was doing that day, but Doc was never that forthcoming with me about anything.... It was probably a producer for a more entertainment based show like *HBO* or *Gangland*. The conversation…just doesn't sound like me. Doc was always very cordial to me on the telephone and then – I'm told – ripped me at Church meetings. If I am on any wiretaps – that's news to me. Although it wouldn't surprise me if I was on some."

During the Mongols investigation, Al Cavazos was shot by an East LA street clique named Gage Maravilla. The ATF attributes the shooting to the "war" with the Mexican Mafia and in official documents implies that the shooting of the inoffensive brother was designed to emotionally wound the powerful one. Afterward a surveillance camera mounted on a utility pole recorded the increasingly stressed out and paranoid Doc Cavazos marching back and forth in front of his house with a rifle in his hand waiting for his enemies to arrive, waiting for his moment, waiting to go down in a blaze of glory.

Ciccone knew when Lars Wilson travelled to Daytona on October 20, 2007 to buy guns from some Outlaws. Ciccone was listening when Cavazos and Wilson discussed using those guns to "take out" the Outlaws.

He was listening on August 1 and September 13, 2007 as the Mongols plotted and partied and bragged with the Pagans Motorcycle Club. The Feds were listening on January 10, 2008 as Wilson ordered Mongols (who happened to be undercover ATF agents) to drive the Pagans out of Baltimore.

Ciccone was listening in November 2007 when Doc, his son and brother, Mike Munz and other Mongols met with seven representatives of the Mexican Mafia at a Mexican restaurant on Universal City Walk just outside the theme park. The tapes of that one are buried so deep they will probably never be unearthed. There are several versions of what happened at that meeting (which might have been at least partially brokered by *Fox's* Blatchford). According to witnesses, *La Eme* wanted the Mongols to pay $25,000 a month either because club members were selling drugs in Mexican neighborhoods or because the Mongols were a predominantly *Xicano* club. Doc, because the Mongols have many Anglo members, replied, "You can't tax white people."

"And, those dudes just got up and marched out," a witness said. "They didn't even pay for their beers."

Ciccone was listening as Wilson warned Doc about the formation of a "brotherhood" between the Bandidos and the Sons of Silence. He listened as he counted 20 members of the Henchmen Motorcycle Club in Gary, Indiana. And he was listening as Doc, in a fit of bravado, bragged that everyone in California had to "recognize" him because "the state belongs to the Mongols."

Al Cavazos, a provably innocent man who lives by the street guy's code, still cannot understand how everything happened to his family and to him. Much of what happened was created by the ATF. None of the worst of what happened was prevented by the ATF. Everything that happened was largely fictionalized by the ATF. Al the Suit, a man who looks in your eye when he shakes your hand, cannot quite wrap his mind around the fact that all of modern law enforcement, criminal prosecution and punishment is a heartless, bitter game based on lies.

The alleged criminality of outlaw clubs is mostly an invention, like a novel. And, police exploit this invention for their own cynical means. In the case of outlaws, the purpose of the press is to enable the cops.

All police, not just federal police, create crimes. It is practically the definition of "professional policing" based on the "officer as stranger" paradigm. If the cops can't get you for anything else they can always charge with disorderly conduct.

The arrest of a Harvard liberal named Henry Louis Gates for talking back to a Cambridge cop named James Crowley in July 2009 is an example of police gamesmanship that everybody already knows. Generally, Gates arrest has been cited as an example of residual or incurable racism in America. "See," a thousand commentators harmonized. "Cambridge is just another word for Selma!" What the incident really illustrated was what happens when a Harvard professor thinks he is playing checkers with a cop who knows they are playing chess. Gates seems to have been so innocent and sheltered a man that he did not even realize he was playing a game.

Gates' front door was stuck. Some good citizen noticed a black man forcing open a door in a house near Harvard Square and called the cops. When Crowley arrived Gates was already inside. Gates, the Director of the W. E. B. Du Bois Institute for African and African American Research at Harvard, showed Crowley his driver's license and Harvard identification card but he was bold about it. He was proud. So Crowley gave Gates a lesson in law.

Crowley's transparent objective, after he decided to arrest Gates for pissing him off, was to create a charge. Crowley began by infuriating Gates with fatuous and condescending questions. Gates fell into the trap. He told Crowley the cop had "no idea who he was messing with." He complained that he was being picked on because "I'm a black man in America."

Crowley had to put up with that insubordination as long as Gates was inside his home so he gave the professor a "lawful order" to step outside. He compelled Gates to move from a legally private to a legally public place – Gates' front porch. Gates could only be charged with being disorderly in public if he was in public. If Gates had refused he could have been arrested for failure to obey a lawful order. Once on his porch Gates had no choice but to put up with the cop. Instead the professor continued to run his mouth. Crowley wrote down in his report that Gates exhibited "loud and tumultuous behavior," which is legal in a private place but not a public one. A moment later, Gates was in cuffs.

To this day, Gates seems to have no more idea than Al the Suit what line he actually crossed. But unlike Al Cavazos, Gates was victimized by one of the nice policemen. Crowley could have put Gates face down and stood on his neck. He could have pointed a gun at Gates head. Based on his "experience and training" he could have "interpreted" Gates' behavior as indicative of methamphetamine abuse. He could have "discerned the smell of burned marijuana." He could have wrecked Gates' home. He did not. He simply cuffed Gates up and took him for a ride in his police car.

Still this fleeting incident became national news. The murder Al Cavazos believes he can pin on the ATF will never be news. There are many more murders than Harvard professors. The most bizarre facet of the Mongols case is that so much money was spent and so much effort was expended on a clandestine operation that remains so secret. Most of it remains officially secret even though nobody cares.

President Obama, a former law professor who interjected himself into the Gates matter, also seemed to be utterly clueless about what line Gates actually crossed which made him a criminal or how he came to cross it. Obama also seemed to think the cop's behavior was about race rather than police procedure. Even distinguished professors and legal scholars are often ignorant of the games cops play. Yet, ignorance of the law is no excuse.

Motorcycle outlaws, meanwhile, are unusually aware of the technicalities and nuances of American criminal law because they have such frequent contact with the police and when they do they are so frequently framed. Virtually any outlaw can insightfully explain the fine points of Terry stops, consent searches or the plain sight doctrine. Any outlaw will tell you to carry your contraband in your saddlebags because it is always reasonable to argue that you don't know how it got there. Criminal law is part of the folk wisdom of outlaw clubs. One of the missions of any motorcycle club is to ensure that its members do not behave as stupidly as Professor Gates did. Any motorcycle outlaw would have instantly recognized Crowley's game and closed his mouth. Consequently, when it comes to outlaws, because they are so hard to get, elaborate criminal entrapments must be constructed.

Operation Black Rain was contrived with virtually limitless resources. The ATF knew everything. The undercovers heard all the gossip. They knew how long Doc liked to cook his microwave popcorn. They knew he was a street kid with street kid dreams. They knew he liked to brag. So assembling the case was mostly a matter of selecting what to include and what to ignore. The very first element of the case that Ciccone and Assistant U.S. Attorney Brunwin decided was what the principal charge against each defendant would be. In big biker cases like the ones that resulted from Black Rain the defendants are always charged with racketeering under a statute called the Racketeer Influenced Corrupt Organizations law, or RICO. Everybody knows the name but most people don't know what that law means.

RICO was the centerpiece of the Organized Crime Control Act of 1970. The law was written by a

Senatorial aide named G. Robert Blakey, who is now the William and Dorothy O'Neill Professor of Law at Notre Dame. And, it is named for the fictional character Rico "Little Caesar" Bandello who was inhabited on film by Edward G. Robinson.

Robinson's Rico character, in turn, was a parody of a notorious entrepreneur named Alphonse Gabriel "Scarface" Capone. "Every time a boy falls off a tricycle," Capone once lamented, "every time a black cat has gray kittens, every time someone stubs a toe, every time there's a murder or a fire or the Marines land in Nicaragua, the police and the newspapers holler 'get Capone.'"

Capone regretted his reputation as a criminal. Starting in 1926 he tried to diversify into legitimate businesses. Eventually he discovered milk. "Honest to God, we've been in the wrong racket right along," Capone exclaimed when he discovered that the profit margins were higher in milk than in whiskey. In February 1932, three months before he went to prison, Capone invested $50,000 in a legitimate business named Meadowmoor Dairies. In the 1960s the descendants of Capone liked to invest in bowling alleys because they were a good way to explain where the money came from. The upshot of that was that the main supplier of automatic pin setting machines, the AMF company, became prosperous enough to buy, and almost ruin, the Harley-Davidson company.

The original intent of the RICO statute – at least by the Congressmen who voted for it – was to protect legitimate dairies, bowling alleys and other businesses, from investment by thugs like Al Capone. That did not work because the threat posed to the nation by the Italian-American Mafia was always overblown and because as years went by the very same acts the Mafia had always been condemned for doing began to be accepted as standard business practice. The Mafia used to sell sin. The gangsters profited from gambling, usury, prostitution, liquor, drugs and theft. Now states, the nation, Indian tribes, rural counties in Nevada, credit card brands, mortgage lenders, banks in general and asset confiscating police all profit from exactly the same sins.

This may or may not be a good thing. It is certainly not something new in the American pageant. Wyatt Earp enforced the law for big banks and mining companies. Before that he was "muscle." Before that he was a pimp. Honore de Balzac said, "Behind every great fortune there is a crime." Crime used to be understood as a kind of cheating for personal gain. Now a crime is anything. Racketeering is anything. The point is to find an excuse to make people suffer.

RICO, as it has evolved, is not intended to punish what most people consider to be crimes, which is to say actions like murder, robbery or what Roman Polanski did to that 13-year-old girl – crimes that lawyers call *malum in se*. RICO is designed to punish crimes lawyers call *malum prohibitum* which is Latin for actions that are illegal because they are illegal – like possessing illegal intoxicants or talking on the telephone about illegal intoxicants or smoking in a public place or having a loud and embarrassingly ugly argument with your wife on a Saturday night.

RICO prosecutions virtually ignore *malum in se* crimes, the actions you have always thought to be a "crime," although at least a dozen of those did occur or emerge during the Mongols investigation. The predicate crimes that RICO exploits are often trivial and are always state crimes that until 1982 would have been prosecuted in state courts. For example, after the Labor Day Murders, none of the Hells Angels who were charged were ever found guilty of the murders. They confessed to talking about the murders. They confessed to hating Mongols.

The *Turkette* decision changed the meaning of "criminal enterprise" away from a legitimate bar, bowling alley or labor union that had been corrupted by "the mob." The *Scheidler* decision a decade later decreed that the "criminal enterprise" no longer had to exist for the purpose of making money. After *Turkette* and *Scheidler*, a class reunion could be a criminal enterprise. A federal prosecutor only had to imagine it.

There are several obvious reasons for the federal prosecution of state crimes. First, RICO allows the investigation of these local crimes by vast police bureaucracies like the ATF. These bureaucracies are self perpetuating and have virtually unlimited resources. All they need to persist are crimes to investigate and RICO provides that. Secondly, RICO allows federal prosecutors a legal fiction that can be used to connect what are actually, in reality, unconnected crimes into a vast, imaginary, criminal conspiracy. Additionally, RICO prosecutors do not have to prove beyond a reasonable doubt that defendants actually committed the "predicate crimes" of which they are accused. State prosecutors do but RICO allows federal prosecutors to prove crimes by the civil standard which is a "preponderance of the evidence." Finally, RICO provides a nice, secure, recession proof way for many lawyers, policemen, and prison guards to make a good living.

Under RICO, if Barack Obama, Henry Louis Gates and Angelina Jolie all like to attend an annual seminar together, and if three people at the seminar have committed two or more criminal predicates, like making a false statement to a federal official or shoplifting, they may be collectively and individually charged with racketeering. They could all be convicted of "the affecting interstate commerce" clause in the RICO law if they sent each other Christmas cards. And the penalty for that racketeering is twenty years in a federal prison.

Many bright and cynical people who should know better still blindly assume that what police do is investigate and solve real crimes. The opposite is true in racketeering investigations. What the ATF, particularly in biker investigations, does is find a way to tie crimes to many related individuals and then create crimes that can be used to prosecute them all. This law enforcement approach is called the "Enterprise Theory of Investigation" and it has a long and twisted history.

A sociologist named Edwin Sutherland coined the term "white collar crime" in the 1930s and wrote a book on the subject in 1949. Sutherland in essence, believed that all businessmen were criminals. With all the best of intentions, after the heartbreak of the Great Depression, Sutherland thought unethical businessmen should be treated worse than murderers. He thought they should be punished for their economic crimes so he advocated that a "person of respectability and high social status in the course of his occupation" should be presumed guilty until proven innocent. Sutherland also attacked the legal concept of *mens rea*, or guilty mind, which states that a person cannot be guilty of a crime unless he intends to commit a crime. Sutherland's theories became popular in two seemingly disparate communities – academia and the FBI.

A Sutherland protégé named Donald Cressey created the "enterprise" concept that quickly became the Enterprise Theory of Investigation. Cressey was particularly not talking about bands of anti-materialistic, socially alienated bikers. He intended to oppose what he saw as social injustice. "The people of the business world are probably more criminalistic than the people of the slums," he wrote in a book he co-authored with Sutherland. The idea of factoring wealth and privilege into the criminal justice equation was attractive to intellectuals. The federal police liked the parts that made prosecutions easier. Of course, in the manner of police bureaucracies everywhere, lest the amateurs know what the professionals are talking about, the Enterprise Theory of Investigation has become simply the ETI.

"The ETI has become the standard investigative model that the FBI employs in conducting investigations against major criminal organizations," an FBI author explains. "Unlike traditional investigative theory, which relies on law enforcement's ability to react to a previously committed crime, the ETI encourages a proactive attack on the structure of the criminal enterprise. Rather than viewing criminal acts as isolated crimes, the ETI attempts to show that individuals commit crimes in furtherance of the criminal enterprise itself. In other words, individuals commit criminal acts solely to benefit their criminal enterprise."

The current idea of the criminal enterprise is very close to what Hannah Arendt meant when she wrote, "Classical totalitarianism *predicts* possible crimes on the basis of one's status as an 'objective enemy.'"

By "criminal enterprise," the FBI author means any group any Federal Prosecutor decides to prosecute. The Catholic Church and the Boy Scouts of America have not yet been prosecuted as rackets because to do so would create a terrible public backlash. But there is no backlash when the organization is an outlaw motorcycle club. The *Scheidler* decision completed the legal magic trick by making the "financial motive" disappear.

In motorcycle club cases, in general and against the Mongols in particular, the government uses RICO to enforce a de facto "Bill of Attainder." Bills, sometimes the word is "writs," of Attainder are specifically prohibited by Article One, Clause three of the Constitution. This prohibition appears so early in the principal American law because it was one of the "rights" for which the revolutionaries fought and died. Technically, in America it is not illegal to belong to Al

Qaeda, the Nazi party, the Ku Klux Klan, La Cosa Nostra, the Communist party or even a motorcycle club. In a case named *Uphaus v Wyman* in 1959, the Supreme Court called guilt by association "a thoroughly discredited doctrine."

But RICO allows prosecutors to turn that ruling on its head. It is the same when mass media leads the general public to believe that motorcycle clubs, right wing militias and "cults" are criminal.

Motorcycle clubs are particularly prone to prosecution under RICO because that are so blatantly "organizations" and because their members tend to believe, as Harley-Davidson's ad agency put it, "in bucking the system that's built to smash individuals like bugs on a windshield." More than tribes, more than thugs, motorcycle clubs are an American ideology. And, also for better or worse, a national consensus seems to be building that America is better for renouncing this ideology.

Under RICO, state crimes punishable by months or a year in jail can be punished like murders. RICO also allows the seizure of assets like motorcycles because, the indictments always allege, no motorcycles no motorcycle gang. The enterprise theory also allows *indicia* searches, which are searches for proof that someone actually belongs to a motorcycle club. In effect, these searches are house wrecking parties. They are inevitably very terrible. Doors and windows are blown open with explosives. Threats like pets are eliminated. Men are beaten and sometimes executed. Wives and children are roughed up. Much glass is broken. Family photo albums, computers and mementos are confiscated.

The nature and practice of modern policing and particularly of racketeering law may help readers understand the trivial nature of many of the charges made in the indictment against the Mongols. The fact that the Mongols are a gossipy family also worked against them because the men who infiltrated the club wrote down all of the gossip. The "preponderance of evidence" rule in RICO cases made that gossip more damning than it would ever be in an ordinary criminal case. The fact that club members often disagreed about Doc Cavazos gave undercover investigators an excuse to get members talking. And, in the end RICO meant that prosecutors didn't have to use any of the mountains of "evidence" they had collected. They only had to threaten defendants with it. Actually, in many cases they didn't even show defendants the "evidence." In many cases prosecutors only alluded to the "evidence" or spread their arms wide and told public defenders the evidence was in two boxes "this big."

This repudiation of Jeffersonian ideology "officially" began when John Ciccone interviewed a Mongol who had been caught selling steroids to cops through the mail. In the course of that interview Ciccone offered the Mongol a deal. The charge would be reduced and after helping to entrap his friends the Mongol could start a new life. ATF infiltrations always begin with trusted traitors. This traitor's name was T.J. Stansbury. He was a member of the Mongols Camarillo chapter, west of the San Fernando Valley and East of Oxnard.

Confidential Informants are paid to be criminals. In actual praxis, the crimes for which motorcycle outlaws are usually prosecuted in federal court are usually incidents where an informant convinces someone who is honor bound to treat him as a "brother" to sell him a gun or guns, or sell him some amount of an illegal drug, or to store some contraband for him or help him win a fight that the informant actually starts.

Confidential Informants are paid up to $3,000 a month plus expenses and they are allowed to keep the profit that accrues from their crimes. It is standard operating procedure in many federal investigations. For example in a Pagans case in West Virginia, a mentally deranged, drug addicted, convicted murderer and confidential informant named James R. "Ronnie" Howerton was encouraged by the government to run and profit from a business in stolen motorcycles and stolen motorcycle parts. On multiple occasions, Howerton sold a stolen motorcycle to a customer after assuring the customer that the bike was not stolen then reported that that customer was riding a stolen bike. Howerton would then be paid for reporting that crime. Howerton fabricated numerous other crimes including at least one murder plot in which he was to be the killer. He was encouraged by his handlers and the subtleties of federal law to withhold evidence of the actual innocence of his victims.

Confidential Informants must be criminals because – the prosecutorial arguments always go – tolerance for the CI's criminality proves the criminal intent of his friends. It does not prove their loyalty to a friend or a club brother. It proves criminality. Professional *agents provocateur* are frequently paid bonuses for the crimes they help create. Hence Pops Blankenship's recorded comment to Jay Dobyn's, "We're going to make, we're going to make our quota."

Some of the "evidence" in motorcycle club cases are simply accusations, made by professional informants or field agents that are then memorialized as official Reports of Investigation. Some evidence is incriminating audio and video recordings. But the "evidence" is never contested because only grand juries ever see or hear any of it. Judges and juries never do because the cases never go to trial. The goal in these cases is to get a federal indictment. What the grand juries never know, however, is which outlaws on a video recording are actually outlaws and which are undercover

Agents or Confidential Informants playing a role. In many cases, it is the flamboyant actions of the government employees that convince the grand jury to indict everyone they see.

Stansbury did not want to go to jail. He was only selling steroids in the first place because he was under financial stress. Ciccone showed him a way to make more money than he had before. It took Ciccone less than a day to close the deal. For the remainder of the investigation Ciccone would refer to Stansbury in all court documents as CI-1.

Ciccone turned Stansbury, "in or about June, 2005." As part of deal, Stansbury pleaded guilty to mail fraud and that confession was one of the tools Ciccone used to control the snitch. Stansbury transferred to the Cypress Park chapter in February 2006. It was the same chapter to which the Los Angeles ATF undercovers would later belong. It is common for the ATF to control or create its own chapter or a whole motorcycle club. In one Warlocks investigation, the Fort Lauderdale chapter was all undercover cops. In the Sons of Silence investigation the ATF created its own motorcycle club. In Operation Black Rain, the Cypress Park chapter had more ATF employees than outlaws.

One of the first people Stansbury betrayed was his old friend and club brother in Oxnard, William Target Owens. Owens was the Mongol for whom the party had been given the night Hitman Martin died and who had argued with Kozlowski about going to war with Toonerville the next day. He was the Mongol who had spotted Kozlowski's photo in Billy Queen's book.

Target Owens, joined the Mongols after riding with a smaller and less notorious, mostly *Xicano* club called the *Carnales*. The name means "the brothers." Owens also had a problem with crystal meth. The drug was his weakness and his adversary. He had stopped consuming crank but he still knew some dealers.

Stansbury knew this. He and Target had known each other for a dozen years. So, Target Owens became T.J. Stansbury's first victim.

Stansbury began begging his old friend to sell him a pound of crank. Stansbury explained he needed the drug to repay a debt to a drug dealer named Russo or else he would be "killed." Russo was ATF agent Greg Giaoni. Owens said no. Stansbury offered to pay a higher than normal price. Owens said no. Stansbury fell to his knees and wept. Owens gave in. He couldn't get Stansbury a pound of the drug but he could help.

On May 4, 2006 Owens managed to get Stansbury 23 grams of meth. He sold it to Stansbury at cost and he helped whittle down his friend's debt with Russo by tattooing "Dirty White Boy" across Giaoni's chest. Soon, somehow, Stansbury repaid Russo and the two became such good friends that Russo started hanging around the Mongols Motorcycle Club. Eventually Stansbury sponsored Giaoni and two other ATF Agents, Darrin Kozlowski and Paul D'Angelo for membership.

At Owens' sentencing four years later the prosecutor, Chris Brunwin, told the judge that Owens had supplied the undercover agent and the confidential informant with "2200 street doses" of the drug and had also promised the two ATF employees that he could use his connection "with the Mexican Mafia" to get them more. What Owens actually told Giaoni was that he had gone to elementary school with a Mexican Mafia member who was a shot caller at San Quentin. Owens was sentenced to five and a half years in prison. He could have been sentenced to life. In order to get this sentence reduced Owens had to admit in writing that "this act was related to his role as a member of the Mongols Gang and was committed in furtherance of the criminal enterprise and knowing that its members and associates, including defendant, would commit racketeering offenses, including narcotics trafficking. The drug trafficking and other crimes of the Mongols organization are offenses which have an effect on interstate commerce."

Confidential informant two was a career snitch named Steven J. Veltus – the brown sheep in a family of accountants from Racine, Wisconsin. He was arrested for the first time in November 1996 with two accomplices, fifteen pounds of marijuana and a gun. "He did his time in St. Croix," an old girlfriend explained, "and it was very stressful for him. The man I knew back in the late 90's would never have turned."

In 2003 Veltus picked up five criminal charges stemming from his possession of about an ounce of crack cocaine and a pound of marijuana. Two days after he picked up the cocaine charges, in November 2003, he agreed to work for the ATF and all his legal problems went away. The ATF gave Veltus a paid job beginning in 2004. He has some history with Darrin Kozlowski and he may have worked with Kozlowski in an investigation of the Warlocks Motorcycle Club in Virginia in 2004. Most of that case remains secret. Veltus was paid $2,500 a month and given immunity from prosecution so he could keep what he stole and he could continue to do drugs. His wife Anna Veltus was also paid as a confidential informant.

Steve Veltus' road name in the Mongols was "Kaos." He liked to pretend that he had once been a Chicago mobster. In various documents in the case, Ciccone states that "CI-2 agreed to become a documented ATF informant in or about October 2005. At the time, CI-2 was a prospect of the Mongols Las Vegas chapter." Actually, Ciccone had assigned Veltus to the Mongols case much earlier in 2005. Veltus was only prospecting with the Mongols in Vegas because that was his job. He might have still been accounted for in the ATF payroll department as part of the 2004

Warlocks or some other investigation but he was probably the first paid snitch to start working the Mongols case. The names and dates of various participants in ATF investigations is always confused to make it as difficult as possible for defense lawyers to try to determine what actually happened. The tactic always succeeds.

Confidential Informants three, four and five in the case were all paid $2,500 a month to pay above market price for guns and drugs. Word got around. Like everybody else, the Mongols are drawn to easy money and many of the gun transactions were actually legal. Number three was the Sergeant-at-Arms of the Mongols San Diego chapter. He was fired from the case on March 28, 2007. Number four was a drug dealer who was not a member of the Mongols. He went to work on the case in June 2007 as part of a plea deal. He sold drugs at a very affordable price that could then be sold to the Cypress Park ATF agents at a premium price. He was paid to seduce Mongols into small gun and drug deals. He also introduced a Montebello, California police officer named Chris Cervantes to the club. Cervantes, who aspired to be an ATF undercover agent, was able to supplement his regular pay with his informant's compensation. He went to work on the case, according to Ciccone, in February 2006. He made a number of drug buys and he often worked with a fourth ATF undercover agent named John "Hollywood" Carr. Carr and Cervantes had worked together on another ATF entrapment in 2004. Throughout the investigation, Carr worked closely with Steve Veltus, CI-2, in Las Vegas.

Confidential Informant Six was another career snitch named Daniel "Coconut Dan" Horrigan. Horrigan was a large powerful man and martial artist. He was the Mongol who supposedly beat a member of the Sons of Silence in Indianapolis. Although in another

186

version of the story that Horrigan liked to tell he talked Mike Munz out of beating the Son to death. In a third common version of the story, Horrigan warned the Son so he wouldn't be killed. The version that counts is the one that made it into the indictment which is officially described as an attempted murder in furtherance of a racketeering enterprise.

Horrigan got his nickname because he liked to break coconuts with his fists. He explained that it was practice for breaking men's skulls. Horrigan became a professional informant after his first serious arrest for cocaine possession at the urging of the man who put him in prison – former Monterey County, California District Attorney Manuel "Manny" Ameron. Horrigan had always wanted to become a cop. After he spent two years in San Quentin, Ameron told Horrigan he would "make a good detective." So with Ameron's help, Horrigan became a freelance professional snitch.

Horrigan's first connection at the ATF was a now retired special agent named Jimmy Packard. Horrigan infiltrated and prospected with the Nevada Nomads charter of the Hells Angels from 2000 into 2002. He was rejected by the Angels in April 2002 after a member of the club recognized him as a police informant. Horrigan would later brag to the Mongols that he had "beaten down" 17 Angels.

After Laughlin, some Hells Angels charters and neighboring Mongols chapters in some locations, like the central coast of California, established liaisons with each other to avoid future violence. Neither club is monolithic, however, so that didn't happen everywhere. For example, it didn't happen in Los Angeles although Doc Cavazos and Sonny Barger did talk, and it didn't happen in Nevada where Horrigan had been identified as a police informant by the Angels but he was still able to join the Mongols.

Horrigan joined the Mongols in 2006 and became an important and ludicrously influential member. He partnered with Lars Wilson who seemed to have worked for the ATF for free in developing grandiose plans for the expansion of the club. Wilson was later indicted and spent more than two years in protective custody cooperating with federal authorities. Doc Cavazos considered Wilson and Horrigan to be his right hand men. Horrigan became the "World Chapter Sergeant-at-Arms" although there never actually was a World Chapter of the Mongols. Most of the more grandiose charges against the Mongols were actually only lies Horrigan told.

One of the new Mongols chapters Horrigan formed was in Oregon. A Mongol there described Coconut Dan as unable to "read or write...addicted to pain pills and thinks he talks directly to God." Naturally, Ciccone suggested to Horrigan that he write a book. Horrigan called it *Iron Warrior: The True Story of an Outlaw Biker Who Infiltrated Both the Hells Angels and Mongols Motorcycle Club*s. *Iron Warrior* almost made it into print. A former BMW saleswoman, casting director and studio executive named Lauren Lloyd liked the idea so much that although the book was never written she tried get a publishing deal and tried to sell the movie rights. That dream died with Horrigan in July 2011.

Together this cast of characters gathered what they could on the Mongols. Several of the eventual charges were spectacular if not new.

"On March 16, 2002, in Riverside County, California, defendants W. Ramirez, and Zuniga, and multiple other members of the Mongols gang attended an ultimate fighting match at the Morongo Casino in Cabazon, California, dressed in Mongols colors, and provoked a riot."

"On April 27, 2002, defendants W. Ramirez and Leyva and other Mongols gang members engaged in an armed confrontation with Hells Angels gang members at the Harrah's Casino in Laughlin, Nevada."

In early December 2005, Mongols opened fire on Hells Angels at a Christmas toy run in Norco, California. Three civilians, including a fire fighter were wounded.

Two Mongols named John "Weto" Newman and Christopher "Punk Rock" Loza beat and stabbed two Hells Angels supporters at a Mobil gas station in Pasadena, California on April 6, 2008. Two months later at the Mongols National Run the two men were given "Respect Few Fear None" patches for fighting for the club. All of this, including the knife fight and the national meeting, was recorded and examined by the ATF. Newman and Loza's attack became one of the charges against the Mongols. Newman was eventually sentenced to 27 months. Loza got 37 months.

The alleged "April 8, 2007 shooting" and the alleged "November, 2007 murder of two City Terrace gang members whose bodies were set ablaze in the desert after being shot," by a Mongol named Thomas Savala was part of the evidence gathered by the ATF but it was never a criminal charge. Savala was charged with selling meth. The dramatic image of the Mongols burning bodies in the desert may be entirely fictitious. It may have simply been intended to be part of some future book or movie. Or it may have been completely true and been a crime the United States simply decided not to prosecute.

In February 2007, two Mongols beat a 26-year-old Pizza Hut dishwasher named Leon Huddleston to death at Young's Bar and Grill in Lancaster, California. The crime was sensational in Los Angeles for a day or two. One Mongol hit Huddleston over the head with a pool cool cue and then both Mongols kicked him in the ribs. The blow to the head turned out to be fatal. The motive for the killing has always been obscure. One

189

witness said it started when Huddleston claimed to be a Hells Angel. In September 2008, Kozlowski tried to get the two Mongols to confess the crime to him but they would not. The two were indicted for the murder in the federal indictment anyway and eventually confessed.

The circumstances and method by which Doc was thrown out bad were all documented by ATF Special Agent Gregory Giaoni.

"Largo indicated his chapter put a plan into effect that separated Doc from his entourage thereby assuring he was alone at the National President's Meeting. Largo and several other Mongols had agreed to confront Doc in the meeting about certain issues. Largo felt there was a possibility that Doc would get defensive and angry from the comments and he feared that Doc would 'make a move.' (Special Agent Giaoni understood this to mean Doc would be armed and attempt to use his firearm as a way of intimidation.) Largo said he had two firearms on his person.... Largo said Richard "Blanco" Ramirez told Daniel "Big Dog" Medel, who is also in Doc's entourage, that if Doc and his crew make a move on the Mother Chapter then Blanco and his crew would "smash" (attack) Doc and his crew.... Largo said Doc is greedy and still wants power in the Mongols.... Largo explained to Special Agent Giaoni about how Doc recently stole money from the Mongols. Largo said Doc has been taking money from the Mongols for years."

This Report of Investigation goes on for hundreds of words. It does not mention the possibility that Largo Gonzalez' accusations may have originated with Giaoni. None of this drama made it into the indictment. Some or all of it may appear in the book Giaoni or Ciccone must eventually "write." Some of it may eventually appear in slightly overexposed sepia tones in the film Tony Scott or Steve Gaghan may make from that book.

There is no way to tell Al the Suit, "Who can really get these bastards." For one thing he doesn't know Tony Scott and for another it is hard to decide who the bastards are. The press can never be allowed to learn details like these. The public must not be exposed to this information because it might, using the traditional phrase, "compromise an ongoing investigation."

So most of the indictment wound up being a dreary account of daily life on the motorcycle outlaw frontier.

"On November 2, 2005, defendant A. Lopez possessed a short-barrel, 12-gauge shotgun, ammunition, methamphetamine and Mongols paraphernalia at a residence in Montebello, California."

"On November 10, 2005, in Los Angeles, California, defendant Viramontes sold stolen stereo equipment to a confidential government informant and two undercover law
enforcement officers, who were then posing as potential Mongols members."

"On August 12, 2006 in Arleta, California defendants Shawley and (Bouncer) Soto sold cocaine to a customer who identified himself as a football coach for a Catholic high school in the San Fernando Valley."

"On November 11, 2006 in Los Angeles, California defendant Price told an undercover law enforcement officer that he had used a stick as a weapon against a Hells Angels gang member."

On November 17, 2006 in Hollywood, California an unindicted Mongols gang member advised an undercover officer that he had beaten a rival gang member and kept that rival's severed tooth taped to a microwave oven in his kitchen."

"On January 9, 2007 defendants Buss and Wedig and other unindicted co-conspirators attacked a rival Hells Angels gang member at a Chuck E. Cheese restaurant in San Diego, California and forced him to surrender his gang clothing."

"On October 7, 2007, in Palm Springs, California, defendants Cavazos, Munz and (Lars) Wilson issued a 'Respect Few Fear None' patch and a 'Black Heart' patch to a Mongols member (Coconut Dan) as a reward for that member having engaged in a confrontation with a rival gang member on behalf of the Mongols in Indianapolis,
Indiana."

"On October 18, 2007, defendant (Bouncer) Soto possessed two semi-automatic handguns, narcotics, and a scale at his residence in Pacoima, California."

"On October 22, 2007, defendant Morein possessed a loaded handgun and methamphetamine in Los Angeles County, California."

"On November 6, 2007, in Azusa, California, defendants Solis and Trujillo robbed M.R. of home theater equipment, using a knife and handgun." (The robbery may also be characterized as a repossession.)

"On November 6, 2007, defendant Tinoco provided patches to defendant J. Garcia to be awarded to new Mongol members."

"On November 10, 2007, in Whittier, California, defendants R. Martinez and Nieves met with undercover law enforcement officers to explain the requirements of their
prospect status and defendant Price attempted to compel one of the officers to ingest methamphetamine."

"On November 11, 2007, defendant Rodriguez possessed ammunition at the Sportsman bar in Hacienda Heights, California, and an unindicted co-conspirator directed undercover law enforcement officers, posing as Mongols prospects, and defendant Angulo to act as security during a Mongols meeting being conducted in the bar."

"On December 9, 2007, defendant Price directed undercover officers posing as Mongols prospects to arm themselves against rival gang members outside the House Lounge in Hollywood, California."

"On December 16, 2007, an undercover law enforcement officer drove defendant McCauley from Los Angeles International Airport to Cavazos' residence in West Covina, California, and McCauley told the undercover officer that he would lose his
position in the military if his superiors learned that he was a member of the Mongols."

"On December 26, 2007, by telephone using coded language, defendant (Lars) Wilson directed an unidentified Mongols member to beat an individual posing as a Mongol member in Canada."

"On January 19, 2008, defendants Cavazos, R. Cavazos, Jr. and Roseli ejected a former Mongol from the House Lounge in Maywood, California, for his connection to the Mexican Mafia."

"On February 3, 2008, by telephone using coded language, defendant Wilson told defendant H. Gonzalez that defendant R. Cavazos, Jr., had required that all Mongols
applications include serial numbers."

Most of the crimes alleged in the case were minor. Many of the legal predicates were only intended to demonstrate that the Mongols were an outlaw motorcycle club. Some of the allegations were intended to lead casual observers of the case to believe that the Mongols was a hierarchically structured, for profit criminal enterprise with Doc Cavazos at the top. Many Mongols would agree with that which is why the club got rid of Cavazos. Doc, for example was alleged to "negotiate with Mexican Mafia representatives concerning the collection of "tax" payments for the narcotics trafficking activities of Mongols members in areas otherwise controlled by the Mexican Mafia." Doc would "direct Mongols members to travel to different locations and commit acts of violence, including murder, against rival gang members, law enforcement or other persons who would challenge the authority of the Mongols criminal enterprise." Doc would "conduct financial transactions to conceal the proceeds derived from the crimes of the organization and convert those proceeds to promote the crimes of the Mongols and enrich themselves."

The mere investigation, stretching out as it did for years grew ever more expensive. In addition to the male undercover agents the ATF devoted four female agents to the case. One of the problems with the Hells Angels investigation in Arizona had been that various Angels kept trying to fix Dobyns up with women. The job of the female agents in the Mongols investigation was to provide the male agents with excuses not participate in sexual shenanigans. What percentage of these lady agents' salary and benefits was part of the Black Rain investigation and how much was accounted for as some other expense "no one knows." It is one of the few times when neither the ATF nor the Department of Justice are being cute. No one knows because it doesn't strike anyone in the federal government as something anyone who isn't a "biker apologist" would want to know.

One of the more interesting allegations in the indictment stated: "On September 18, 2007, in San Bernardino, California, defendants R. Lozano, Reynolds, and I. Padilla and an unindicted co-conspirator armed themselves with firearms and arranged to purchase 33 kilograms of cocaine with an undercover law enforcement officer and a confidential government informant."

That charge so epitomized what really happened during Operation Black Rain that it deserves to be examined in detail.

Face

After John Ciccone recruited Steven "Kaos" Veltus, in November 2003 or October 2005 or whenever it was, the first thing he did was point Kaos toward Las Vegas and a Mongol named Harry "Face" Reynolds.

Face Reynolds is an honest, loyal, truthful, humble, brave, generous and self-deprecating man. In the millennium in which the foundations of the American economy have become rhetoric, usury, pornography and Facebook, Reynolds is a marble mason. He has the hands, physique and temperament of a man who makes useful things out of heavy, fragile and beautiful pieces of rock. Everything about him is immediately transparent the first moment he smiles at you. He has a wife and two small children and he is protective of his aging father. He describes himself as "a mother hen." The Mongols love Reynolds. Everybody loves Reynolds except the Hells Angels and the ATF. He used to drink with Roger Pinney. He used to ride next to Doc Cavazos.

Reynolds joined the Mongols in Orange County, California. He is devoted to the club, as all members are, because it is his "brotherhood." He started a chapter in San Bernardino, California "just to stick a little needle in the other guys." By other guys he means the Hells Angels whose founding charter is called Berdoo. When Reynolds moved to Las Vegas, during the hotel construction boom, he became the first Mongol there.

The Las Vegas chapter eventually grew to three members and when a biker named Kaos appeared Reynolds let him hang around with the rest of the club. The first thing Reynolds says is, "I liked Kaos when I first met him. I thought he was a cool guy. It was only later when we fell out."

Reynolds has never abused drugs and, like most outlaws, he is reluctant to lie to anyone but cops. Motorcycle outlaws, as part of their culture, are scrupulously honest. That old fashioned prohibition against lying is one of the vulnerabilities the ATF exploits when it investigates and prosecutes bikers. Motorcycle outlaws also have a uniquely pragmatic view of the drug business. In most clubs, including the Mongols, a member can sell drugs because he has an inalienable right to support himself however he can, in either the licit or the underground economy. But at the same time members are never allowed to pressure another member, associate or friend of the club into something like drug or contraband sales. And, that is just what led to the falling out between Face Reynolds and Kaos. The ATF's repeated efforts to turn Reynolds into a criminal was a multi-year, often absurd, charade.

Veltus was a classic *agent provocateur*. His job was to try to criminalize the Vegas chapter of the Mongols and as many other Mongols as he could. He wasn't just allowed by the ATF to break the law. The ATF was paying him to break the law and that was what eventually led Harry Reynolds to kick Veltus out of the Vegas chapter.

Veltus secretly tape recorded one conversation in Reynolds' living room on September 26, 2006, when Reynolds was trying to get his friend to go straight. The conversation lasted for almost two hours and Reynolds clearly could not conceive that Kaos was an informant. Reynolds began by reprimanding Veltus for trying to force a prospective member of the club to break the law.

Kaos: What'd I do bro?

Reynolds: Shit, um....

Kaos: That thing with Milo?

Reynolds: Yeah, you hurt my feelings, you both. You...you were treated shitty as a prospect, and he, last week he asked me if this club...if he would ever be asked to do anything illegal. And, I told him no, dude. The club would never make you do anything. And then what happens? You take him to do something illegal....

Next, Reynolds told Kaos to stop trying to give him money from the crimes he was supposedly committing.

Reynolds: You don't make money off of them, what you do, you turn around and hand it back to them....

Kaos: Yep, yep, yep.

Reynolds: . . .okay. What did you do that day you came here with an envelope for me? You hand me an envelope?

Kaos: Oh?

Reynolds: What'd I do? It ain't mine.

Kaos: Yeah.

Reynolds: I don't make money off you.

Kaos: Yeah.

Reynolds: You know. If we do something together fine. I...I think that's wrong. That hurts. That really fucking hurts. Because I think brotherhood and helping each other is first. Not to mention...okay...I might be taking it a little personal, maybe I'm not, I don't know, but uh…I need a bike. Milo needs a bike. Your bike ain't tuned too good...

Kaos: Yeah.

Reynolds: ...why is he so, you know what I mean? Hello!

Kaos: Yeah.

Reynolds: That... I don't understand that. You know. Nothing can…here first. You're thinking me, me, me. That's all you think about! Me, me, me.

Kaos: Yeah.

Reynolds then told Kaos that the least he could do was not implicate the Mongols in his crimes.

Reynolds: You know what? Mongol no! Mongol no. Not to mention…and this is the other thing I'm bothered with you about…you went to do something that was illegal with your shirt on! You were wearing a support shirt. That makes it a Mongol issue. I'm just pointing it out. I won't tell them that. But, I'm telling you that. I'm not doing nothing about it. I'm telling you....

Kaos: Alright.

Reynolds: So you can think next time. I don't want to see that shit like that again. Because I…think about it.

Kaos: Yeah.

Reynolds: (inaudible.) You got a shirt, they ever pull you over…whatever…and they find out? Bam! Okay? They can run your name (inaudible). Oh, you were (inaudible) Mongols. (You say) I don't know what you, you are talking about. (Cop says) Well you're wearing that. I know you got that. Now…you fucking…. Now all the house is gonna be ready cause… now you put all of us, and not just you…. Him too! Because you know what? He seen you wearing the shirt! He's fucking three year fucking member. Should be

198

telling you. You shouldn't be wearing that! What we're doing, 'cause I don't check (inaudible.) When I seen you out here I knew where you were going.

Kaos: Yeah.

Reynolds: So I can't say nothing about your shirt, right?

Kaos: Yeah, yeah.

Near the end of the conversation Reynolds tried to explain to Kaos for about the hundredth time what is important and what is not in an outlaw motorcycle club.

Kaos: Yeah, basically that was my worry. Because I need the money you know?

Reynolds: And I understand that, but you know what Kaos? And, I don't mean to be disrespectful. Brotherhood is first. Money second.

Kaos: Yeah.

Reynolds: I could give a fuck about money. Because you know what? When I'm in...laying in the gutter...my brother's gonna be there. Not, you know.... Money ain't gonna float up to me.

Kaos: Yeah.

Reynolds: You know what I mean? And I'm not saying you're like....

Kaos: But I still gotta pay my bills, bro. You know?

Reynolds: I understand that. But you'd rather hang with a prospect who was a cool dude and stuff.... I understand bills need to be paid. You know what? I don't work. She don't work. But you don't see me going out there fucking over my brothers, just to make a couple bucks.... Like I said...I...I'm disappointed in you but I don't blame you because you don't know your grounds as much. But I'm telling you right now, your grounds are, are a lot, and it's not me.... I understand you're worried about losing a deal but you know what?

Fuck that deal. Fuck that fucking deal. This is more important, I think. And if you don't think it's more important then I can't teach (inaudible). You know what I mean? This club's first.

Kaos: Yeah.

Reynolds: This club is fucking first. I don't care if I could make a million dollars. If it had anything to do...and I swear to God I mean that...and if it had anything to do with putting my brothers in jeopardy or anything like that I wouldn't do it. I would not do it. Cause, I (don't) give a fuck about money. I give a fuck about this club. We're brothers.

Reynolds was reminding Kaos Veltus on the relevant club rule which, taken verbatim from the Mongols' "Constitution," states: "Any member that uses the club for any illegal gain such as (drugs, guns, funny money, etc.) will face immediate disciplinary actions and be expelled from the club."

At the time Reynolds saw Veltus becoming addicted to drugs. He thought most of the crimes his friend was committing were a product of that. And, in the very old fashioned way of motorcycle outlaws, he was obliged by honor to try to straighten his club brother out. And, Reynolds grew frustrated when he couldn't save Kaos from his self-destructive impulses and appetites. Of course Reynolds had no idea what was really going on.

Throughout the investigation, beginning in 2005, Veltus bragged to his non-ATF employer (a jeweler), to his wife's employer (in addition to the ATF she worked for Clinique) and to other non-biker friends that he was an "undercover agent."

"He bragged the ATF handed him guns," one Vegas source said. He bragged, "the ATF allowed him to break the law and would let him do anything." He bragged that the ATF would help him "publish a book."

He bragged he would sell, "way more books than Billy Queen because he was going to have way more busts." On another occasion he bragged he was, "Gonna have the ATF record for the most busts." On multiple occasions Veltus told people he wanted to impress that the investigation of the Mongols was "all a setup."

Most elements of that setup failed because Reynolds is, at worst, cagey or, at best, a heroically admirable man. Veltus stored untaxed cigarettes in Reynolds garage for example, and tried to get Reynolds to move the boxes so they would be covered with Reynolds' fingerprints. Reynolds told him to move his own cigarettes. On another occasion, Veltus reported that he had sold Reynolds "a pound of marijuana." The accusation, which was completely fabricated, was repeated as a truth to the grand jury in the case and was used by Ciccone in testimony to secure wiretaps.

When it became clear to the ATF that Veltus could not turn the Vegas Mongols into a racket on his own, Ciccone had him introduce an undercover agent to Reynolds. The agent was John "Hollywood" Carr.

"I never liked that guy," Reynolds said on the same couch he once shared with Veltus. "He wasn't one of us. You know what I mean. He didn't even like motorcycles very much."

Carr was assigned to the Los Angeles office of the ATF. He was part of Ciccone's original "gang."

When he wasn't infiltrating bikers, Carr recruited men to rob drug safe houses and then arrested them for that. The press releases described Carr's victims as home invasion robbers. Carr won a Federal Bar Association Medal of Valor Award in 2002. According to his commendation "Special Agent Carr earned his award for working undercover to catch violent gang members staging a series of home invasion robberies. Carr transformed his look, acquainted himself with the criminals, and pretended to help them in their operation. Carr gave the criminals false information, which led them to traps planned by the ATF. Thanks to Carr's work, many dangerous criminals were caught and taken off our streets." The commendation characterizes Carr as a hero. "John Carr risked his life working on this assignment," the commendation states. "There are not many people who would make such a great sacrifice for others to feel safe in their homes. Through his courage, bravery and steadfast dedication, Carr prevailed in the face of danger."

Not everyone agrees about Carr's heroism. Immediately before he turned his attention to Harry Reynolds, one of the dangerous criminals Carr took off the streets appealed his conviction on the grounds "that the Government violated his right to due process by…directing the entire criminal enterprise from start to finish and by promoting a crime of violence." What Carr actually did was recruit five men who were "predisposed" to sticking up a drug safe house. He supplied a drug house for them to rob and talked them into the crime in a series of meetings over more than a month. The men demonstrated their predisposition by "meeting with Carr," putting on "bullet proof vests" and "possessing firearms." When they were arrested during their final meting with Carr they were charged with "conspiracy to distribute at least five kilograms of cocaine," "conspiracy to interfere with interstate commerce by robbery" and "possessing a firearm in furtherance of a drug trafficking crime." The Ninth Circuit Court rejected the appeal on the grounds that the one man who was actually convicted should have raised the issue before his trial instead of afterward. "We hold today," the Court wrote, "as have the Second, Third, and Eighth Circuits, that a defendant waives his claim of outrageous government conduct of which he is aware if he fails to assert it in a pretrial motion to dismiss."

The ATF had already seized a warehouse in Los Angeles for Carr to use as a cover. Reynolds thought Carr bought and sold surplus goods. For more than a year, Carr's association with the Mongols was as Steve Veltus' friend. Carr became a source for heavily discounted cigarettes.

Reynolds thought Carr was up to no good and refused to let him formally apply for membership in the club. Eventually Veltus was allowed to start another chapter – with the assistance of Lars Wilson and Coconut Dan – in nearby Henderson, Nevada. Carr patched into that chapter without going through the process of prospecting. Carr was allowed to "P-Patch" which is what the Mongols called a probationary membership. Carr paid Doc Cavazos $750 and Cavazos let him put on a patch.

"I never cared for Henderson," Reynolds said. "I thought all those guys were scandalous and dirty." Reynolds thought he was rid of both Veltus and Carr. He almost was. He would have been if it wasn't for the complicated obligations of honor that are integral to belonging to an outlaw club.

Motorcycle outlaws have their own rigid set of laws. Just as you can get thrown out bad for sleeping with a club brother's woman or lying or refusing to fight members are also honor bound to observe an unbreakable paternal relationship between the man who sponsors someone for membership in the club and the man who is sponsored. For as long as both remain in the club they call each other "my Dad" and "my Kid." Bouncer Soto, for example, was Hitman Martin's Dad. T.J. Stansbury was the father to all three ATF undercovers in Cypress Park. Harry Reynolds was "Dad in the club" to Mongols in both Vegas and San Bernardino.

Hollywood Carr, Face Reynolds would eventually learn, had set up "some sort of deal" in Vegas for September 2007. Reynolds learned that Carr had recruited his "kid" from San Bernardino, a young Mongol named Raphael Vargas "Peligrosa" Lozano, to provide "security" for whatever the deal was. Carr had also recruited a young member of Reynolds' Vegas chapter named Ismael "Mouth" Padilla. Peligrosa was going because he owed Veltus for two cases of Carr's discount cigarettes and this was a way to repay the debt. Padilla was offered a thousand dollars. That much money is only two days pay for an undercover ATF agent but it is a significant amount to working class men.

Reynolds, who insists he was mostly concerned about what Carr might be trying to involve his kids in, called Veltus and asked him about the deal. Veltus told Reynolds it was "just a deal" and told him if he was worried he could attend and Carr would pay him a thousand, too. So Reynolds finally took the bait.

"My wife always said she would stick by me as long as I didn't do anything stupid" Reynolds said. "Then I did this. Which was stupid." It was the month when the economy in Las Vegas was just starting to crash.

Since Carr was passing out cash Reynolds even brought his wife's cousin's boyfriend because he needed money, too.

The complete drug deal, in a room at an off strip hotel called the Silverton Casino, was caught on three hidden video cameras. In total, the footage is about six hours long and probably fewer than a 100 of people have ever seen it all. It was never intended to be evidence at a trial. It was always meant to be evidence to present to a grand jury to get an indictment. At least four things stand out about the video.

First for a case that probably cost $150 million the quality of the footage is ridiculously bad. One camera was placed right over the television so the only audio on that feed is from the Ultimate Fighting Championship Fight Night 11 which was broadcast live from the Palms Hotel and Casino over on the strip. Over and over viewers of the surveillance video hear about the amorous triumphs of Bob, and the delights of very many women, after Bob discovered Enzyte male enhancement. The footage from other feeds is either very dark or the audio is difficult to understand without listening over and over. The time stamps on the three feeds are unsynched. Events that are captured on one camera occur up to ten minutes earlier or later on the other two cameras. So much for forensic science.

It is impossible not to notice how performative both Carr and Veltus are. Carr turns the air conditioner on and off depending on whether he wants his voice to be recorded or not. Carr also seems to be a narcissus. He takes off his shirt and flexes for the grand jurors. Veltus practically leans against one camera with an automatic pistol shoved in the small of his back. He ties a bandanna around his head and theatrically announces "Change my look a little bit in case I got to pop one of those fools." The grand jury transcripts in this case will never be released but it seems pretty obvious that the grand jury thought they were indicting Veltus and Carr.

Both Carr and Veltus drop Face Reynolds' name as many times as possible because he was, in fact, the main target of the Vegas investigation. The first Mongols to enter the room are Lozano and Padilla and the depth of their criminality is betrayed by what they talk about. "Is this smoking or non-smoking. As soon as we walked through the door we saw these three gorgeous, like fine ass bitches in skirts, I guess they work over there at that little restaurant."

Carr replies, "Is it just you guys coming? Or Face."

Veltus says, "Face is coming. Yeah, Face is down."

One of the young men asks "what is the deal?"

Carr replies, "I'll explain when Face gets here." Then he starts pulling bullet proof vests out of a duffel bag, hands them out and instructs the young men how to put them on. Carr then tries to establish for his grand jury audience that the Mongols armed themselves for this deal. "Now hey, did somebody need a strap? Who needs one? Yeah I'm covered. You covered? Who needs one? Uh, Face's boy?"

Lozano tries on his bullet proof vest and says, "Hey, this is nice. It even covers your fucking *huevos.*"

Then Face Reynolds and Caspar, his wife's cousin's boyfriend enter the room. Face gives Carr a very pro forma hug. Their bodies never touch. Face puts his left arm briefly around Carr while he holds him away with his right hand, pats him on the back and moves on. Face nervously, immediately lights a cigarette. Carr offers Face a gun and says "You want one? You got one?" Reynolds makes a sour face and shakes his head no. Carr asks, "Are you sure?" Anyone can see, even on the terrible video, that the economy is failing, Reynolds is out of work, he is there to keep an eye on the younger men for whom he feels responsible and he could really use a thousand dollars. Face mumbles, "I'm cool." And turns his back on Carr who he clearly cannot stand. One of the video feeds says the time in Vegas is 8:49:57 and Carr immediately moves close to one of the hidden microphones. "Come here, fellas." Then Carr tells Veltus, "Tell them what we're going to do." He orders the confidential informant to do it in order to weaken the defense of entrapment. It is calculated. Veltus jerks his hand as if he is setting a hook in a fish.

Then Carr, who is also clearly nervous, goes ahead and explains anyway. When he talks Face Reynolds has been in the room for exactly 30 seconds. "Here's basically, the deal. This dude, I've dealt with him two prior times. I've bought like two or three from him. He's been cool. You know, like we're on a personal, like friend level but Anthony stepped it up. I'm gonna pick up 33 from the guy today." In the corner of the screen Face Reynolds cocks his head to the left and crosses his arms. The video is too dark to recognize his expression. "So when I talked to him two days ago he was cool, you know. There was nothing unusual but he was like 'you know I'm gonna bring my boys, you know,' which is kind of unusual because usually it's just me and him. So that kind of gets me thinking because you know because we're talking 33. I'm paying 16. I mean, we're talking 500 grand."

That is the first hint any of the Mongols have that Carr is talking about a big drug deal.

"So that just gets me thinking in my head, you know," Carr continues, "that maybe this dude's, you know, that this dude...I just want...I don't want too skinny a palm tree with this guy...you know on the outside chance that he wants to get like squirrely with me...I figured, you know...the presence of you dudes is gonna stand up and down. The way I'm gonna play it to him is he's gonna come here. He's gonna bring the shit here. We're gonna look at all of it. We're gonna cut every one. Make sure its all straight." Reynolds wipes his face with one big hand then and turns his back to Carr.

"I've got the money in another room," Carr says. "I'm gonna take him and me. The only two. I'm not gonna let him bring anybody else. We're going to the room. I got a counter. We're going to count our money. The money's straight. We'll come back. Adios. He goes. Pack up the shit. Walk me to the car. Cause I have no doubt this dude's is gonna bring other dudes. I mean, I would. I mean, I can understand that. But he may post them up, you know, outside or something like that. See I just want to make sure that one of two things is gonna happen. (And here Carr become histrionic.

Face Reynolds notices it.) I'm gonna come up out of here with 33 keys or I'm gonna come up out of here with my money." He says this like bad television. Like he is auditioning for a role. It is 8:51:57. Face has been in the room for 2 minutes and ten seconds. Caspar has spent most of the time looking at pictures on the wall.

Carr continues, "And there's nothing other than those two things that are going to happen. I just want to make sure that he's straight with me on this. I just want to make sure that everything counts out right, you know. Like I've said I've dealt with him before. I have no issues with the dude. He's always been straight with me so I'm not anticipating any problems. "

Carr gets up.

Veltus hands Caspar a gun. Caspar looks at it like a child with a toy and promptly drops one of the bullets on the floor. Carr continues to drone on about "I don't anticipate any problems."

Reynolds wears a puzzled look. Years later he explains, "I'm thinking, you are gonna go into another room alone? Then what are we doing here?"

Carr tries again to get Face to take a gun. Here you go Face. Face again refuses. In the official report of this event, Report of Investigation 430, Ciccone writes. "Reynolds implied he had his (gun.)" About five minutes after he entered Face goes to watch the UFC fight on television. "A thousand bucks is a thousand bucks," he said later. "I'll sit on a couch and watch the fight for a thousand bucks."

At 8:57:50, according to the video feed with both audio and video, Carr gets a phone call from his "drug supplier." The drug supplier, Carr announces, looks "Mexican but he's like part Sicilian." So he could be affiliated with at least two of the more well known Mafias. Carr says, "It's show time." The drug supplier was actually a Los Angeles County Sheriff's Deputy named Tino Brancato who had a part time job as a Task

Force Officer, which is to say amateur actor, for the ATF.

While Carr and Veltus brag to each other about the pending drug deal Padilla and Lozano continue to chatter excitedly to anyone who will listen about the pretty girls they almost talked to downstairs. "…three fine ass girls with skirts and everything! And I was like, fuck! I just died and went to heaven! Out loud, you know, like right in front of them. I go like, I don't give a fuck. So those girls, they start talking in Spanish and I go like *Que chulas* (which is a demure and almost old fashioned pickup line in Spanish.) So they go "Oh shit. You speak Spanish." And Kaos was dragging us back like, no, you gotta go that way."

So Padilla and Lozano were literally dragged to the drug deal. And Reynolds was only there because he thought Carr and Veltus were reckless and stupid enough to put the young men in danger. Reynolds got up and asked Veltus about the door to an adjoining room. Reynolds, now that he knew he was there to provide security for a drug deal, was afraid thugs might rush in from the adjoining room and murder them. Reynolds tested the door. There was a Las Vegas Metro SWAT team on the other side of that door. Veltus told Reynolds it was not a problem and talked him out of taking the other two Mongols and leaving. Carr and Veltus laughed about it later.

Sheriff Brancato knocked on the door eleven minutes later. He and Carr jawed at each other like a campy, community theater remake of *The Good, The Bad and The Ugly*. "Are we gonna do this thing," Carr asks as he poses for the hidden camera.

"We gonna do this thing," Brancato improvises.

"I mean we're gonna do business right," Carr asks. "I mean business is business."

"I'm gonna walk out of here with 528," Brancato glowers, "and then everybody's happy. Okay?"

Reynolds says he knew it all sounded so amateurish that he thought it couldn't really be dangerous. "Like, I never went to one of these things before," he said. "I thought, well maybe this is what they're like, you know." He stopped worrying and concentrated on the fight. As far as he knew, Carr was buying $528,000 worth of corn starch and he did not like Carr enough to care.

Carr and Brancato come and go for the next 45 minutes. Another undercover Sheriff and amateur thespian named Jake Hickman played the role of Brancato's muscle. Reynolds cousin asks him if he has seen the sporting goods store that adjoins the casino. The undercover cop agrees it is, "bad ass. Yeah, they got a fish pond and shit in there. You should check it out."

Carr spread all the bundles of cocaine out on the bed. It was actually 70 pounds of police cocaine, checked out of official custody to make this drug deal a real crime. Carr sticks a knife in each of the kilo packages. Veltus samples some of it to make sure it is real. Like all confidential informants, he must be willing to consume drugs. He is the only man there who samples any of the drug. Throughout the deal, Reynolds is sullen, unhappy and uncooperative. Several times Carr goes over and pats him on the shoulder or tries to engage him in talk about the deal. Mostly Reynolds looks like a size 54 man shoved into a size 42 tuxedo for his daughter's wedding to a man he cannot stand. When the deal is finally completed Reynolds' wife's cousin's boyfriend Caspar gives Carr his gun back. Reynolds takes his thousand dollars. Carr tries to give Caspar only $500. Reynolds tells him, "He sat on the couch the same as me. Give him the thousand." Carr agrees.

Reynolds seems to intimidate Carr. Not because Reynolds is a big, tough looking guy but because of Face Reynolds' moral force. Reynolds is not a trivial

210

man. He makes a contract when he shakes your hand. He attended Carr's deal, which turned out to be a cocaine deal, because he said he would. He insisted that Caspar be paid the same as everyone else because that is what Carr said the job paid.

When Carr and Veltus were alone in the room again Carr turned up the air conditioner to muffle their voices. Carr keeps pointing to the place where Reynolds was sitting as they two men seem to discuss whether they have enough to frame Reynolds. "See...no," Carr says. His affect changes when he is himself. He stabs his finger at Veltus and then at the couch over and over. Veltus looks afraid. The two of them are getting their stories together. Finally Carr declares, "He had access." Veltus nods and Carr tells him. "Okay. Now we're gonna walk down there." Reynolds and the other Mongols are supposed to be waiting for Carr in the parking lot but Reynolds had already stuffed the thousand dollars in his pocket and driven home.

A federal prosecutor, a subordinate of Chris Brunwin named Reema M. El-Amamy, would later tell a judge that what happened in that room at the Silverton was "guerilla street theater."

Carr pulled the same stunt another time in the Mongols investigation and tried to set up a third big drug deal. The participants in the second deal were all indicted. At Hitman Martin's funeral, a few days after Brunwin asked the grand jury to return the indictment, Carr approached a Mongol from Oregon named Mooch DeLoretto and asked him to help sell cocaine there. DeLoretto told him "no" then reported the offer to Mike Munz. Munz reported Carr to club president Largo Gonzalez. Gonzalez was furious that even after Doc had been voted out bad this sort of thing was still happening in the club. Largo told Carr to take off his patch, leave and never come back. A few days later both

Largo and Munz were arrested and charged with drug dealing, too.

That drug deal was the last time Face Reynolds spoke to either Veltus or John Carr.

Three weeks after the guerilla theater production, the ATF moved Steve Veltus and his wife to Missoula, Montana. Whenever Veltus needed to make an appearance in Las Vegas or California, the ATF would fly him to Vegas. (Extensive air travel was one of the ways the investigation and prosecution of the Mongols came to cost so much.) Veltus was almost out of control under the big sky. He broke laws with impunity. "The ATF knew it," a source said.

Multiple sources saw him flash a gun multiple times. Ciccone always intervened with local police on Veltus' behalf. Veltus pulled a gun on a University of Montana student. He assembled a portfolio of photographs for his pending memoir. At the same time he was introducing himself to the Helena chapter of the Mongols, Veltus seemed to have decided to tell everybody in Missoula that he was secret agent. He bragged with alarming openness that he was about to join the witness protection program under the assumed named William Lazara (the similarity to Lazarus who rose from the dead has Ciccone's fingerprints all over it) and that he was going to retire on his "bonus money" from the Mongols case. At that time, Veltus also had a cell phone with a Boston telephone number.

He used his status with the ATF to get away with more crimes. He announced that his retirement plan was to buy a restaurant from an old woman in Sula, Montana. He gained the woman's trust and moved into but did not operate her restaurant. Late in 2008, two months after shaking hands with the restaurant owner on the deal Veltus and his wife disappeared. He attempted to burn the restaurant down when he left but the arson was not successful. Inside, firemen and police found several pounds of marijuana and the carcass of an illegally taken elk. Veltus also stole kitchen equipment and at least $2700 in cash. The total loss to the restaurant owner was $18,000.

The owner tried to track down Veltus to sue him for the damage he had done. Since Veltus had bragged about his connections with the ATF it was a comparatively easy chase. "What do you want us to do," John Ciccone asked the restaurant owner's son when he called. The son said he wanted to sue either Veltus or the ATF for the damage Veltus had caused. Ciccone replied, "Well that's not gonna happen."

The son complained to the local ATF office in Missoula and threatened to sabotage the government case against the Mongols by testifying to statements Veltus had made about it "all being a big setup." The agent threatened the man with "prison" if he tried to publicize what he knew.

Thirteen months after the guerilla theater performance, on October 21, 2008, the day of the televised Mongols bust, five cops came for Face Reynolds at work at the soon to be completed Encore at Wynn in Vegas.

That was the day a Los Angeles television reporter said to the ATF spokesman, "And, we always hear, you know I've done stories on some of these biker gangs before and they say we're clubs. We're not a gang. What do you say to that?"

And, the ATF spokesman replied, "That's a joke. The Mongols are a gang. They recruit from the most vicious street gangs here in Los Angeles. They're nothing but a criminal syndicate on wheels. Uh, they're a motorcycle clu...gang and that's what they are. They're criminals."

That day the cops rushed at Face Reynolds from behind, threw him to the ground and chained him. He was immediately fired and banned from all Wynn resorts for life.

Simultaneously, his house was wrecked by a task force of Metro Las Vegas police officers and ATF Agents. His furniture was overturned. Every drawer in the house was pulled out and emptied. His sick father's room was sacked. His motorcycle was seized. His father's old motorcycle was seized. Every piece of Mongols memorabilia in the house was seized. Photo albums and computers were seized. It took two trucks to haul everything away. His wife, his father and his two children aged five and seven were all threatened. ATF Agents took the pictures off his little girl's wall and smashed them on the floor. "There was glass everywhere," he said. When Face Reynolds bailed out three days later the house was uninhabitable.

And that was only the beginning of the nightmare.

Justice

If Operation Black Rain was cynical, contrived, unfair or corrupt, the prosecution of the case was worse. Even if the investigation can be dismissed as an aberration or an exception to the way the "good guys" usually "get" the "bad guys," even if the investigation can be defended by arguing that it has been unfairly described here, the prosecution of the Mongols still exemplifies the terrible reality of modern American justice.

The United States no longer has an adversarial system of criminal law. Trials are rare. America now has an administrative system of criminal justice. On the bottom in America, on the fringes, among the humble, once you are indicted it is all over. The only question is what somebody like Assistant U.S. Attorney Christopher Brunwin is going to do to make you suffer and how much it will hurt.

More than 96 percent of all federal defendants plead guilty. Ninety percent of the four percent who insist on inconveniencing the system with a trial are found guilty. Once they indict you, you have less than one chance in a hundred of being exonerated. Practically none of the federal defendants who get away are part of a production as important to the Department of Justice as the Mongols prosecution.

Depending on where you draw the lines, there were at least four Mongols racketeering cases although subsequent RICO cases against the Pagans and the Outlaws resulted from the same investigation. The main case which began in one Los Angeles courtroom and eventually spread to another Los Angeles courtroom and a courtroom in Orange County, was named *United States versus Cavazos and Others*. A much smaller case called *US versus Maestas and Others* was adjudicated in Denver. The smallest racketeering case, against a lone Mongol, is called *US versus Christopher Ablett* and years after the Mongols bust it is still being contested in Oakland. The fourth case, a civil case over the matter of whether any cop can simply seize what he believes to be "Mongols paraphernalia" when he sees it, was called *Ramon Rivera versus Ronnie A. Carter, Acting Director, Bureau of Alcohol, Tobacco, Firearms and Explosives (ATF); John A. Torres, Special Agent in Charge, ATF Los Angeles Field Division; and Eric H. Holder, United States Attorney General.*

The obvious clumsiness of even naming the main court cases hints at, but does not begin to explain, why so little was written about the Mongols after the raids in October 2008. None of the usual biker experts has written about the investigation. The prosecution has been, for all practical purposes, secret. But the case is still important enough that even people who detest the Mongols and "their ilk" should know about it because it is a bright marker on the road of flight from the old to the new and improved America.

The point of Operation Black Rain was to put every outlaw in America out bad – to seize his cut, his motorcycle and his memorabilia, to rough him up, wreck his home, scare him and tell him "don't come around this club no more." It was, simultaneously

216

emotionally, financially and legally devastating for the men involved. The point of the "enforcement effort" described in this book was never to punish "criminals." The point was to crush a set of seductive, romantic, dangerous, and maybe obsolete, ideas.

Seventy-seven of the 79 men who were named in the Mongols indictment that was returned the day Hitman Martin was autopsied had pled guilty by November 2011.

One defendant named Jorge Cottini died in custody. He was sick when he was arrested. He did not have to die. He died as sick men always die in jail. He died because nothing compelled his jailers to try to save him. So he never copped a plea and he was sentenced to the stiffest penalty of any of the defendants.

Peter Bouncer Soto who had been Hitman Martin's "Dad in the club," avoided arrest for 33 months. During an interview in the summer of 2010, Soto remembered his invitation to Martin. "Let's fuck bitches. Let's ride motorcycles. Let's be brothers." Bouncer kept his motorcycle and he kept his Mongols cut. He mourned for his days in the club. Almost two years after he went on the run he still liked to put on his vest and ride his bike. He confessed that some nights he "dreamed" about the Mongols. He felt guilty that he was "not locked up with the brothers." He was eventually arrested by *La Policía Estatal Preventiva* in the *La Sierra* section of Tijuana, Mexico on July 26, 2011 in what Mexican police described as a routine sweep. Late in 2011, Soto was still demanding a trial.

All the other defendants in the case pled guilty to something. Most of them pled guilty to Count One of the racketeering indictment which (in the clumsy cant of American justice) read:

"Beginning on a date unknown, and continuing to on or about October 9, 2008, in Los Angeles County, within the Central District of California and elsewhere,

217

(the) defendants and others known and unknown to the Grand Jury, being persons employed by and associated with the Mongols criminal enterprise, which enterprise engaged in and the activities of which affected interstate and foreign commerce, unlawfully and knowingly combined, conspired, confederated, and agreed together and with each other to violate Title 18, United States Code, Section 1962, that is, to conduct and participate, directly and indirectly, in the conduct of the affairs of the enterprise through a pattern of racketeering activity, as that term is defined in Title 18, United States Code, Sections 1961(1) and 1961(5), consisting of multiple acts involving murder, in violation of California Penal Code Sections 31, 182, 187, 189, 217.1, and 664; robbery, in violation of California Penal Code Sections 211, 212.5(a), and 213; distribution of controlled substances, including methamphetamine and cocaine, in violation of Title 21, United States Code, Sections 841(a)(1) and 846; and multiple acts indictable under Title 18, United States Code, Sections 1956 and 1957 (money laundering). It was a further part of the conspiracy that each defendant agreed that a conspirator would commit at least two acts of racketeering in the conduct of the affairs of the enterprise."

The stated objective of the main Mongols case, the one named for Doc Cavazos, was to prove that the Mongols were a hierarchically structured, criminal racket, in competition with other criminal rackets for illicit profits and with the money moving up a pyramid from the street to Doc Cavazos' bank account. The tacit but more important objective in the government's view was to prove the allegations made in the Cavazos indictment by rounding up all the most knowledgeable Mongols, threatening them all with 20 years to life, and keeping up the pressure until they admitted in writing that the Mongols Motorcycle Club was a criminal syndicate.

There could never be any entrapment defense because entrapment can only be used as a defense at a trial and from the beginning there was never going to be a trial. Most of the accused in *Cavazos* had to evaluate their plea deals without ever seeing most of the evidence, or "discovery," against them. Many federal district courts have what is called an "open file" policy which means that prosecutors reveal their evidence to defenders as soon as the accused is arraigned. None of the federal courts in which the Mongols cases were contested does that. The American Bar Association has proposed that there should be an open file policy for plea bargaining. There is no such policy in any of the courts that handled any of the Mongols cases. Defenders had to guess what the government might be able to prove.

It became a kind of game theory laboratory. Even the names of the confidential informants were revealed reluctantly in order to hinder defenders from evaluating the veracity of ATF contractors like Steve Veltus and Coconut Dan. The plea bargaining process was actually part of the investigation. The investigation used the threat of continued imprisonment to help investigators search for proof of what had already been charged and for proof of additional crimes. The story about the bodies burning in the desert was, among other things, a rumor to pressure defendants into pleading guilty. The defendants knew who the traitors had been. But they had no idea what Veltus, or Coconut Dan, or Hollywood Carr or Kozlowski might have alleged or how they might have contrived those allegations.

The government is supposed to disclose evidence that impeaches its *agents provocateur* and that proves "actual innocence" but in practice this never happens in federal court. A prosecutor can only be accused of withholding this evidence during an appeal of a conviction and defenders usually do not know or care what a prosecutor withholds.

The discovered evidence in the case grew by the week even though most of it had been gathered long before. Eventually the discovery in Cavazos amounted to more than 10,100 pages of documents, 356 Compact Discs and 110 Digital Video Discs. This discovery is not the evidence against any one particular defendant. Because all the defendants were charged with racketeering the discovery is what the prosecution claims is evidence of racketeering. Any defendant may be in only one page of it. In November 2011, the *Cavazos* case also included more than 4,600 official court filings. A large fraction of those filings are sealed.

The prosecutors were not required to disclose any of the discovery until seven days before any trial. Prosecutors and defenders call these last minute disclosures "evidence dumps." Brunwin, Ciccone and their associates had years to consider and arrange all this information to fit their theory of the case. Defense attorneys did not. If a defendant insisted on a trial instead of a plea deal, he would have a week to examine what the government had been looking at for years.

In federal court, as one scholar put it, a prosecutor "can effectively dictate the terms of the 'deal'" After the Nixon Administration decided to get tough with soft judges, prosecutors became the most powerful officials in federal court. Innocent observers often assume that prosecutors act fairly on behalf of the interests of the whole community but in general that is not the case. Usually, prosecutors advocate the interests of their allies the police.

At the beginning of the case most of the defense attorneys simply assumed, based on what they had read or seen on television, that their clients must be guilty. In the Pagans case a year later, some of the attorneys moved to strike "surplusage," or inflammatory language, about the Pagans criminal enterprise, from the indictment. None of the Mongols defenders did. The Mongols defense attorneys could have moved for an evidentiary hearing on the allegation that the Mongols was a criminal enterprise. None of them ever contested that allegation.

Face Reynolds' lawyer tried to sever his client from the racketeering charge and failed. When he tried to force that separate trial he was threatened with an evidence dump.

The evidence in *Cavazos* was basically everything that at least 18, highly motivated, domestic spies equipped with state of the art electronic surveillance and an army of assistants could learn about everybody connected to a 500 member motorcycle club over three years. There could never be a journalistic or legal narrative of the case except what the ATF and the DOJ insisted it must be because the narrative needed an author. All that information could be arranged the way footage is arranged to make reality TV. And, of course, the author of this show could only be John Ciccone.

Virtually all of the Mongols took the plea because the punishment for not taking the plea was 20 years to life. The punishment for pleading guilty was always something less.

The first Mongol to plead out was Lars Wilson, which probably only formalized an agreement that had been made with the ATF years before. The deal couldn't have been made directly with Brunwin, because legally, technically, that would have been unethical. But there was no ethical issue at all if Ciccone made the deal and Ciccone and Brunwin just happened to think exactly the same thing.

The next Mongols to confess to being racketeers were the three Cavazos – Doc, his son Lil Rubes and his brother Al. Ciccone went to Doc Cavazos cell and dictated the plea deal to him. Doc had to confess to being a racketeer, cooperate with Ciccone and Brunwin in debriefings and agree to surrender ownership of the Mongols name and patch to the U.S. Government. Ciccone said he would "hang Lil Rubes" if Doc didn't go along. So Doc took the deal. Christopher Brunwin immediately requested that all plea agreements be made secret. The request was made, Brunwin would argue, on the sage counsel of Ciccone. In a sworn declaration the ATF agent told the court:

"I, John Ciccone, declare as follows: I am a Special Agent of the Bureau of Alcohol, Tobacco, Firearms and Explosives, United States department of Justice, Los Angeles, California. I have been employed as a Special Agent of the ATF for approximately eighteen years...."

"A number of defendants have entered. guilty pleas and offered to cooperate with the government. Other defendants have also provided information to the government, and have requested that their plea agreements be filed under seal, in order to protect them and their family members from possible retaliation. Based on my knowledge of the Mongols gang and the facts learned during the course of the investigation, I believe that the concerns about physical retaliation to defendants are credible. The Indictment describes a number of acts of violence, threats, and intimidation by the Mongols organization. I believe that some of the defendants would have a greater concern for possible retaliation than others, based on the nature of the organization and the defendant's role within the organization.

"Agents have coordinated with the Marshal's Service in order to assist with the safety and security of inmates, particularly with regard to housing issues that might address the danger to inmates. However, I anticipate that the government will continue to need to file some documents under seal as a protective measure, particularly when defendants intend to cooperate...."

"I declare under penalty of perjury under the laws of the United states that the foregoing is true and correct to the best of my knowledge and belief."

Actually, at that point only two defendants in the case, Lars Wilson and Doc Cavazos, had promised to cooperate but no one could know that. It could have been all of the score of Mongols who quickly agreed to take pleas. Defendants had no way to know which of the plea deals were sealed because the pleaders were snitching and which were sealed as part of a prosecutorial strategy. Someone in the ATF, maybe Ciccone but more likely it was Ciccone's boss John Torres, leaked the news that lots of Mongols rats were jumping off the Mongols ship to an ATF friendly paper, the Whittier California *Daily News*. *The Associated Press* ran the story nationally.

Then the *AP* sued to find out what those pleas were. The *AP* thought the people had a right to know. "The scope of the relief sought by the government in the past, sealing all plea agreements, is too broad and is not supported by specific facts that would warrant the extensive relief being sought in their motion. (The only support they offer for the relief they sought was the declaration of Agent John Ciccone, which is devoid of any
specific facts.) The government did not just make the claim that cooperating plea
agreements should be filed, under seal, and in camera, but that the mere fact that a
defendant has plead guilty, all plea agreements whether the defendant is cooperating
or not, and all cooperator plea agreements, should be filed under seal," one motion argued.

That suit dragged on for months and was eventually dismissed. It was dismissed on the naïve judicial assumption that all the plea deals would eventually be revealed on "closure" of the case after a trial. Of course, there would never be a trial, or closure, and the majority of those early pleas were unsealed after most of the defendants who had entered them joined the *AP* in suing to have their agreements made public.

All the defendants, except Lars Wilson, held out for some period of time. Doc held out for almost two months. But inevitably, one after another, month after month, Mongol after Mongol finally said "fuck it" and caved. One Mongol who caved later regretted it. "Do you know who I really admire now" he said. "The HA. Their shit is tight. None of them would have given in." The official, *pro forma* confessions in court were Stalinesque.

"How far did you advance in school," a judge would ask sweetly, or sternly or jocularly, as he or she began the interrogation that verified the "competence" of the confessed criminal.

And before he would answer the wise defendant would always whisper something to his lawyer. And, only after the lawyer whispered back would the defendant dare to say, "High school." Or, "Ninth grade." Or, "I dropped out of college."

"And, are you aware that you may be giving up certain of your rights, like the right to vote or own a gun or serve on a jury?"

Whisper, whisper. "Yeah, probably astronaut is also out of the question," the lawyer would advise confidentially.

Whisper, whisper, nod. The defendant answers the judge, "Yeah, right."

"And are you in fact actually guilty?"

Whisper, whisper. Bitter, little laugh. And then the slight smile that means that the defendant is about to turn forever to stone. "Yeah. Guilty."

The judge would decree that the confessed criminal was "in fact" guilty and then the defense attorney would always say, "Thank you, your honor."

The prosecutor would always say, "Thank you, your honor."

That was always the best part: As the Deputy Marshalls led the "convicted" man away in his orange jump suit, in a belly chain and cuffs and sometimes in shackles; as the opposing sides stuffed files back into their expensive leather cases; before they would go out into the hall to smile about last summer in Rome or on the Costa del Sol; the opposing lawyers would always thank the judge.

Meanwhile the *Ablett* racketeering case stalled because the prosecutors there simply refused to disclose most of the evidence against him. The prosecutors also refused to disclose any evidence that the Mongols were a criminal racket or any of the evidence in the *Cavazos* case.

Ablett was the Mongol charged with murdering Hells Angels Frisco President Marc "Papa" Guardado outside a bar called Dirty Thieves at the corner of 24th Street and Treat Avenue in San Francisco. Ablett was socializing with a woman he had known in high school and one of her friends. He was wearing a Mongols tee shirt with a Virginia bottom rocker which is worth noting because the Virginia Mongols had been invented by Coconut Dan Horrigan and Lars Wilson. The Virginia Mongols were led by three ATF undercover agents named Jeff Grabman, Rick Hankins and Mark Kelly.

Guardado had been told by some secret someone that there were "Mongols down on Treat." The Dirty Thieves was an Angels hangout and it is likely Ablett didn't know that. Guardado found Ablett talking to the two women outside the bar. Guardado was probably not alone. A few months after the murder,

Gangland, one of the ATF's favorite news outlets, reenacted the killing in a television episode that reported that five Hells Angels had attacked Ablett. The information would have come from the ATF. However many combatants there were, an argument quickly escalated into a fight. Guardado's last words were "He keeps stabbing me!" A witness told the FBI she saw Ablett shooting Guardado. Ciccone learned of the killing almost as soon as it happened. He appears to have known about the homicide before Guardado's family.

Ablett is charged with multiple counts of racketeering. His indictment claims, "...the Mongols biker gang was a criminal organization whose members and associates engaged in among other things, murder, conspiracy to commit murder, attempted murder, conspiracy to traffic in narcotics, narcotics trafficking, robbery, extortion, money laundering and witness intimidation."

"The Mongols gang is a nationwide organization that has made efforts to expand internationally. The gang is believed to have 500 to 600 members. The Mongols organization is comprised of approximately 68 identified chapters. The chapters are located in different geographical regions throughout California as well as Oklahoma, Florida, Nevada, Oregon, Maryland, Virginia, New York, Utah, Washington, Montana, Arizona, Colorado, Mexico and Canada"

"On or about September 2, 2008...as consideration for the receipt of and as consideration for a promise and agreement to pay anything of a pecuniary value from the Mongols and for the purpose of gaining entrance to and maintaining and increasing his position in the Mongols...the defendant Christopher Bryan Ablett unlawfully and knowingly did murder Mark Guardado...."

That boiler plate was written by John Ciccone.

The most important of the civil cases – there are multiple civil cases attached to the Mongols prosecution – was *Ramon Rivera*. It was brought by a San Diego Mongol represented by David Blair-Loy of the San Diego branch of the American Civil Liberties Union. It was important, because it challenged the government's method of outlawing motorcycle clubs.

The first judge in the *Cavazos* case, Florence Marie Cooper, had granted an injunction at the beginning of the case that prevented the Mongols from transferring ownership of their insignia. Her rationale was that if the existence of a "Mongols criminal enterprise" was ever actually proved the "trademarks" might be valuable assets subject to forfeiture. Then, like a good judge, Cooper ignored all television and press coverage of the case so she never heard the claim that she had authorized police to rip forbidden shirts off people's backs.

The Department of Justice and the ATF interpreted Cooper's injunction differently. They believed the injunction meant it was open season on the word "Mongols." At the time, even some Mongols actually felt embarrassed for Ciccone. "The little fella is losing it," one Mongol said in June 2009.

Ciccone crashed a Mongols party and stole a box of tee shirts. A week later he sent a Los Angeles County Sheriff's Swat team into the home of a former Mongol named Mauricio Montano. Montano had been in a wheelchair for 20 years but he was an ex-Mongol who sympathized with the club so the Sheriffs tossed his home and confiscated a Mongols clock, a Mongols picture, his ancient Mongols cut, three Mongols tee shirts, two beanies, two bandannas and a Mongols belt buckle.

In June 2009, Ciccone shut down the crappy motel in Lancaster where the Mongols had planned to hold their national run. The club made other plans.

Ciccone tracked them down, stood outside their new residence and "screamed" that he had seen "two shirts and a belt buckle" that day and he wanted them. Later, Ciccone started breaking into Mongols cars using a lockout tool. He claimed he had "a warrant." When Mongols asked to see it Ciccone said he "lost it."

"This dude seems crazy and doesn't seem to care about the law," a Mongol complained. Judge Cooper was distressed when she finally heard about some of this in July 2009.

Cooper was easily the most sympathetic official in the case. She followed an unconventional path to the federal bench. As a young mother, she attended San Francisco City College for five years but never got her degree. She worked as a legal secretary. She got coffee for important people. She ran their errands and was not rewarded when she did their work for them. Eventually she was admitted to what is now Whittier College of Law as part of a special program for bright people who lacked college diplomas. She graduated first in her class.

She was a maverick judge. She infuriated the George W. Bush Administration when she told the United States Navy to stop testing a kind of sonar that environmentalists were afraid might hurt whales.

She ruled on behalf of the family of a rapper named Christopher Wallace. Wallace performed under a couple of names including The Notorious B.I.G. and Biggy Smalls before he was gunned down outside the Petersen Automotive Museum in Los Angeles in 1997 – just about the time Ciccone was investigating Death Row records. A Los Angeles cop named David Mack, who was simultaneously a member of the Compton Bloods, was widely implicated in the shooting. Wallace's family sued the LAPD for information and when the Los Angeles police ignored the suit Judge Cooper ordered the city of Los Angeles to pay the Wallace family $1.2 million.

The government told Cooper that its claim to the Mongols name and patch was part of Doc Cavazos' plea deal. The government said that Cavazos "has admitted as part of his plea (and the undisputed evidence conclusively confirms) that the Mongols Registered Trademarks were acquired and maintained by defendant (Doc Cavazos) during and in the course of the operation of the RICO enterprise." They cited the guilty pleas that had been entered as evidence that the Mongols was a criminal syndicate. Cavazos' "admissions also establish that the Mongols Registered Trademarks afforded a source of influence over the RICO enterprise that (the) defendant admits he established, operated, controlled, conducted and participated in the conduct of, rendering the marks subject to forfeiture."

In her ruling on the forfeiture of the Mongols patch, Judge Cooper sounded a little like Captain Renault in *Casablanca*.

"At the June 22 hearing," she wrote, "the Government revealed for the first time that the mark it sought to forfeit was a collective membership mark. Previously...the Government (in this case ATF Case Agent John Ciccone) referred to the mark simply as a trademark, which was 'purportedly for use in commerce in connection with promoting the interests of persons interested in the recreation of riding motorcycles.' In contrast to commercial trademarks, which are used in commerce and generally not entitled to full First Amendment protections, collective membership marks are used by members of an organization to 'indicate membership in a union, an association, or other organization.' The use and display of collective membership marks therefore directly implicate the First Amendment's right to freedom of association. The Supreme Court has recognized that 'implicit in the right to engage in activities protected by the First Amendment' is 'a corresponding right to associate with others in pursuit of a wide variety of political, social, economic, educational, religious, and cultural ends.' This right is crucial in preventing the majority from imposing its views on groups that would rather express other, perhaps unpopular, ideas.' Furthermore, clothing identifying one's association with an organization is generally considered expressive conduct entitled to First Amendment protection.... If speech is noncommercial in nature, it is entitled to full First

Amendment protection, which prohibits the prior restraint and seizure of speech-related

materials without a judicial determination that the speech is harmful, unprotected, or otherwise illegal."

"Even if the Court were to accept the Government's evidence that Ruben

Cavazos controlled the use of the mark during his tenure as National President," Cooper wrote, "there is no support for the notion that a defendant's control of property belonging to a RICO enterprise is sufficient to establish a forfeitable ownership interest in the property. In addition, there is no evidence that Ruben Cavazos owned a majority interest or any interest in the Mongol(s) that would equate to an ownership interest in the mark."

In a direct rebuke of the ATF Agents who had been stealing patches, tee-shirts and memorabilia from Mongols members and sympathizers the judge wrote, "...even if the Court were to assume that the collective membership mark is subject to forfeiture, the Court finds no statutory authority to seize property bearing the mark from third parties.... only defendants' interests in the RICO enterprise and the proceeds from their racketeering activity are subject to forfeiture."

The ruling blew apart the government's plan to outlaw specific motorcycle clubs but the real loser was Doc Cavazos who could not then deliver on what he had promised in his plea deal – which was to turn over the Mongols insignia to Ciccone.

A month later, the U.S. Attorney in Los Angeles and Chris Brunwin's boss, Thomas P. O'Brien, resigned after a small controversy over his expense account. He announced that he was "seeking new challenges" and took a job defending white collar criminals.

Judge Cooper died in January 2010. Before she actually died, while she was on her deathbed, John Torres told another ATF friendly newspaper, The San Gabriel Valley *Tribune* that Judge Cooper's ruling had not been definitive and was only a temporary setback for the prosecution. "That process (of outlawing Mongols insignia) is still moving forward," Torres told the *Tribune*. "No one has 'won' the case. It's just the message that we want to put out to them and other gangs that may use the same type of *indicia* to identify themselves."

When asked for clarification at the time, U.S. Attorney press officer Thom Mrozek stated: "The government continues to seek the forfeiture of the Mongols trademarks. The issue is the subject of ongoing litigation in the courts, and we will continue to fight to prevent anyone from using the trademark to indicate any affiliation with the criminal organization."

Prosecutors filed motions that called Cooper's ruling "premature adjudication" because she had noticed a Constitutional issue in a lower court. The idea was that Cooper's death gave the government a second chance to outlaw a motorcycle club and the government raised the issue again and again for almost two years before it finally lost again and was forced to appeal the proposed forfeiture to the Ninth Circuit. The appeal is pending but the Ninth Circuit is unlikely to overrule the lower court judges.

After Judge Cooper's death two new judges, David O. Carter and Otis D. Wright, each inherited about half the case. Wright, a former L.A. County Sheriff's Deputy and a former prosecutor, was the less esteemed of the two judges. He was inclined toward calling the Mongols a "motorcycle gang" in court. "You know what it is," he explained one time. "I keep seeing Mongols OMG in all the government filings. Mongols OMG."

Some of the Mongols refused to take plea deals. One of them was an average sized, easy, talkative, likable, neat man who looks like a real estate agent from the San Fernando Valley. His name is Alfonso "Lil Grande" Solis and he is a real estate agent in the Valley.

He was rounded up with the rest of his "criminal co-conspirators" on October 21, 2008 and he rotted away in a federal lock up until Judge Cooper finally granted him bail, just before she died, on December 16, 2009. Solis simply refused to plead guilty to a crime he did not commit. That so frustrated his first lawyer that the lawyer quit and for six months Solis was forced to represent himself. The law library in his prison was inadequate and he did not have computer access.

He eventually found a sympathetic lawyer who arranged a plea deal for a crime with which Solis could live – misdemeanor possession of 8.8 grams of marijuana. The legal term for eating a charge is "acceptance of responsibility." After he made bail he was placed on "supervised release" which is the legal term for being technically free but having someone remind you constantly that you are not. His was one of the cases assigned to Judge Carter.

"Why do we have him under supervised release," the judge asked Brunwin. "It seems like a waste." Carter seemed unaware of how expensive getting the Mongols had been.

Brunwin paused, nervously before he gritted his teeth and mumbled, "Defendant could do better."

"What?"

"Defendant could do better."

Carter decided to let Solis be free of supervision. "No stopping at Mongols functions."

"Oh no," Solis promised.

"No flying of colors."

"Yes, your honor."

Marijuana is gradually becoming legal to possess in California. It is legal to have small amounts, up to eight ounces or about 226 grams, of the drug for medicinal use. The maximum federal penalty for the charge to which Solis pled guilty is a year in prison although nobody actually does a year for 8.8 grams. Solis did fourteen months. Because he was a Mongol.

A year and a half later he was still suing the government to try to get his motorcycle back. It was one of the ones John Walsh had used as a theatrical prop.

Shawn Monster Buss, who had tried to save Hitman Martin's life by the side of the freeway, took his plea deal in June 2009. Buss formally agreed that the "Mongols Gang" was a criminal enterprise and specifically that: "on April 29, 2006, defendant Buss and other members of the Mongols gang armed themselves and attended a Mongols party in Temecula, California. On December 10, 2006, defendant Buss and other members of the Mongols gang beat an African-American patron at the Tokio Lounge in Hollywood, California, while shouting racist slurs at the victim. On January 9, 2007, in San Diego, California, defendant Buss and other members of the Mongols gang assaulted a Hells Angels supporter and forced him to surrender his Hells Angels clothing at a Chuck-E-Cheese restaurant. On October 26, 2007, defendant Buss went to a location in Hollywood, California when another member of the Mongols gang informed defendant Buss that members of a rival gang might initiate a confrontation with other members... (and he)

participated in Mongols leadership meetings. Defendant agrees that his conduct was related to his membership in the Mongols and was committed in furtherance of the criminal enterprise and knowing that its members and associates, including defendant, would commit racketeering offenses, including narcotics trafficking. The drug trafficking and other crimes of the Mongols organization are offenses which have an
effect on interstate commerce."

Judge Cooper sentenced Buss to 24 months in prison, three years of supervised release and the RICO special assessment which is a fine of $100.

Big Dog Medel, who smiled shyly when he stood next to Heidi Murkoff at Alan Nevins' publishing party, pled guilty to racketeering 15 months later. He confessed that he: "was a member of the Mongols Gang, and was known in the gang as 'Big Dog.' Defendant Medel was Sergeant-at-Arms of the Northeast Los Angeles Chapter of the Mongols gang. On October 6, 2007, co-defendant Cavazos awarded defendant Medel and other members of the Mongols gang 'Respect Few Fear None' patches. Additionally, on May 31, 2007, defendant Medel told a co-defendant that he was going to inform another co-defendant and other members of the Mother Chapter that a member of the Northeast Los Angeles Chapter of the Mongols gang was not paying dues. On December 18, 2007, a co-defendant informed defendant Medel that the co-defendant believed that his house was about to be raided by law enforcement. Defendant Medel instructed the co-defendant to contact him right before his house was raided so that defendant Medel could advise other members of the Mongols gang." And it was all in furtherance of the "racketeering criminal enterprise." Judge Wright gave him five months.

Another defendant was Bryan McCauley who was accused of doing what Dirty Jim (Jesse Ventura)

Janos had done in the early 70s. McCauley was in the Navy, he was a member of the Mongols in San Diego and he lawfully possessed guns and government surplus ammunition. Coconut Dan, had reported that he thought McCauley looked like a "domestic terrorist." The guns and ammunition annoyed the federal magistrate, Margaret Nagle, who arraigned him.

"Your Honor, what we have here is a nineteen and a half year veteran of the United States Navy," McCauley's attorney began.

"Bought himself a pack of trouble it sounds like," the judge replied.

"Well your Honor, if the court notes that all of these weapons are legally registered to him. They were legally purchased by him."

"Government ammo is not a good thing."

"Well, you know, the government made the allegations. I don't know if that's true or not."

"My father was a mailman," the judge lectured the defendant and his lawyer. "The guy who worked at the window at the post office he worked at borrowed five bucks for lunch from somebody in the office but it just so happened that the inspector came in when he was out and said, 'you're five dollars short.' And he said, 'Oh, I borrowed it for lunch but I was going to pay it back.' That was the end of 23 years of his career. The government takes these rules and regulations pretty seriously…. And, Mr. McCauley, if you are hanging with guns and leather vests with this crowd, you know, you sometimes wind up in the position of being judged by the company you keep, as I tell my children. And, you've got a long service in the Navy but, again, you may find yourself in a bit of trouble one way or the other on this one….. You know, it's late on Friday. I probably shouldn't say what I'm about to say on the record. I suppose the Second Amendment isn't my favorite Amendment when it comes to allowing people, in Washington D.C. as the Supreme Court has held that it does, to have semi-automatic assault weapons."

On September 6, 2009 McCauley confessed that he "has been a member of the Mongols criminal enterprise. Defendant was also an officer in the Mongols and was elected Sergeant-at-Arms of the gang's San Diego chapter, and participated in leadership meetings with co-defendant Cavazos and other Mongols leaders. Defendant further agrees that his conduct was related to his membership in the Mongols Gang and was
committed in furtherance of the criminal enterprise and knowing that its members and associates would commit racketeering offenses. The racketeering offenses of the Mongols organization are offenses which have an effect on interstate commerce."

Two months later Judge Cooper sentenced him to three years probation and the $100 RICO tax. And, he was kicked out of the Navy.

Target Owens held out for more than a year. After he was arrested his lawyer told him to take what he could get. "You're a member of the Mongols motorcycle gang. What do you expect?" By his bail hearing on January 27, 2009 the attorney had begun to come around. Ciccone attended the hearing. Ciccone attended most of the hearings.

"The substantive crimes that Mr. Owens has been accused of involved sales to undercover agents," Owens lawyer said. "These were gentlemen who were friends of Mr. Owens who took advantage of the trust that he had with them as fellow members of the club and allowed them to induce…induced him to make these sales which is not something he does. He's not a drug seller.

"Specifically, he says that many of the statements that they're attributing to him were either made by other people or were made by the confidential informant himself; in that there's a consistent effort by the confidential informant in this case and perhaps by the government to blow up statements that may have been made by him to make him look like a dangerous individual. For example, there's a meeting that happens at the beginning of the investigation, and the statements talk about how Mr. Owens is threatening an individual. Well, if you look at the facts of the case the individual who had the beef was the confidential informant. He was the one who wanted the violence to happen against the other individual and he's literally putting his own words in Mr. Owens' mouth.

"They are making allegations that he sold methamphetamine on one occasion to somebody who apparently came to him in tears because he said he was going to get killed by somebody else. And, he needed the methamphetamine to make something good. Okay?

"And, there's no disputing the aggressiveness of this investigation." The lawyer who had begun to catch on stabbed his finger at Ciccone. "There's no disputing the historical aggressiveness of the agent who's here and prosecuting the Mongols! Prosecuting them and persecuting them!"

In February 2010 Owens formally confessed that as "part of his role as a member of the Mongols criminal enterprise, defendant knowingly and intentionally distributed methamphetamine. Specifically, on May 17, 2006, defendant William Owens sold approximately 23.0 grams of actual methamphetamine to a confidential government informant that defendant believed was a member of the Mongols gang and an undercover law enforcement officer that defendant believed was an associate of the Mongols gang. Defendant further agrees that this act was related to his role as a member of the Mongols Gang and was committed in furtherance of the criminal enterprise and knowing that its members and associates, including

237

defendant, would commit racketeering offenses, including narcotics trafficking."

Judge Carter sentenced Target Owens to 46 months in prison followed by three years of supervised release. Two weeks before he went to prison he said, "You can't beat RICO. My lawyer said he would fight it as long as I wanted but he thought I was going to lose and if I fought it I was looking at 20 years.... At least the one good thing about the deal is I'll get my motorcycle back."

Face Reynolds confessed on March 23, 2010 that he "is a member of the Mongols. As part of his role as a member of the Mongols criminal enterprise, defendant Reynolds and other co-defendants and members of the Mongols, as well as another individual that defendant Reynolds brought with him, provided security for an undercover law enforcement officer that defendant believed was an associate of the Mongols and a confidential government informant that defendant believed was a member of the Mongols. The purpose of defendant Reynolds and co-defendants providing this security was to provide the UC and CI with protection while the UC and the CI purchased thirty three kilograms of cocaine from other undercover law enforcement officers that defendant Reynolds believed were narcotics suppliers. In exchange for providing this security, defendant Reynolds was paid $1000 by the UC. Defendant further agrees that this conduct was related to his role as a member of the Mongols and was committed in furtherance of the criminal enterprise and knowing that its members and associates, including defendant, would commit racketeering offenses, including narcotics trafficking. The drug trafficking and other crimes of the Mongols organization are offenses which have an effect on interstate commerce."

Reynolds said he confessed because there was "no way to fight the charge that I was a Mongol. Every step of the way, they could prove I was in the club. And, that was 20 years."

Reynolds confessed to a "Level 31" charge. In modern, federal sentencing practice a Level 31 charge carries a sentence of 108 to 135 months in prison. On February 7, 2011 Judge Wright, the ex-cop and ex-prosecutor, and a black man who had heard all about the Mongols racism for months, sentenced Face Reynolds to supervised probation for five years. Reynolds also had to forfeit some of his rights as a citizen including the right to federal benefits like unemployment compensation. His confiscated goods and motorcycles were not returned.

Mike Munz pled guilty to racketeering on December 15, 2009. He confessed that he was "a member and officer of the Mongols criminal enterprise." He "regularly led meetings of Mongols officers and members and directed Mongols members about the requirements and responsibilities of the organization, including conducting armed attacks on rival gang members. Specifically, defendant, along with co-conspirators, led a meeting on April 6, 20 2006 in which they addressed a confrontation with rival Hells Angels gang members. On April 26, 2006, and August 16, 2006, defendant led Church Meetings of the Mongols San Diego chapter. On June 16, 2007, defendant, along with co-conspirators, addressed Mongols at an all members meeting in Los Angeles, California. Defendant also participated in Mongols functions. For example, defendant attended a Mongols party in Temecula, California on April 29, 2006, with co-conspirators."

The confession continues for pages. "Defendant participated in membership decisions within the organization. Defendant recruited members into the organization and collected funds from them for the organization. In June 15, 2007 defendant directed a polygrapher to administer a polygraph examination to three undercover law enforcement officers, posing as prospective Mongols members, as a condition to their membership in the organization. The polygraph examination was intended to determine whether the undercover officers were in fact law enforcement officers or cooperating with law enforcement. Defendant also addressed conflicts between the Mongols organization and rival organizations, and defendant, along with co-conspirators, participated in a meeting at Universal Studios City Walk during which representatives of rival organizations demanded monthly tax payments from the Mongols to reimburse the rival organization for losses suffered as a result of a confrontation with the Mongols. Defendant admits that these acts were related to his role as a leader and member of the Mongols organization, and his actions were committed in furtherance of the criminal enterprise and knowing that members of the criminal enterprise would commit multiple racketeering acts, including armed attacks on rival gang members, attempted murder and narcotics distribution. Defendant also admits that the crimes of the enterprise are offenses which have an effect on interstate commerce."

On December 13, 2010 Judge Carter sentenced Munz to 70 months and three years of supervision after his release.

Hector Gonzalez, who threw both Doc Cavazos and ATF Agent John Hollywood Carr out of the Mongols because he thought they were criminals, took his plea deal on June 6, 2011. He confessed that, "The Mongols organization has long participated in armed conflicts and violent confrontations, including riots at casinos in Laughlin, Nevada and Cabazon, California. During the time period charged in the indictment, defendant was an officer of the Mongols organization. He served as an officer, as the National Treasurer and, later, National President for the Mongols and was known in the organization as Largo. In his role, defendant directed some of the activities of the Mongols organization. He participated in and led Mother Chapter meetings of the Mongols, as well as Presidents meetings, Sergeant-at-Arms meetings, All Members meetings and Mongols National Runs along with other Mongols members and leaders, and provided some direction to Mongols members about the conduct of the organization and told them to keep your house clean."

Largo's confession also continued at length. Anyone who has read this far in this book could write most of it.

As soon as his brother and son secured their plea deals, Doc Cavazos appears to have stopped cooperating with Brunwin and Ciccone. Doc and Lil Rubes were sentenced *en camera*, in a secret court session, on September 8, 2011. Doc got 14 years and Lil Rubes got 51 months. The sentences are sealed. Zacarias Moussaoui, John Gotti, Timothy McVeigh, leaders of the Mexican Mafia and leaders of the Aryan Brotherhood were all sentenced in open court but Doc's sentencing was secret. After he was sentenced Doc wanted to give an interview to a reporter but he was prevented from doing so by Brunwin and the U.S. Marshalls.

Most of the "voluntary" guilty pleas were public. Each time the ritual began with the judge determining the competency of the defendant to enter a guilty plea. Christopher Brunwin was present for almost all of these public confessions. He usually read the confession aloud.

Brunwin is a prince in this hell. He went to the prestigious Boalt Hall School of Law at Berkeley but he still, probably, only makes about $120,000 a year – which must be less than Ciccone – at least until he gets his book deal. He is a small man who does not lift weights. He wraps dark framed glasses around his Supercuts head and he wears the same suit every other criminal lawyer wears. It has two pieces. The jacket has two buttons and it is a shade without color. If it had a color it would be the color of rich dirt or new born bullshit.

He is friendly and helpful to the defense lawyers. He gives one visitor, who must not be very professional because he is wearing a recognizably khaki suit, advice on the judge. He reminisces pleasantly about his undergraduate days at UCLA and every so often he steals a glance at the poorly dressed stranger who stares at him and takes notes.

Brunwin doesn't "really give interviews."

"Do you really think you could prove the Mongols are a criminal conspiracy?"

"Oh absolutely."

"Really."

"Without a doubt."

"Okay. How would you prove the Mongols is a criminal conspiracy?"

"It's already been proven over and over," he tells his feet.

"How?"

"What?"

"How have you proven over and over that the Mongols are a criminal conspiracy?"

"I guess you don't know the case."

"Yeah."

"We have had defendant after defendant come into the court and admit it over and over."

Risky

On July 9, 2009, at an unusually well orchestrated press conference, Los Angeles Chief of Police William Bratton announced that the murder of Manual Vincent Hitman Martin had been solved. Bratton told the eager press that 20 members of the Toonerville Rifa clique were in custody. Four people, the Chief explained, had been arrested for murder, four for attempted murder and twelve more had been arrested on suspicion of violating drug or gun laws.

The implication was that the four murder suspects were involved in the Martin shooting. The Glendale police spokesman, Tom Lorenz said, "Obviously since that shooting, it's been nine months of a grueling investigation."

The arrests were carried out by Swat team members of the Los Angeles Police Department, the Los Angeles County Sheriff's Department, the Glendale Police Department and other unnamed agencies at two that morning. Martin's murder, the press was told, had actually been solved by the Glendale police. That murder, the official account went, had prompted Glendale to put up a wiretap which led to the "discovery of key evidence." That key evidence, whatever it was, "led to the arrests." Lorenz said

Martin's killer had been arrested by another, unnamed police agency on charges unrelated to the murder but he had not yet been charged with killing Martin. Thoughtful reporters were left to assume that first there was the murder, then there was the wiretap, then whoever did it was caught bragging about it on the phone.

There were no names released at the press conference. Nobody in the Los Angeles press seemed to mind. All of the local press ran with the headline, which was basically the same story Kozlowski had told exactly nine months before – Toonerville did it. No reporter at the conference questioned how the murder could be solved without a named suspect.

The man who would eventually be charged, Richard Dean "Risky" Clayborn was not arrested for the murder until 2:10 p.m. on August 12, 2009. Clayborn is neither Mexican nor a resident of Glendale. His eyes are blue and he lived in Chatsworth. He was arraigned at 8:30 a.m. on September 11. It is a state case. State cases in California are, in general, less transparent than federal cases.

More than three years after Martin's murder and more than two years after Clayborn's arrest the suspect still doesn't have a trial date. Although it was possible to interpret the press conference as announcing that there was a Toonerville case, as there has been a Mongols case, there is no Toonerville case.

The Clayborn case has been arranged to frustrate press scrutiny. The basic document that begins police reporting is called an "arrest log." It is one of the few official police documents in California that is considered "public." Announcing that the alleged shooter had been arrested somewhere for something that was not the murder made it virtually impossible for most reporters to even learn Clayborn's name. If any reporter tried to look he could not possibly succeed.

There are many local and federal arrests in Southern California every day and the best place to hide a leaf is in a forest.

No one wondered why the police would bother to hide Hitman Martin's killer. There was too much obvious news for any rational reporter to pursue an old, solved murder case. The day Clayborn was arrested for murder Ted Kennedy was sick, the Feds raided two medical marijuana dispensaries in the city, there was a news conference about a toxic waste dump in Pacoima and the home foreclosure crisis was the big local and national story.

Chief Bratton may have been lying – depending on what the meaning of lying is. He may have been lied to. The Glendale police had been telling tall tales about the Martin murder all along. For example the statement that, "Coroners were unable to determine if Martin died from the gunshot wound to his chest or injuries sustained in the subsequent motorcycle crash...."

Risky Clayborn had been taken into custody on June 30, 2009 – more than a week before the press event – by the Los Angeles Police Department Gang Activity Section on three counts of possessing drugs for sale and one count of being a felon in possession of a gun. His bail was set at $1.2 million. So, at the time of Bratton's announcement there certainly was a pool of possible suspects from which to choose and Clayborn was in that pool.

Clayborn had 29 prior convictions so he was not likely to be a defendant who would arouse much sympathy or interest. He was charged at his arraignment – two months after Bratton spoke – with murder, attempted murder and two counts of discharging a gun from a vehicle. Clayborn pled not guilty to all four charges and his bail was raised to $3.2 million. He has been in jail ever since. The details of the assassination, like who was driving the car, whether Clayton had been at The Mix, or if he had even been in Glendale and how and why he managed to single out Hitman Martin have never been disclosed. Evidence that has been made public includes "aerial photographs" and a "traffic ticket." Specific details of the shooting are unlikely to emerge because there will probably never be a trial.

Bratton resigned as Los Angeles Police Chief at the end of October 2009 and took a job with a private security firm in New York. He became a consultant to Scotland Yard in August 2011. He has been unavailable to comment on why he announced the Martin murder had been solved a month before a suspect was charged.

According to his booking documents Clayborn, who was already in custody, was arrested for the murder by the Glendale police. Four Glendale cops and one female prisoner testified at Clayborn's preliminary hearing on May 6, 2010. Fifteen days later one of the cops, Detective Arthur Frank, was named Glendale Officer of the Year for his, "investigative work regarding the murder of a Mongols motorcycle gang member on the Glendale (2) Freeway in 2008, which was eventually linked to a Toonerville gang member." Frank, along with 52 other Glendale cops, was awarded a "Toonerville 187PC Campaign Ribbon" to wear on his uniform. The number 187 is the California Penal code statute that forbids murder.

If Detective Frank recovered a murder weapon, it has not yet been surfaced in court. Wiretaps seem to point at Clayborn. He also apparently implicated himself in the murder in multiple interviews with Detective Frank. So far in the case, there has been no mention of the "Los Angeles High Intensity Drug Trafficking Area Intelligence Architecture Plan," the War Room, the ATF or any of the undercover ATF agents who rode to the party at The Mix with Martin the night he died.

Clayborn will never get out of jail. He is unlikely to ever be interviewed by a reporter. In addition to his three original drug charges, his original weapons charge and the four charges resulting from the Martin murder, he faces additional attempted murder charges from an incident while he was in Los Angeles County Jail on January 2, 2010.

He is also now charged with murdering another inmate in county jail on February 28, 2011. That murder will be a death penalty case. After his arraignment on that charge on August 31, 2011 his bail was revoked. Clayborn's lawyer knows, even if Clayborn does not, that his best chance to avoid the death penalty is to refrain from wasting the court's time and confess to Martin's murder.

And, when that happens the Hitman Martin murder case will finally be officially closed.

30449787R00154

Made in the USA
Lexington, KY
04 March 2014